CONSIDERING COMPASSION

CONSIDERING COMPASSION

Global Ethics, Human Dignity, and the Compassionate God

Edited by
Frits de Lange
and
L. Juliana Claassens

☙PICKWICK *Publications* • Eugene, Oregon

CONSIDERING COMPASSION
Global Ethics, Human Dignity, and the Compassionate God

Copyright © 2018 Wipf and Stock Publishers. All rights reserved. Except for brief quotations in critical publications or reviews, no part of this book may be reproduced in any manner without prior written permission from the publisher. Write: Permissions, Wipf and Stock Publishers, 199 W. 8th Ave., Suite 3, Eugene, OR 97401.

Pickwick Publications
An Imprint of Wipf and Stock Publishers
199 W. 8th Ave., Suite 3
Eugene, OR 97401

www.wipfandstock.com

PAPERBACK ISBN: 978-1-4982-8152-2
HARDCOVER ISBN: 978-1-4982-8154-6
EBOOK ISBN: 978-1-4982-8153-9

Cataloguing-in-Publication data:

Names: de Lange, Frits, editor.| Claassens, L. Juliana M., editor

Title: Considering compassion : global ethics, human dignity, and the compassionate God/ edited by Frits de Lange and L. Juliana M. Claassens.

Description: Eugene, OR: Pickwick Publications, 2018 | Includes bibliographical references and index.

Identifiers: ISBN 978-1-4982-8152-2 (paperback) | ISBN 978-1-4982-8154-6 (hardcover) | ISBN 978-1-4982-8153-9 (ebook)

Subjects: LCSH: Religious ethics | Compassion | Religion and ethics

Classification: LCC BJ1475 C7 2018 (print) | LCC BJ1475 (ebook)

Manufactured in the U.S.A.   09/17/18

Contents

Contributors | vii
Acknowledgments | xi
Introduction | xiii

Rethinking Compassion

1. Affect, Empathy, and Human Dignity? Considering Compassion at the Intersection of Theology and Science—*Dion Forster* | 3
2. The Event of Compassion—*Frits de Lange* | 17
3. Compassion as a Virtue of Love—*Pieter Vos* | 31

Retrieving Compassion

4. Rethinking the Ethics of Compassion with Levinas and Badiou—*Renée van Riessen* | 49
5. Ways of Teaching Compassion in the Synoptic Gospels—*Annette Merz* | 66
6. Compassion of and with Christ in the Late Medieval Spirituality of the Bloodied Pen and Paint Brush—*Len Hansen* | 87

Enacting Compassion

7. Justice as/and Compassion? On the Good Samaritan and Political Theology—*Dirk J. Smit* | 109
8. Poverty and Inequality in South Africa: What's Compassion Got to Do with It?—*Nadine Bowers-Du Toit* | 129
9. Mercy and Justice: A Diaconal View on Compassion in a Changing Welfare State—*Herman Noordegraaf* | 145

Cultivating Compassion

    10.   Cultivating Compassion? Abigail's Story (1 Samuel 25) as Space for Teaching Concern for Others—*L. Juliana M. Claassens* | 157

    11.   "To the Wonder": Finding God in the Most Unexpected Places—*Charlene van der Walt* | 170

    12.   *Passio—Compassio*: J. S. Bach's Passions Transformed into a Passion Transcending Christianity—*Mirella Klomp* | 187

Contributors

Nadine Bowers Du Toit
Associate Professor of Practical Theology
Director of Unit for Religious and Development Research
Faculty of Theology
Stellenbosch University
Stellenbosch, South Africa

L. Juliana M. Claassens
Professor of Old Testament
Chair Department of Old and New Testament
Head of Gender Unit
Faculty of Theology
Stellenbosch University
Stellenbosch, South Africa

Frits de Lange
Professor of Ethics
Protestant Theological University
Amsterdam/Groningen, The Netherlands
Extraordinary Professor Systematic Theology and Ecclesiology
Faculty of Theology
Stellenbosch University
Stellenbosch, South Africa

Dion A. Forster
Associate Professor in Systematic Theology and Ethics
Chair Department of Systematic Theology and Ecclesiology
Director, Beyers Naudé Center for Public Theology
Faculty of Theology
Stellenbosch University
Stellenbosch, South Africa

Len Hansen
Research Development and Support
Director of NETACT
Faculty of Theology
Stellenbosch University
Stellenbosch, South Africa

Mirella Klomp
Assistant Professor of Practical Theology
Executive Manager of Institute for Ritual and Liturgical Studies (IRiLiS)
Protestant Theological University
Amsterdam/Groningen, The Netherlands

Annette Merz
Professor of New Testament
Protestant Theological University
Amsterdam/Groningen, The Netherlands

Herman Noordegraaf
Professor of Diaconia by Special Appointment of Diaconia
Protestant Theological University
Amsterdam/Groningen, The Netherlands

Dirk J. Smit
Professor of Reformed Theology and Public Life
Princeton Theological Seminary
Princeton, New Jersey, USA
Extraordinary Professor of Systematic Theology
Stellenbosch University
Stellenbosch, South Africa
Honorary Professor Theology Faculty
Humboldt University, Berlin, Germany

Charlene van der Walt
Associate Professor of Gender and Religion
School of Religion, Philosophy, and Classics
University of KwaZulu Natal
African Coordinator for the Network SRHR, Church of Sweden

Renée van Riessen
Associate Professor of Philosophy of Religion
Protestant Theological University
Amsterdam/Groningen, The Netherlands
Endowed Professor for Christian Philosophy
Leiden University,
Leiden The Netherlands

Pieter Vos
Assistant Professor of Ethics
Director of the International Reformed Theological Institute (IRTI)
Protestant Theological University
Amsterdam/Groningen, The Netherlands

Acknowledgments

Considering Compassion: Global Ethics, Human Dignity, and the Compassionate God is the culmination of a remarkable international collaboration with multiple representatives from our two institutions meeting yearly—one year in Stellenbosch, and one year in Groningen/Amsterdam/Kampen—with the purpose of reflecting on various aspects and dimensions of human dignity. This collaboration in part also offered the impetus for the Faculty of Theology of Stellenbosch University's Hope project, which consisted of some generous funding, which allowed us the space to foster and cultivate exactly the type of interdisciplinary and intradisciplinary conversations with regard to the intersection of theology, human dignity, and other fields of inquiry reflected in this book. This funding also in part made possible this current publication, representing the labor of two of these consultations on the theme of Compassion and Human Dignity and Global Ethics, respectively in May 2015 and May 2016.

In this regard, we want to acknowledge the vision of people like the former dean of the Faculty of Theology, and now Vice Rector Social Impact, Transformation and Personnel, Prof. Nico Koopman. Our joint research collaboration on Human Dignity started on his initiative, way back in 2005, and his commitment to a global public theology and an ethics of dialogue between North and South on justice and human dignity has given a strong and indispensable impetus throughout these years.

Our thanks also go to all the members of our respective faculties who over the years have contributed to these consultations and helped foster a collaborative ethos in addition to daring to cross the narrow disciplinary boundaries that often mark our scholarly enterprise.

We want to thank Pickwick Publications for offering a home to *Considering Compassion*. It has been a pleasure working with you. And to Ria Smit, who under often challenging circumstances that involved moving to a new home in a new continent, has done a stellar job in language editing and copy editing the manuscript into the correct format.

Frits de Lange, Protestant Theological University, Amsterdam/Groningen, The Netherlands

Juliana Claassens, Faculty of Theology, Stellenbosch University, Stellenbosch, South Africa

Introduction

Considering Compassion: Global Ethics, Human Dignity, and the Compassionate God

FRITS DE LANGE AND L. JULIANA M. CLAASSENS

GLOBALIZATION MAKES THE WORLD bigger than human moral imagination can afford. We do not seem to be prepared for coping very well amidst a world where we are increasingly challenged by the interconnectedness of all to all and everything to everything on this globe; not economically, politically, socially, ecologically, nor religiously. Some decades ago the German philosopher Günther Anders (1902–1992) wrote a book about the "Outdatedness of the Human Race" ("Die Antiquiertheit des Menschen"), asserting that human nature cannot keep pace with the algorithmic speed of the technological revolution.[1] His title also seems applicable to the challenges globalization holds for the planetarization of human consciousness. Living together as humanity on one planet needs to be reinvented in the twenty-first century. The challenge to create a new, peaceful, just, and sustainable world order is vital to the survival of us all.

As theologians who are particularly skilled in doing theology amidst ever-changing and challenging contexts, we are inclined to ask: What, if anything, can theology contribute? This question has been, already for more than a decade, at the center of the collaboration between the Faculty of Theology of Stellenbosch University, South Africa, and the Protestant Theological University in the Netherlands; institutions from the northern and

---

1. The first volume of the two-volume work *Die Antiquiertheit des Menschen* (*Outdatedness of Human Beings*) was first published by C. H. Beck in Munich in 1956. The work has seen several editions in German but has not been translated into English.

the southern hemisphere, committing themselves to an ongoing research project on human dignity in a globalizing world.[2]

The question is, even for anti-globalists, not whether and when we will move toward one interconnected world, but how. Lifestyles and cultures that once lived in splendid isolation are exposed to one another, not only by the search for economic markets, but also by migration and travel, communication technology, and social media. Humankind will have to grow toward a planetary consciousness, and expand the limited scope of our moral imagination beyond the borders of family, tribe, class, religion, nation, and culture.

Here theology can play a constructive role. "The Empire"—a capitalist world order based on greed, aggression, and power[3]—regardless of how powerful and all-encompassing, does not necessarily need to be our common fate. The future still depends on choices to be made. The outlooks, though, are not reassuring. Traditional communities are breaking apart, inequality increases,[4] nations fall apart, and millions of migrants are adrift across and between continents. Religions no longer seem to bind people together, but disperse them in various kinds of fundamentalism. And even more disconcerting, religions worldwide function as a legitimization for worldwide terrorism of extremist groups. On a scale as never seen before, people suffer from the violence of civil wars.

Globalization is creating new winners and losers, privileged and disadvantaged, powerful and vulnerable individuals and communities. Is it a question of how one continues to uphold and believe in the ideal of human dignity *for all*? It seems that a more compassionate culture and politics might be of help in the cultivation of a global culture that endorses the equal human rights of all. Philosopher Martha Nussbaum, in particular, is an author committed to the values of compassion and human dignity, both in the academic arena as well as in public debate. In her work on classical and modern moral philosophy, Nussbaum shows the crucial role that moral emotions such as empathy play in upholding an inclusive morality which does not divide the world into "us" and "them." She argues that "[r]espect grounded in the idea of human dignity will prove impotent to include all citizens on terms of equality

---

2. Some of the fruits of this rich collaboration were published in the collection of essays by Claassens and Spronk, *Fragile Dignity*.

3. The *Accra Confession*, adopted at the meeting of the World Alliance of Reformed Churches in Accra, Ghana (2004), inspired by Hardt and Negri in their book *Empire*, defines the "Empire" as the new global order, as "the coming together of economic, cultural, political and military power that constitutes a system of domination led by powerful nations to protect and defend their own interests"; see World Communion of Reformed Churches, http://wcrc.ch/accra.

4. Piketty, *Capital in the Twenty-First Century*.

unless it is nourished by imaginative engagement with the lives of others and by an inner grasp of their full and equal humanity."[5]

Nussbaum moreover maintains that cultivating compassion both on a personal and an institutional level will contribute to a more just world. Narrow forms of patriotism and nationalism limit compassion to an in-group, excluding those on the outside. What we need in a globalizing world is the promotion and endorsement of what she calls a "compassionate world citizenship." She argues as follows:

> Most of us are brought up to believe that all human beings have equal worth. At least the world's major religions and most secular philosophies tell us so. But our emotions don't believe it. We mourn for those we know, not for those we don't know. And most of us feel deep emotions about America, emotions we don't feel about India, or Russia, or Rwanda. In and of itself, this narrowness of our emotional lives is probably acceptable and maybe even good . . . Nonetheless, when we observe how narrow and partisan our compassion usually is, we must ask how it can be educated and extended, so that the equal worth of all human beings becomes a stable psychological reality for us.[6]

According to Nussbaum, it is vital that the education in the commonality of human weakness and vulnerability should become a profound part of the education of all young people. She argues that literature in particular ("stories and dramas, history, film") is well suited in helping people in what she calls "decoding the suffering of another," opening up the lives of others near and far so as to foster a greater sense of understanding and insight into what others are experiencing. Rigorous study in global economics combined with philosophical and religious ethics may further contribute to foster compassion beyond one's narrow circle of concern.[7]

The plea for cultivating compassion with a broader reach is also at the core of the Charter for Compassion, a worldwide movement started in 2009 by the science of religion scholar Karen Armstrong. Individuals, groups, but also institutions and political organizations are all invited to sign and support the Charter.[8] While Nussbaum focuses on education, Armstrong points to religion as the source for a compassionate politics. In her view,

---

5. Nussbaum, *Political Emotions*, 380.
6. Nussbaum, "Compassionate Citizenship."
7. Nussbaum, "Compassionate Citizenship."
8. Seattle, Washington, USA, became the first city in the world to affirm the Charter, followed by many others. In the Netherlands: Leiden, Groningen, Apeldoorn, and Rotterdam.

the Golden Rule is the ethical core of the great world religions Christianity, Buddhism, Islam, and Hinduism. The conviction that one should treat others as one wants to be treated oneself, gives a tangible moral backbone to the flesh of compassion. It turns emotion into a principle. As the Charter of Compassion outlines their objectives:

> The principle of compassion lies at the heart of all religious, ethical and spiritual traditions, calling us always to treat all others as we wish to be treated ourselves . . . Compassion impels us to work tirelessly to alleviate the suffering of our fellow creatures, to dethrone ourselves from the centre of our world and put another there, and to honour the inviolable sanctity of every single human being, treating everybody, without exception, with absolute justice, equity and respect.[9]

The Charter of Compassion furthermore admits that religion in the past rightly can be said to have had a bad reputation when it comes to compassion. Religious traditions often functioned as the source and legitimatization of interreligious violence and colonial oppression. Therefore, Karen Armstrong contends that we engage in an act of retrieval: compassion has to be restored as the center of morality and religion; cultural and religious diversity has to be appreciated and encouraged, and an informed empathy with the suffering of all human beings, even those regarded as enemies, has to be cultivated. As the Charter of Compassion maintains, "We urgently need to make compassion a clear, luminous and dynamic force in our polarized world . . . Born of our deep interdependence, compassion is essential to human relationships and to a fulfilled humanity."[10]

In her worldwide movement for the promotion of a global interreligious culture of compassion, Karen Armstrong can count on the support of various religious world leaders such as His Holiness the Dalai Lama. He too travels around the world as a committed ambassador of borderless compassion. The Dalai Lama defines compassion as "the wish for another being to be free from suffering," and distinguishes compassion closely associated with a personal attachment from that of genuine compassion. It is quite natural that we want the people we love to be free from suffering. But this can be described as compassion that emerges from personal need. His Holiness the Dalai Lama rather proposes that "genuine compassion is based not on our own projections and expectations, but rather on the needs of the other: irrespective of whether another person is a close friend or an

---

9. The Charter for Compassion.
10. The Charter for Compassion.

enemy."[11] Hence, the goal of the Buddhist practitioner is to expand his circle of concern and develop true compassion. The Dalai Lama is convinced that this task is not limited to Buddhist monks or religious believers in general, but that it is part of a new, global ethic. "Given patience and time, it is within our power to develop this kind of universal compassion."[12]

A global movement to cultivate and extend compassion beyond the immediate circle of concern may indeed find inspiration from many different religious sources. In Judaism, compassion is considered to be one of the central attributes of the divine, and one of the core obligations of humanity. The Hebrew Bible describes God as both compassionate and merciful: "The LORD! The LORD! A God merciful and gracious, slow to anger, and abounding in steadfast love and faithfulness" (Exod 34:6). Israel has to take the Lord as an example for its own ethical behavior. "Just as God is called compassionate and gracious, so you too must be compassionate and gracious, giving gifts freely" (Sifre Deuteronomy 49). To "walk in God's ways" is to respond with compassion to the suffering of others.[13]

Compassion, or *Rahman* and *Rahim* in Arabic, is also at the heart of Islam. Each of the 114 chapters of the Quran, with one exception, begins with the verse, "In the name of Allah the Compassionate, the Merciful", and a good Muslim starts each day, each prayer and each significant action by invoking Allah the Merciful and Compassionate by reciting *Bism-i-llah a-Rahman-i-Rahim*.

Christianity is rooted in the biblical story, which started with a merciful God who was moved by the suffering cries of the Hebrew people, and culminated in the narrative of Christ as the icon of a compassionate God. The paradigmatic role that the story of the Good Samaritan played in Christian spirituality and ethics shows the pivotal role of compassion throughout its history. In early Christianity the renowned, unselfish care for the poor and destitute organized by churches, moved Julian, the Roman emperor from 355 to 363, to the jealous exclamation, "Nothing has contributed to the progress of the superstition of the Christians as their charity to strangers . . . the impious Galileans provide not only for their own poor, but for ours as well."

The question at the heart of this book that has brought colleagues, who have over the years have become friends, from two universities on two different continents, together is the following: Do the religious teachings, the biblical stories, and Christian traditions of compassion still provide us with

11. Dalai Lama, *Compassionate Life*, 17.
12. Dalai Lama, *Compassionate Life*, 23.
13. Compassion in Judaism.

the sources of moral imagination needed to guide us into the global era? Jonathan Sacks holds that the "central insight of monotheism—that if God is the parent of humanity, then we are all members of a single extended family—has become more real in its implications than ever before." Sacks suggests that the Enlightenment concept of universal rights remains a "thin" morality, when it is not fueled with moral imagination. Here, the biblical idea that "those in need are our brothers and sisters and that poverty is something we feel in our bones" is far more powerful. "The great faiths do more than give us abstract expression to our shared humanity; they move us to action and give compelling shape to the claims of others upon us."[14] In order to adjust this rather bold assertion, this book critically investigates the Christian legacy. *Can the Christian practice of faith really contribute to a more compassionate world, and how?*

Once we started talking and reflecting and writing, an even more critical question arose, and that is whether compassion is really the answer. *Is it true that more compassion is what we need for upholding human dignity in a global world?*

During two stimulating consultations respectively held in Stellenbosch, South Africa and Groningen, Netherlands,[15] colleagues from different theological disciplines reflected on the question of compassion from a variety of angles.

To our mind, a hermeneutics of compassion is an integral element of Christian ethics. Retrieving the meaning of compassion transcends the question of how to define it. Aristotle defined compassion as "a painful emotion directed at another person's misfortune or suffering."[16] Compassion is sorrow *for* and *with* the other, or as Augustine puts it in one place, "on behalf of" the other. But meanings never exist in the abstract; they are embedded in shifting contexts and practices. Other words and concepts are closely related or sometimes used synonymous with compassion, such as mercy, pity, neighborly love, *medeleven* (Dutch), *meelewing* (Afrikaans), *Mitleid*, empathy, fellow-feeling. The linguistic distinctions made, or the affinities uncovered, often do reflect a normative agenda.

The least one can say, however, is that *com-passio* always entails a fellow-feeling: one human being shares the suffering of another and has the desire to alleviate it. But how should one understand this phenomenon? Does it belong to our human—or primate—nature and is our brain

---

14. Sacks, *The Dignity of Difference*, 112.

15. Held on May 6 and 7, 2015 in Stellenbosch, South Africa; and May 19 and 20, 2016 in Groningen, The Netherlands.

16. Quoted by Nussbaum, *Upheavals of Thought*, 306.

evolutionary "wired" to be compassionate? Then the question of how to expand our human circle of our concern, and how far it can be stretched in the context of global humanity, becomes of primordial importance, as the work of Nussbaum but also of the Dalai Lama shows.

In the first section of this collection of essays, "Rethinking Compassion," Dion Forster shows in his contribution how contemporary cognitive neuroscience invites us to take a naturalistic view on compassion as a common moral emotion, given with human nature. "From the perspective of cognitive neuroscience, empathy is that ability within the human person to identify, understand . . . and partially feel or experience the suffering of another person . . . Empathy, and ultimately compassion, is thus a neurological state that can be identified in the brain activity of the individual who witnesses the suffering of the other. These neurological states are coupled with associated behaviors." Nevertheless, a distinction has to be made between empathy and compassion. While empathy involves the feeling of co-suffering, compassion takes a further step, it moves from experience to action. The capacity for understanding the emotion of another may be hardwired into the brain, as it is activated by shared experience of the pain of another, or by observing their pain. But the decision to act on the pain of the other, however, is, Forster concludes, a cognitive process and implies a voluntary choice. Therefore he embeds his naturalistic understanding of compassion theologically within the framework of a Christian humanism.

That the compassionate act in favor of another's distress is a conscious affair, is questioned in his turn by Frits de Lange, who takes the perspective of contemporary phenomenology as a starting point for his reflection. He interprets compassion as a contingent event, a phenomenon neither a self-evident part of our biological make-up, nor in our cognitive faculties. We do not consciously decide to become compassionate. As the parable of the Good Samaritan illustrates, compassion is a power that transcends and overcomes us. It starts in our belly, as a kind of gut-feeling,[17] rather than in our head. "In the *decision to stay* and not to flee, a decision often taken pre-reflexively with the body, the 'we' of common suffering transforms itself into a responsible 'I' taking care of a unique, irreplaceable 'Thou'. 'Moi voici,' 'here I am,' is the place of birth of the ethical self. 'It is *you*, and no one else, who should stay with me,' the call summons. Suffering binds us together in a primordial commonality, but suffering also individualizes, in making our presence irreplaceable."

---

17. The verb used in Luke 10:33, "he took pity on him," *splagchnizomai*, can also be translated as "to be moved in the inward parts." See Annette Merz's contribution in this volume.

A non-naturalistic view on compassion is also defended by Pieter Vos, who argues that compassion should not be seen as a morally indifferent emotion shared indistinctively by every human being, but as a virtue of love, to be developed and cultivated in concrete educational practices. Compassion as a natural thing should sometimes even be mistrusted. Imaginative empathy, as Nussbaum writes, can also be deployed by sadists. Therefore, as she stipulates normatively, "the type of imaginative engagement society needs . . . is nourished by love."[18] Vos agrees with Nussbaum in that respect, but in order to overcome Nietzsche's argument that compassion is rooted in resentment and egoism, he relates compassion out of love firstly to the joy in another's well-being. "Not sadness about unfortunate circumstances as such is the driving force of compassion, but love and joy that unite us with our fellow people."

When compassion is understood within the framework of neighborly love, it becomes a matter of freedom. The hermeneutics of compassion, though informed by the natural sciences, enters the realm of ethics. Compassion is a good thing, but after a moral evaluation not all kinds of compassion are judged as good. From a Christian, ethical point of view, compassion needs to be other-regarding, not solely an expansion of self-love. It should be directed at the concrete alleviation of the other's suffering, not to the raising of someone's self-esteem and feelings of moral superiority.

A distinction should be made between good and bad, weak and strong, false and genuine compassion. St. Augustine was the first to make this distinction in theology. He spoke of malevolent compassion, *malivola benevolentia*, remembering himself watching the suffering of actors in the Roman theaters, wallowing in his own tears. The audience of stage plays enjoys its own pity, though it is aware that it is only *mise-en-scène*.[19] Augustine, however, would not agree with Nietzsche's radical disqualification of all compassion as self-indulgent *Mitleid*. He speaks of a "truer mercy," caused by the suffering hardship of others, but without any pleasure or delight. On the contrary, true compassion is, as the fulfilment of the commandment of neighborly love, directed to eliminate the suffering of the other (Confessions, III.2.2/3). Apparently, compassion needs the discourse of obligation and love as a command in order to be "good."

In the second section, "Retrieving Compassion," contributors delve deeper into the question of the complex nature of compassion in the church's religious traditions. Renée van Riessen questions how contemporary authors Karen Armstrong, Martha Nussbaum, and Roman Krznaric

---

18. Nussbaum, *Political Emotions*, 380.
19. Housset, *L'Intelligence de la Pitié*, 24, referring to Augustine, *Confessiones* 3.3.

present compassion as a natural and politically useful inclination, and *therefore* as good, in an ethical sense. The current philosophical rehabilitation of compassion as a moral emotion after Enlightenment's rationalism occludes what is really happening between persons when they become each other near in suffering. She refers especially to Emmanuel Levinas, who points to the radical strangeness of the other, also and particularly in proximity, in which the taking of responsibility is rooted.

"Being connected to responsibility, the phenomenon of nearness or proximity does not necessarily imply empathy or *Einfühlung*. On the contrary: Levinas seems to argue that experiencing responsibility or ethical engagement *precedes* empathy. It has its origins rather in a shared vulnerability, a being exposed, as beings of flesh and blood to the same condition." Alain Badiou's critique on Levinas touches the heart of the matter: is what compassion means only understandable with the help of Greek philosophical sources, or do we have to listen—with Levinas—to biblical, prophetic sources from Judaism? In the discussion of compassion, a distinction becomes visible between "an ethics of the other that cannot but refer to religion as its last horizon of meaning (as Levinas does), and a more general ethics of otherness that stays within the human being and therefore *refuses* such reference to the religious."

As a biblical scholar, Annette Merz takes up that challenge as she focuses in her contribution on the New Testament narratives about the compassionate Jesus against the background of Hellenistic Judaism and classical Greek thought. Especially in the gospel of Mark an explicit connection is made between the narratives about Jesus' compassion in his public presence and the coming of the Kingdom of God. "The Kingdom of God becomes present . . . where people feel the closeness of God through Jesus' teaching, healing, and an over-abundant communal meal. Compassion is the motive behind Jesus' actions of proclaiming, healing, and inviting people to the table," as Merz summarizes her findings. Characteristic of Jesus' compassionate practice is its aim to create new kinds of community or to restore damaged relationships with the socially excluded. In the gospels of Luke and Matthew, this aspect of Jesus' eschatological mission is emphasized even more. Jesus' programmatic solidarity with the weak can be characterized "as a subversive political strategy: compassion as an antidote against the usual divide and rule."

Len Hansen explores the etymological background of the concept of compassion in the iconography and theology of the late European Middle Ages, since the term "compassion" itself originates in that context. The neologism *com-passio* was coined in order to express how Christian believers, in their affective spirituality, shared the suffering of Christ. Medieval art served as a vehicle for expressing but also teaching this compassion. Hansen writes that the depictions and descriptions of the violence which Christ had to endure "were clearly understood as being formative for spiritual growth and moral education. One of the primary emotions to evoke was compassion. On the one hand, it was to evoke compassion *with* the suffering Christ. However, on the other hand, it was to intensify the consciousness *of* the extent of the compassion of the crucified Christ with sinful humanity that was to be experienced, but also to be imitated." As far as the sharing of Christ's compassion for the sick and the poor, there is no greater example for the medieval believer than Francis of Assisi's embrace of the leper.

But does the sophisticated disentangling of all kinds of compassion in the end lead us anywhere? Is it not a misnomer that compassion is the solution for all of our global woes? Do we really need more compassion for enhancing a global culture of human dignity? The lingering questions in this regard were quite evident in the fact that some of the scholars involved in the two-year research project on "compassion" suggested that we add a question mark. The complexities of "Enacting Compassion" is evident in the third section of the book when three contributions in this volume, centered on the concrete enactment of compassion, show that compassion as such may not be enough of a foundation on which to build a global ethic. Three case studies from our respective countries of South Africa and the Netherlands are presented: an analysis of the political struggle against apartheid in South Africa (Smit); then, after 1994, the development of a democratic society striving for social justice and equality (Bowers Du Toit); and finally the way in which the Protestant Church in the Netherlands is committed in its diaconate to overcome poverty and social exclusion (Noordegraaf). These practical manifestations of compassion (or at least the lack thereof) show the pitfalls of building morality solely on mercy and moral emotions.

As Dirkie Smit writes in his contribution on political theology in this volume, it is one thing to agree with sociologist Zygmunt Bauman that law alone is not sufficient to help us face the challenges of globalization, and that we need compassion; but "to understand what that compassion would and could entail, to imagine the necessary practical implementation, and to find the necessary motivation" is another. He reminds us of how during the years of the struggle against apartheid, especially Reformed church leaders and theologians were deeply skeptic about an exclusive focus on compassion as the essential Christian attitude towards oppression. "For many the struggle was not primarily one of morality, ethics, love, and compassion; in fact, ideals of reconciliation and forgiveness were often seen as personal virtues focused on interpersonal relationships only and therefore regarded with deep skepsis and even rejected out of hand, for example in the case of the influential

Kairos Document, but the struggle was rather about questions of structure and power, of law and justice. Love was to be seen in law; compassion had to show the face of justice." Informed by Calvin's theology of law, they proposed an alternative reading of the parable of the Good Samaritan (Luke 10:25–37). The spontaneous and self-sacrificing act with which the Samaritan cared for one victim in the ditch, abandoned all the others on this dangerous road to their fate. Would he have acted more responsibly if he had approached the local government, influenced public opinion, if necessary organized protest and public support? "Would the better response not have been to employ and strengthen a police force, secure the lonely road, build hospitals to care for victims, raise taxes to help fund all these public services, create jobs for the poor, curb unemployment, improve education, better integrate the robbers into community life and society?" Compassion is not enough; it can make things even make worse, covering up systemic injustice.

As Nadine Bowers Du Toit then points out in her contribution, even in post-apartheid South Africa, compassion continues to have a dubious reputation. "For many years (and still to a large degree today), it is in the mode of compassionate acts of charity that the church in South Africa has largely been operating in response to the challenges of poverty and inequality. However well-meaning this response may be, it is widely recognized that welfare projects which merely attend to the symptoms rather than the root causes of poverty do not and cannot address the nature of systemic disadvantage . . . Compassionate relief is, therefore, not sufficient to engage the complex nature of poverty and inequality, and brings into sharp relief the issue of power (and its intersectionality with race and class) in an unequal and radicalized society." As the South African participants of our two consultations admitted, most of their colleagues in the ministry do not like to preach on Sunday about the Good Samaritan in their congregations, because of the colonial burden its exegesis carries with it. The image of white church ladies visiting poor black children on Sunday afternoon kept looming during our sessions on compassion, even though the work of Martha Nussbaum and others confirm the already deep-rooted conviction, already expressed by John Calvin and elaborated by Dirkie Smit in his contribution on political theology, that a just law needs to be acted out in love. Justice then is what we need, more than compassion!

This certainly seems the case in the southern hemisphere, where most of the people face extreme inequality. But it also applies in more affluent countries in the north, where a neoliberal social order has increasing poverty and social exclusion as its consequence. Herman Noordegraaf points out in his contribution that the diaconal role of the churches in this context includes both: assisting persons in need, and participating in the public debate by raising awareness for social needs and injustice in the churches and society at large. Over centuries, he writes, "the term 'justice' was not used in older church orders; only 'mercy' was taken up as a defining term for *diaconia*. It was only in . . . "the new church order" of the *Nederlands Hervormde Kerk* of 1951 that the concept of justice was used for the first time, referring to the task of the church to remind, if necessary, the government and society to practice according to their calling."

This became clear to our mind during our last consultation in May 2016 in the Netherlands, when the country was faced with thousands of refugees fleeing the civil war in Syria for a safe haven in Europe. Dutch churches are actively involved in the reception of and care for refugees driven out of their countries. We invited some young refugees into our conference to share their stories with us. We experienced a valuable moment of mutual understanding and recognition for the distress they, their families, and their country, went through. But the encounter also induced a feeling of uneasiness: should churches not first and foremost raise political protest against the dictatorial regimes that may be at the origin of these massive migrations? We were reminded again of the words of Dietrich Bonhoeffer that the church should not only "bandage the victims under the wheel, but . . . jam a spoke into the wheel itself."[20] The question mark behind compassion (?) kept intriguing this project until the end, making the participants aware that in their plea for cultivating and enacting compassion they should be well aware of not falling down three traps in which fellow-feeling with the suffering others can result.

Genuine compassion should not be *sentimentalized*. Though it does not go without emotions, it does not depend on them. Victims of injustice are not always touching or moving; they can leave us indifferent because they are too many, or they can even raise disgust. This is why the Bible presents neighborly love as a command, an inescapable obligation even when we do not have any warm feelings for our neighbor.

The second trap is *paternalism*, exemplified in many representations of the Good Samaritan, bowing himself from above over the victim. Genuine compassion does not regard the other as an object of benevolence, does not expect gratitude of the one being cared for. This is why compassion needs justice as equal treatment.

The third pitfall for compassion is *arbitrariness*. Of course, we are attached to our friends, attracted by our partner, and have invested ourselves in our family. Our moral emotions have preferences for people we like in our close neighborhood. The test of genuine compassion therefore is whether it

---

20. Bonhoeffer, "The Church and the Jewish Question," 132.

can be expanded to strangers and—in the radicalization Jesus proposed—even to our enemies. Justice needs warm compassion in order to be loving; but compassion needs cold justice as well in order to be good for all.

However, despite all the complexities and the concerns regarding the act of defining and especially enacting compassion, some of us still believe in the importance of at least trying to foster a greater sense of compassion in individuals and in groups.

Guided by these caveats the fourth section of this volume called "Cultivating Compassion" opens ample space for exemplary practices of compassion. As Nussbaum points out, circles of concern can be expanded by reading, telling, and playing out stories in which compassion is dramatically enacted. The way in which biblical narratives and spiritual works of art inform and fecundate the teachings and liturgy of Christian communities and consequently contribute to the cultivation of compassion is shown by Mirella Klomp, Juliana Claassens, and Charlene van der Walt in their contributions.

As an Old Testament scholar, Juliana Claassens believes that biblical texts are "wonderful tools for forging what Nussbaum calls participatory imagination. Biblical stories, and perhaps specifically the tragic ones, possess the ability to draw the reader in, creating the space for conversation about what is good and what is right. In this encounter between text and context, the individual is bound to look anew not only at the narrative world created in the text, but also at the world in which the reader finds him-/herself." The story told in 1 Samuel 25 about Abigail's hospitality to David, after her husband Nabal refused to feed him and his four hundred men, exemplifies what she means. In a close reading of the story in the context of the violent rivalry between Saul and David, Claassens shows how the gracious act of Abigail not only breaks the circle of violence and revenge between David and Nabal, but also seems to have a transformative effect on the rivalry between David and Saul. The story raises important questions for readers many centuries later: "Can we respond to the history of others with gentleness? Can we receive their life story into our imagination? May we actively seek to cultivate perceptions and capacities of mercy so that we may live and live well?"

Charlene van der Walt proposes a parallel reading of the biblical narrative of the prophet Jeremiah and the 2013 film of Terrence Malick, *To the Wonder*. According to Van der Walt, "the world of these interconnected narratives becomes a safe space for readers to confront complex and painful life realities. In the encounter with the characters, who find themselves to be isolated within the narrative, interpreters may be encouraged to reflect on their own experience of isolation." Compassion shows itself in these narratives only in a negative mode as vulnerability, isolation, the absence of community, a suffering God, expressed in acts of prophetic lament.

As noticed earlier, the very concept of compassion originates in medieval theology and spirituality, where the performance of the passion of Christ served as a model and mirror for the Christian believer (see Len Hansen's contribution). In the Netherlands, the yearly performance of J. S. Bach's Passions in the time before Easter echoes this practice, though in a thoroughly secularized context. In her contribution, Mirella Klomp analyses her own ambivalent experience of attending a contemporary passion play, *Passio-Compassio*: a piece created in 2010 that draws from Johann Sebastian Bach, Oriental Early Christian Songs, as well as Turkish Sufi Songs (i.e., expressions of Islamic mysticism). In a personal theological reflection she asks how to evaluate the move that contemporary artistic expressions of compassion are making when they turn the Christian passion into a passion that transcends Christianity. Her reflection reads like an existential learning process, a trajectory all Christian theologians have to go through, opening themselves up for the global experience of the many and the manifold, building bridges, crossing borders. "'Compassion' is the act of connecting with the suffering other—and in that, by that, and through that, with the love of the suffering Other—reaching out and allowing or even welcoming her/him with their pain into one's own life." Compassion is not a word with a fixed meaning, but it is a practice of discovery.

Perhaps this final sentence is an "answer" to the unresolved question of the why and how of compassion in our world that by the day seems to be in more desperate need of kindness, gentleness, graciousness, empathy, and, yes, compassion. Ultimately, it is up to ordinary men and women to decide, or perhaps even in stronger terms, to be compelled to act in terms of genuine compassion in each and every exceedingly complex and messy situation where human beings are suffering from terrible poverty and injustice.

Bibliography

Anders, Günther. *Die Antiquiertheit des Menschen*. Vol. 1, *Über die Seele im Zeitalter der Zweiten Industriellen Revolution*. Munich: Beck, 1956.

———. *Die Antiquiertheit des Menschen*. Vol. 2, *Über die Zerstörung des Lebens im Zeitalter der Dritten Industriellen Revolution*. Munich: Beck, 1980.

Bonhoeffer, Dietrich. "The Church and the Jewish Question" (1933). In *Testament to Freedom: The Essential Writings of Dietrich Bonhoeffer*, edited by Geffrey B. Kelly, and F. Burton Nelson, 130–33. Rev. ed. New York: HarperCollins, 1995.

Charter for Compassion. https://www.charterforcompassion.org/charter.

Claassens, L. Juliana, and Klaas Spronk, eds. *Fragile Dignity: Intercontextual Conversations on Scriptures, Family, and Violence*. Atlanta: Society of Biblical Literature, 2013.
Compassion in Judaism. http://what-when-how.com/love-in-world-religions/compassion-in-judaism/.
Dalai Lama. *Compassionate Life*. Somerville, MA: Wisdom, 2003.
Hardt, Michael, and Antonio Negri. *Empire*. Cambridge, MA: Harvard University Press, 2000.
Housset, Emmanuel. *L'Intelligence de la Pitié: Phénoménologie de la Communauté*. Paris: Cerf, 2003.
Nussbaum, Martha. "Compassionate Citizenship." Commencement Address, May 16, 2003, on the occasion of receiving an honorary degree. Georgetown University, Washington DC. http://www.humanity.org/voices/commencements/martha-nussbaum-georgetown-university-speech-2003
———. *Political Emotions: Why Love Matters for Justice*. Cambridge, MA: Belknap, 2013.
———. *Upheavals of Thought: The Intelligence of Emotions*. Cambridge: Cambridge University Press, 2001.
Piketty, Thomas. *Capital in the Twenty-First Century*. Translated by Arthur Goldhammer. Cambridge, MA: Belknap, 2014.
Sacks, Jonathan. *The Dignity of Difference: How to Avoid the Clash of Civilizations*. London: Continuum, 2002.
World Communion of Reformed Churches. *Accra Confession*. http://wcrc.ch/accra.

Rethinking Compassion

Affect, Empathy, and Human Dignity?

Considering Compassion at the Intersection of Theology and Science

Dion Forster

Introduction

WHAT DOES IT MEAN to be fully human? This question aims at helping us to understand not only the phenomenon of the human person but also the existential reality of being a person. Because of our social reality, true humanity is nested in the complexity of being a person in relation to other persons. My humanity is tied to the humanity of other persons and theirs is intricately linked to mine. As such, I cannot be fully human without showing care and concern for the full humanity of others—this necessitates compassion.

The purpose of this essay is to engage the subject of the dignity and wholeness of human persons within the ambit of theological ethics. A number of specific conversation partners have been chosen to provide focus and texture to this intersectional theological dialogue. These partners come from two quite different approaches to the study of the dignity of the human person. First, we shall consider some recent contributions from the perspective of Christian humanism. This aspect offers a thick theological consideration of what some traditional and contemporary schools of Christian thought consider important when engaging the topic of true humanity in community. Next, we shall engage with some contemporary contributions to the understanding of what it means to be human from the perspective of cognitive neuroscience. This bourgeoning field of study has a great deal to offer to our understanding of what it means to be human, particularly when one considers the experiences that shape our sense of humanness. How do we experience true humanity within ourselves? How do we experience and express such humanity in relationship with other human persons?

By means of this interdisciplinary conversation it will be shown that both the discourse of Christian humanism and current neuroscientific explorations on the experience of humanness point to the importance of compassion as a critical characteristic to being fully human, even rehumanizing our shared existence. Without a clearly developed theological understanding of what shared humanity means and an intentional choosing for compassionate awareness, we may quickly fall into inhumane, selfish, and abusive patterns that deny the dignity of other persons and so inadvertently deny our own dignity in the process. Gender violence, racial animosity, environmental exploitation, religious hatred, economic abuse, and political manipulation are but a few contemporary examples of failures in compassion that deny our shared dignity and impinge upon our capacity to flourish as human persons.

Toward an Understanding of Human Dignity and the Fullness of Humanity

A first important consideration regards recent theological reflections on the nature and significance of human dignity for a conversation on what it means to be human. In other words, in what ways would one characterize the fullness of humanity—from various perspectives, including a theological perspective? We shall approach aspects of this complex subject from a variety of vantage points that help us to gain some understanding of what the dignity of the human person may entail in relation to shared humanity and compassion.

Nico Koopman problematizes the notion of human dignity when he notes that contemporary approaches to the discourse have tended to draw upon two very different sources in their reasoning and articulation. First, he writes that for Christians the

> Trinitarian faith that Christians confess has a strong human element. This faith has at its heart and core, the flourishing and wellbeing, worth and value, esteem, honour and dignity of all humans—and indeed the whole of creation. Human beings are created in God's image. We are saved by Jesus Christ, and we are renewed by the Holy Spirit. This Trinitarian work in our lives is the deepest source and foundation of our dignity.[1]

---

1. Koopman, "Human Dignity in Africa," 240.

There is a clear direction to the reasoning expressed above—it begins with a belief that the Trinitarian God has a claim upon creation in general (and human persons in particular). This understanding of human dignity moves from a position of conviction (thought or belief) towards action; thereby giving both content and expression to what it means to be truly human and even humane. One could argue that such a view begins with the subjective and works toward objective realities. This movement can also be evidenced in the work of other contemporary Christian theologians who have written on the subject of human dignity.[2] Jürgen Moltmann's eschatological view of reality invites Christians to live in hope. Christians, as bearers of hope in the present world, are to live in anticipation of the fullness of hope that will come for all of humanity and all of creation in the fullness of time.[3] Frits De Lange's notion of the "hermeneutics of dignity" is another example of this movement. The belief in the dignity of the human person, based on the person, claim, and work of God in creation, directs the way in which Christians are to make sense of their daily lives and the world.[4] Naturally, these are just two examples of a myriad of theological approaches to human dignity—but they are nonetheless illustrative of the move from the subjective to the objective, which is common among contemporary theologians who engaged discourses of human dignity.

Koopman next mentions the secular philosophical approach to human dignity, citing the examples of Immanuel Kant and Ronald Dworkin which "are mostly based on human capacities."[5] The human capacities that are most commonly referred to are rationality and creativity. Such an approach posits dignity in the human person in relation to an identifiable, even measurable, aspect of objective reality. The movement of this form of reasoning is thus largely from the objective perspective toward the subjective content of the concept of human dignity.

This theoretical divide between subjective and objective approaches to human dignity remains the source of a great deal of disagreement and debate in academic circles. It is here where an ethical approach to compassion and affect[6] allows for some richer and more textured conversation between

---

2. See the following examples: Moltmann, *On Human Dignity*; Ackermann, *Human Dignity*; De Lange, "Hermeneutics of Dignity"; Sporre, *In Search of Human Dignity*.

3. Moltmann, *Theology of Hope*; Moltmann, *The Living God and the Fullness of Life*; Harvie, *Jürgen Moltmann's Ethics of Hope*; Vorster, "An Ethics of Hope."

4. De Lange, "Hermeneutics of Dignity."

5. Koopman, "Human Dignity in Africa," 240.

6. Within this chapter, "affect" refers to a form of emotional experience by the individual. In psychology, the concept of "affective emotion" is most frequently related to an emotional experience evoked in relation to, or in response to, persons or events;

the religious and philosophical, the subjective and the objective views of full humanity. An approach to human dignity within the ambit of ethics brings the real experience of the human person into focus; in other words, what is the good and the right, for me and for all persons, in our experience? We may not always be able to agree on the theoretical content (or approach) to human dignity; however, we can show, by experience, where our dignity is being threatened.

Wolfgang Huber helps us to understand the possibilities contained in such an approach when he writes, "The concept of human dignity is among the most controversial in the language of ethics and politics. Yet those whose dignity has been disregarded or even trampled on know full well what human dignity means. Its meaning is established by the denial of it."[7]

Koopman extrapolates Huber's contention above by pointing to the work of the Nigerian scholar Wole Soyinka, who "describes this violation of dignity with words like 'anti-humanism' (Soyinka, 2007:xiii), 'reduction in self-esteem' (Soyinka, 2007:6), 'nullification of human status' (Soyinka, 2007:104), 'humiliation' (Soyinka, 2007:104), 'assault on dignity' (Soyinka, 2007:8)."[8] Koopman goes on to speak about the "faces of the violation of human dignity."[9] Thus, what Huber, Koopman, and Soyinka are emphasizing is that we come to understand something of what full humanity, indeed human dignity, is when we witness its denial or minimization in other persons. Stated simply, a shared experience (empathy) of the denial of human dignity can evoke emotional concern for the other (empathy), and this emotion can lead to compassion and even action. Thus, there need not be an agreed set of values or some mutually articulated notion of human dignity for a person to respond compassionately to the suffering or abuse of another.

The use of the language of recognition by Soyinka, and in particular Koopman's use of the notion of the "faces of the violation of human dignity" illustrates the importance of the discourse of compassion in relation to intersectional understandings of human dignity (subjective and objective approaches).

A further important line of thinking that is helpful for our understanding of human dignity comes from the ethicist Emmanuel Levinas, who employs the image of "the face" as that engagement between the self and the

---

Swart et al., "The Impact of Crossgroup Friendships," 311–12. For a powerful example of affective empathy in the South African Truth and Reconciliation Commission, see also Gobodo-Madikizela, "Trauma, Forgiveness and the Witnessing Dance," 170.

7. Huber, *Violence*, 10.

8. Soyinka, *Climate of Fear*, xiii, 6, 104; Koopman, "Human Dignity in Africa," 241.

9. See also Koopman, "Some Theological and Anthropological Perspectives"; and Koopman, "Human Dignity in Africa," 242.

other which not only frames our view of the world, but our very identity as human persons.[10] The emotion (affect) that accompanies the recognition of the absence or denial of human dignity in the other allows for the possibility of the emergence of new language, perhaps even new directions of movement, toward what it means to be fully human. What this suggests is that compassion may in fact be a new language toward the shaping of the fullness of humanity.

In the next section, we shall show that compassion precedes reason and language since it is a prerational emotional state (or process). Our capacity to recognize the humanity (or denial of humanity) in another is not based upon reason or intellect. It stems from a very basic emotional state; indeed, even animals (who do not share in human rationality and reason) have the capacity for compassion.[11] Levinas's ethics of "the face" found its genesis in an act of compassion that was shown to him by a dog named "Bobby" while he was a prisoner in a Nazi concentration camp.[12] He writes of Bobby,

> about halfway through our long captivity, for a few short weeks, before the sentinels chased him away, a wandering dog entered our lives. One day he came to meet this rabble as we returned under guard from work. He survived in some wild patch in the region of the camp. But we called him Bobby, an exotic name, as one does with a cherished dog. He would appear at morning assembly and was waiting for us as we returned, jumping up and down and barking in delight. For him, there was no doubt that we were men.[13]

For Levinas, the recognition of humanity does not primarily require reason or human intellect, but rather it begins with compassion (a recognition of "the face" of the other). He wrote of Bobby,

> [I]n this corner of Germany, where walking through the village we would be looked at by the villagers as *Juden*, this dog evidently took us for human beings ... We were the condemned as the contaminated carriers of germs [by the villagers]. And this little dog welcomed us at the entrance of the camp, barking happily and jumping up and down amicably around us.[14]

---

10. Robbins, *Is It Righteous to Be?*
11. See Panksepp, *Affective Neuroscience*; Panksepp, "At the Interface of the Affective, Behavioral, and Cognitive Neurosciences"; Panksepp, "Affective Consciousness."
12. Levinas, "The Name of a Dog."
13. Levinas, "The Name of a Dog," 153.
14. Robbins, *Is It Righteous to Be?*, 41.

Bobby the dog had recognized his humanity, his "face," as a human person. This compassionate act of recognition was for Levinas an affirmation of his human dignity, even when rational human persons could not recognize it (perhaps even denied it because of their reasoning and intellect). This is an important point to hold onto. What was it that hindered the villagers from acting with compassion? As we shall see in the discussion of the neuroscientific functioning of compassion, it is quite possible that the villagers were suffering from compassion fatigue, or had simply been conditioned not to recognize the suffering and humanity of Levinas and his fellow prisoners. Bobby, on the other hand, was operating from a much more basic emotional state which was not susceptible to social manipulation and political propaganda. Bob Plant sums it up succinctly when he says, "Bobby lacked both the linguistic and cognitive capacities required to 'universalize maxims' . . . Bobby was, in an important sense, 'the only one who recognized' Levinas and his companions 'as men'[sic] . . . While his reactions may indeed be 'primitive,' they nevertheless manifested a certain level of goodness."[15]

Thus, in line with Levinas's reasoning above, when a person encounters another person from the primary perspective of compassion, the theoretical and methodological barriers are superseded in an attempt to move toward full humanity. One is moved to participate with others, regardless of their approach or perspective, because of a shared set of emotions (affect and empathy). Indeed, this could lead to a shared grammar, a new ethical language or perspective, on human dignity that could challenge and even reshape beliefs and practices that deny human dignity.

In this regard, Paul Ricoeur suggests that what is needed for such a process to take place is an act of translation[16] that can bridge the differences in language (or belief) and the very ontological nature of difference between self and other.[17] Kearney, writing in the context of reconciliation with the other, helps us to further understand the possibility that emotion (affect) and compassion have in this process of translation, when he writes that it "is only when we translate our own wounds in the language of strangers and

---

15. Plant, "Welcoming Dogs," 54.

16. "Translation can be understood here in both a specific and a general sense. In the specific sense—the one in common contemporary usage—it signals the work of translating the meanings of one particular language into another. In the more generic sense, it indicates the everyday act of speaking as a way not only of translating oneself (inner to outer, private to public, unconscious to conscious, etc.) but also more explicitly of translating oneself to others"; Kearney, "Introduction," xiv–xv.

17. Ricoeur and Brennan, "Reflections on a New Ethos for Europe," 7. Ricoeur and Brennan write as follows: "The identity of a group, culture, people or nation, is not that of an immutable substance, nor that of a fixed structure, rather, of a recounted story."

retranslate the wounds of strangers into our own language that healing and reconciliation can take place."[18]

Martha Nussbaum shares this perspective in saying, "the ability to imagine the experience of another—a capacity almost all human beings possess in some form—needs to be greatly enhanced and refined if we are to have any hope of sustaining decent institutions across the many divisions that any modern society contains."[19]

In this regard, compassion (as affect or emotion) could illicit shared understandings of human dignity that could move diverse groups of persons toward a shared goal, namely the intention of achieving the fullness and flourishing of humanity. This is where new discoveries in neuroscience may help us to develop greater understanding of the importance of compassion in relation to human dignity.

Cognitive Neuroscience, Compassion, and the Movement toward Human Dignity

Recent developments in contemporary neuroscience offer helpful perspectives in a conversation on compassion and in particular on how this can contribute toward a thicker and more nuanced understanding of human dignity.

Greg Miller suggests that one of the common starting points for scientific enquiry is a "clear definition of the object of study."[20] He notes, however, that recent research by the Center for Compassion and Altruism Research and Education (CCARE) at Stanford University, which includes neuroscientists, philosophers, psychologists, and theologians, concluded that it is very difficult, if not impossible, to come to a scientific definition of compassion. As he writes: "If the participants had chosen, they might have drawn up a Venn diagram of overlapping terms—sympathy, empathy, and altruism, to name a few—preferred by scholars from different disciplines."[21] Indeed, it is unlikely that one would be able to offer a scientific definition of compassion; that does not mean, however, that one cannot gain significant insights on what compassion is, and how it operates, from the natural sciences.

As part of this collaborative research project Paul Ekman, a University of California neuroscientist who specializes in facial expression and body language, indicated that his research shows a strong correlation between observation of the pain of another and the emotion of compassion. This

18. Kearney, "Introduction," xx.
19. Nussbaum, *Not For Profit*, 10.
20. Miller, "A Quest for Compassion," 458.
21. Miller, "A Quest for Compassion," 458.

would seem to resonate with Levinas's notion of "the face" discussed above. In particular he noted "that the sight of suffering causes pain in those who observe it."[22] This aspect of human emotion is best characterized as a form of empathy; i.e., recognizing the pain of another.[23] Tania Singer, a cognitive neuroscientist from the University of Switzerland, shows in her work that one can clearly identify the neurological activity associated with empathic functioning in the human brain.[24] Miller comments that Singer's work shows that "one particular area, the anterior insula, has a key role in empathy." This neural mechanism, however, is just "one facet of compassion, which, by most definitions, requires not just recognizing suffering in others but feeling compelled to do something about it."[25] This is the ethical imperative.

From the perspective of cognitive neuroscience, empathy is that ability within the human person to identify, understand (to some extent at least), and partially feel or experience the suffering of another person—what is known as "the affective states of others"—while still being able to identify that the feeling arose in the other person or persons.[26] Empathy, and ultimately compassion, is thus a neurological state that can be identified in the brain activity of the individual who witnesses the suffering of the other. These neurological states are coupled with associated behaviors. Empathy is coupled with "recognition, understanding, emotional resonance, and empathic concern for another's concerns, distress, pain and suffering."[27] Whereas compassion takes a further step, it moves from the experience of the emotion to action in that it is coupled with "their

---

22. In Miller, "A Quest for Compassion," 459.

23. Of course, the concept of empathy is in itself a contested and complex subject of academic study. There is a growing awareness of the reality that it is unlikely that any person will ever be able to fully understand or experience what another person is experiencing. In truth, most people cannot even fathom the complexity of their own experiences, let alone those of others. At best, we try to reinterpret the witnessed or imagined experience of another in our own cognitive empathetic and affective empathetic terms. See Paolini et al., "Effects of Direct and Indirect Cross-Group Friendships"; Barlow et al., "Rejected!"; Levine and Hogg, Encyclopedia; Swart et al., "The Impact of Grossgroup Friendships"; Goosen, "Comparing Cross-Group and Same-Group Friendships"; Lewis, "A Between-Subjects Comparison of Same-Group and Cross-Group Friendships." Also see the excellent study by Gerhardt, "Why Love Matters" and Williams's unpublished address at the Global Network for Public Theology meetings in Stellenbosch, October 24, 2016, entitled "Ethics, Empathy and Imagination."

24. See Hein and Singer, "I Feel How You Feel"; Lamm and Singer, "The Role of Anterior Insular Cortex"; Klimecki et al., "Functional Neural Plasticity"; Singer and Klimecki, "Empathy and Compassion."

25. Miller, "A Quest for Compassion," 459.

26. Lown, "A Social Neuroscience-Informed Model," 333.

27. Lown, "A Social Neuroscience-Informed Model," 333.

acknowledgement, and motivation and relational action to ameliorate these conditions."[28] Thus, empathy involves feeling *as* another; compassion involves feeling *with* another.

This is an important distinction for cognitive neuroscientists since the subject/object distinction between the suffering person and the empathic person is not always resolved in compassionate action. For example, it is possible that the villagers in Levinas's narrative may have recognized the human suffering that he and his companions faced, yet something prevented them from acting on that recognition of suffering and injustice.

Neuroscientists suggest that the capacity for understanding the emotion of another is hardwired into the brain and it is activated by an imagined shared experience of the pain of another, or by observing their pain, and mentally reconstructing it within one's own mind and experience.[29] In most instances this process is precognitive—in other words, the affective empathetic experience is realized before one can process what it means or where it comes from. The encounter with the other, or the event of the other, elicits an internal psychological reaction. The decision to act on the pain of the other is, however, a cognitive process—it accesses the reasoning centers of the brain and is most often a choice which activates the "dopamine-related reward processing areas in the ventral striatum."[30] However, if the choice to act is not made, or cannot be made, there can be psychological and physical consequences for the self. There are numerous instances in which people witness the suffering of another and experience their pain (through the involuntary activation of the pain-empathy network of the brain in the anterior insula (AI) and medial and anterior cingulate cortex (MCC, ACC)). Yet, they do not have the capacity to act, or the will to act, which would be the natural move from empathy to compassion. This can leave latent feelings of pain, anxiety, stress, and guilt within the observer.

Neuroscientists identify this as the difference between involuntary process of "affective empathy" and the voluntary process of "cognitive empathy."[31] Affect is what we feel in the moment. We have very little control over this. Cognition is how we process or make sense of the feeling. The cognitive process and response is something which we can manage; either in the moment, or by preparing ourselves to respond in a certain manner over time. An example of this is the phenomenon known as "compassion fatigue" suffered by people who are frequently exposed to the unresolvable

28. Lown, "A Social Neuroscience-Informed Model," 333–34.
29. Goetz et al., "Compassion."
30. Lown, "A Social Neuroscience-Informed Model," 334.
31. Lown, "A Social Neuroscience-Informed Model," 334.

suffering and pain of others (such as palliative care nurses and doctors). It can lead to suffering and burnout in the person, or even in the community (such as the hospice) if there are not sufficient resources to move from affective empathy to cognitive empathy.[32] It is worth observing that there is a distinction between the objective reality (the involuntary neurological activity that occurs when observing the pain of another) and the subjective reality (whether one has the capacity, or indeed the will, to move from the experience of pain to the choice, and ultimately the action, to resolve the pain of the other).

Research shows that the activation of the neural networks associated with compassionate action are sensitive to a number of influences. These include "attention, valuation of others, ability to experience and respond to one's own and others' emotions, contextual issues such as repetitive exposure to pain, perspective-taking, self-boundaries and regulation of emotions."[33]

It has been shown that repetitive exposure to the suffering and pain of others not only alters the cognitive capacity for compassion (i.e., the subjective choice to act), but it may even alter the neurophysiology of the brain (i.e., those neurological pathways and areas associated with affective empathy). Such neurobiological change is known as neuroplasticity. There is not yet agreement about the plasticity of the "compassionate brain."[34] What is clear, however, is that there are clear neurological consequences to not making the move from affective empathy to cognitive empathy and compassion. The result is that a number of significant projects have been launched by highly reputable academic institutions, to investigate the importance of "compassion education" as an attempt to rehumanize a world which is suffering from "compassion fatigue."[35]

When one reviews the activities which are undertaken in such projects it is interesting to see that a great deal of empirical evidence about the functioning of the brain is encouraging scientific research into the importance of understanding what it takes to move toward a shared and full humanity. Research shows that acts of service and justice seem to be more common

---

32. Not only individuals can suffer burnout and loss as a result of an inability to move from affective empathy to cognitive empathy. See the recent study by Train, *Compassion in Organizations*, for a detailed empirical study of organizational compassion. See also Madden et al., "Emergent Organizational Capacity for Compassion." Some have argued that whole nations suffer from compassion fatigue due to the normalization of dehumanizing acts such as rape, murder, starvation, and depravation.

33. Lown, "A Social Neuroscience-Informed Model," 334.

34. Hein and Singer, "I Feel How You Feel," 158.

35. See Miller, "A Quest for Compassion"; Klimecki et al., "Functional Neural Plasticity"; Singer and Klimecki, "Empathy and Compassion"; Lown, "A Social Neuroscience-Informed Model."

among persons with religious convictions.[36] This holds great potential for a theological ethics of compassion.

What is important in the context of this essay is that the recognition of the other (and their suffering) is a core aspect of the functioning of the human brain. This seems to concur with the argument presented earlier in this paper that a primary emphasis in discussions of human dignity is the capacity to recognize, identify, and associate with instances where the dignity of human persons is being denied.[37] Moreover, when we experience empathic emotion for the other, we are confronted with the ethical imperative of whether we will choose to act with compassion.

A Plea for an Ethics of Compassion: Some Conclusions on Affect, Empathy, and Human Dignity at the Intersections of Theology and Science

This essay began by asking: what does it mean to be fully human? In particular, the essay wanted to understand what it means to be fully human in relation to other human persons. It was argued that while it is unlikely that any single study will be able to express what such shared human dignity entails, we can be fairly certain that we are able to identify instances in which the dignity of persons is undermined, denied, or threatened. The importance of this experiential locus was considered from the perspectives of theology (particularly in pertaining to a growing interest in theological perspectives on human dignity) and cognitive neuroscience (particularly in relation to studies on the relationship between empathetic experience and compassionate action).

The neuroscientific data shows that we are "wired" to recognize the pain and suffering of others. While we cannot easily change how we feel in the moment of encounter with the suffering other (empathy), we can, over time, learn how to respond in humane, life giving, ethical, and dignified ways, to such persons and situations, as the references to Koopman, Soyinka, and Huber suggested.[38] This is an ethics of compassion. Such an ethics is built on the foundation of a belief that all persons are created in the image of God. From this theological foundation, an ethics of compassion finds embodiment in a new humanity which is characterized by deep and

---

36. See Jack et al., "Why Do You Believe in God?"

37. See Huber, *Violence*, 10; Soyinka, *Climate of Fear*, xiii, 6, 104; Koopman, "Human Dignity in Africa," 241.

38. See Huber, *Violence*, 10; Soyinka, *Climate of Fear*, xiii, 6, 104; Koopman, "Human Dignity in Africa," 241.

significant solidarity.[39] It recognizes where true humanity is under threat through the social, political, religious, and economic forces of dehumanization which operate in contemporary societies (as suggested by Huber, Koopman, and Soyinka). Finally, the ethics of compassion recognizes that in the light of recent discoveries in neuroscience, a concerted effort needs to be made to turn empathetic concern (affect for the other) into compassionate action. This process should be more than just the isolated actions of individuals; it should find expression in communities, policies, and whole societies that are characterized by compassion. Processes such as envisioning the flourishing of others, imagining solutions to complex social and economic problems, envisioning alternative realities or solutions, and acts of care and service, need to be established in order to facilitate the development of compassionate brains, compassionate persons, compassionate communities, and ultimately compassionate societies.[40]

De Lange beautifully sums up this possibility when he writes: "A shared acknowledgement of the vulnerability of being human and the dependency on others' care may invite us to a mutual recognition of goodness amidst suffering."[41]

Persons, communities, and societies that are shaped by an ethics of compassion, can indeed contribute towards the re-humanization of society.[42] What is required is the rediscovery of the importance and dignity of the human person in Christian theology—as was common in the ancient tradition, which is being reignited in discourses of Christian humanism. Such a theological framework, when considered from the vantage point of insights gained on human experience, in relation to empathy and compassion in cognitive neuroscience, could help both individuals and communities to understand the importance of acting ethically for the common good when confronted by suffering.

Bibliography

Ackermann, Laurie. *Human Dignity: Lodestar for Equality in South Africa*. Cape Town: Juta, 2012.

Barlow, Fiona Kate, et al. "Rejected! Cognitions of Rejection and Intergroup Anxiety as Mediators of the Impact of Cross-Group Friendships on Prejudice." *British Journal of Social Psychology* 48 (2009) 389–405.

39. De Gruchy, "Humanism, Religion and the Renewal of Culture." Please also see Claassens's development of a theology of compassion as an act of solidarity with the pain of another, in Claassens, "'Give Us a Portion.'"

40. Lown, "A Social Neuroscience-Informed Model," 338–41.

41. De Lange, "Hermeneutics of Dignity," 25.

42. Huber, *Violence*; Koopman, "Human Dignity in Africa."

Claassens, Juliana. "'Give Us a Portion among Our Father's Brothers:' The Daughters of Zelophedad, Land, and the Quest for Human Dignity." *Journal for the Study of the Old Testament* 37 (2013) 319–37.

De Gruchy, John W. "Humanism, Religion and the Renewal of Culture: A Review." *Modern Theology* 31 (2015) 195–200.

De Lange, Frits. "Hermeneutics of Dignity." In *Fragile Dignity: Intercontextual Conversations on Scriptures, Family, and Violence*, edited by L. Juliana Claassens, and Frits de Lange, 29–39. Atlanta: Society of Biblical Literature, 2013.

Gerhardt, Sue. "Why Love Matters: How Affection Shapes a Baby's Brain." *Infant Observation* 9 (2006) 305–9.

Gobodo-Madikizela, Pumla. "Trauma, Forgiveness and the Witnessing Dance: Making Public Spaces Intimate." *Journal of Analytical Psychology* 53 (2008) 169–88.

Goetz, Jennifer L., Dacher Keltner, and Emiliana Simon-Thomas. "Compassion: An Evolutionary Analysis and Empirical Review." *Psychological Bulletin* 136 (2010) 351–74.

Goosen, Anneke. "Comparing Cross-Group and Same-Group Friendships amongst White South African Students at Stellenbosch University." Master's thesis, Stellenbosch University, 2011. https://scholar.sun.ac.za/handle/10019.1/6735.

Harvie, Timothy. *Jürgen Moltmann's Ethics of Hope: Eschatological Possibilities for Moral Action*. Farnham, UK: Ashgate, 2009.

Hein, Grit, and Tania Singer. "I Feel How You Feel But Not Always: The Empathic Brain and Its Modulation." *Current Opinion in Neurobiology* 18 (2008) 153–58.

Huber, Wolfgang. *Violence: The Unrelenting Assault on Human Dignity*. Minneapolis: Fortress, 1996.

Jack, Anthony Ian, et al. "Why Do You Believe in God? Relationships Between Religious Belief, Analytic Thinking, Mentalizing and Moral Concern." PLOS ONE 11 (2016) e0149989.

Kearney, Richard. "Introduction: Ricoeur's Philosophy of Translation." In *On Translation*, by Paul Ricoeur, translated by Eileen Brennan, vii–xx. New York: Routledge, 2006.

Klimecki, Olga M., et al. "Functional Neural Plasticity and Associated Changes in Positive Affect After Compassion Training." *Cerebral Cortex* 23 (2013) 1552–61.

Koopman, Nico. "Human Dignity in Africa: A Christological Approach." *Scriptura* 104 (2010) 240–49.

———. "Some Theological and Anthropological Perspectives on Human Dignity and Human Rights." *Scriptura* 95 (2007) 177–85.

Lamm, Claus, and Tania Singer. "The Role of Anterior Insular Cortex in Social Emotions." *Brain Structure and Function* 214 (2010) 579–91.

Levinas, Emmanuel. "The Name of a Dog, or Natural Rights." In *Difficult Freedom: Essays on Judaism*, by Levinas Emmanuel, translated by Seán Hand, 151–53. Baltimore: Johns Hopkins University, 1990.

Levine, John M., and Michael A. Hogg, eds. *Encyclopedia of Group Processes and Intergroup Relations*. Thousand Oaks, CA: SAGE, 2009.

Lewis, Cindy Lisa. "A Between-Subjects Comparison of Same-Group and Cross-Group Friendships amongst Coloured South African Students at Stellenbosch University." Master's thesis, Stellenbosch University, 2014. https://scholar.sun.ac.za/handle/10019.1/86223.

Lown, Beth A. "A Social Neuroscience-Informed Model for Teaching and Practising Compassion in Health Care." *Medical Education* 50 (2016) 332–42.

Madden, Laura T., et al. "Emergent Organizational Capacity for Compassion." *Academy of Management Review* 37 (2012) 689–708.

Miller, Greg. "A Quest for Compassion." *Science* 324, no. 5926 (2009) 456–59.

Moltmann, Jürgen. *On Human Dignity: Political Theology and Ethics*. Minneapolis; Fortress, 2007.

———. *The Living God and the Fullness of Life*. Louisville: Westminster John Knox, 2015.

———. *Theology of Hope*. 1st Fortress Press ed. Philadelphia: Fortress, 1993.

Nussbaum, Martha C. *Not For Profit: Why Democracy Needs the Humanities*. Princeton: Princeton University Press, 2010.

Panksepp, Jaak. "Affective Consciousness: Core Emotional Feelings in Animals and Humans." *Consciousness and Cognition* 14 (2005) 30–80.

———. *Affective Neuroscience: The Foundations of Human and Animal Emotions*. New York: Oxford University Press, 1998.

———. "At the Interface of the Affective, Behavioral, and Cognitive Neurosciences: Decoding the Emotional Feelings of the Brain." *Brain and Cognition* 52 (2003) 4–14.

Paolini, Stefania, et al. "Effects of Direct and Indirect Cross-Group Friendships on Judgments of Catholics and Protestants in Northern Ireland: The Mediating Role of an Anxiety-Reduction Mechanism." *Personality and Social Psychology Bulletin* 30 (2004) 770–86.

Plant, Bob. "Welcoming Dogs: Levinas and 'the Animal' Question." *Philosophy and Social Criticism* 37 (2011) 49–71.

Ricoeur, Paul, and Eileen Brennan. "Reflections on a New Ethos for Europe." *Philosophy and Social Criticism* 21 (1995) 3–13.

Robbins, Jill, ed. *Is It Righteous to Be? Interviews with Emmanuel Levinas*. Stanford, CA: Stanford University Press, 2001.

Singer, Tania, and Olga M. Klimecki. "Empathy and Compassion." *Current Biology* 24 (2014) 875–78.

Soyinka, Wole. *Climate of Fear: The Quest for Dignity in a Dehumanized World*. New York: Random House, 2007.

Sporre, Karin. *In Search of Human Dignity: Essays in Theology, Ethics and Education*. Münster: Waxmann, 2015.

Swart, Hermann, et al. "The Impact of Crossgroup Friendships in South Africa: Affective Mediators and Multigroup Comparisons." *Journal of Social Issues* 66 (2010) 309–33.

Train, Katherine Judith. "Compassion in Organizations: Sensemaking and Embodied Experience in Emergent Relational Capability. A Phenomenological Study in South African Service Organizations." PhD diss., University of Cape Town, 2015.

Vorster, J. M. "An Ethics of Hope for Moral Renewal in South Africa." *Journal of Theology for Southern Africa* 140 (2011) 4–19.

Williams, Rowan. "Ethics, Empathy and Imagination." In *Global Network for Public Theology*, 1–43. Stellenbosch: Unpublished, "Tanner Lectures," 2016.

The Event of Compassion

Frits de Lange

THIS ESSAY IS ABOUT ethics and compassion. I do not want to look here at compassion from the perspective of ethics, but conversely, I want to question ethics from the perspective of compassion. My aim, therefore, is not to offer a definition of compassion, enter into a conceptual analysis, and relate compassion to emotions like sympathy and empathy, or principles like altruism and benevolence, neighborly love and mercy. Nor do I want to discuss the normative status of compassion by answering questions such as: Is compassion—as recently defended by Karen Armstrong and others—a new paradigm of doing ethics altogether? Or is compassion a particular moral emotion to be subjected to the rational guidance of the moral law and the principle of obligation, as the Kantian tradition in ethics will uphold? Does compassion really represent a virtue, but one that has to be balanced with others like justice?

These are all relevant questions; however, ones that I will leave aside for the purpose of this essay. Instead of situating compassion somewhere within ethical theory, I rather seek to question the ethical enterprise as a whole from the perspective of compassion. More precisely, my argument is that the event of compassion deconstructs the "ethical subject" as the center of moral agency, i.e., the presupposition of most of the modern ethical theory. I suggest that in ethics, we, as moral subjects, do not know who we are. And *that* is exactly who we are.[1] Instead of defining more precisely our moral identity, ethics benefits of its unsettlement. Precisely in order to become perhaps better people living better lives, we need a negative, apophatic moral anthropology.

In the first part of this essay, I will approach compassion not as an ethical concept, or a moral emotion, virtue or principle, but as a *phenomenon* that,

---

1. Caputo, *More Radical Hermeneutics*, 17–41; Caputo, *On Religion*, 18.

if taken seriously, precludes the possibility of speaking about moral agents as closed subjects, centers of interior reflection on their outward behavior.

In the second part of this essay, I illustrate this perspective with a reading of the biblical parable of the Good Samaritan that is one of the most powerful stories ever told on the subject of compassion. This parable is, though, not to be read as a straightforward appeal to selfless neighborly love. It rather shows that moral identities are fluent, just as the different perspectives characters can have in one and the same story are not fixed. Compassion then should not be considered as the characteristic virtue of a good person, an individual moral capacity, but as an event that overcomes anyone who does not close him-/herself to the risk of being altered by the joy or the suffering of others.

"The Fellowship of Those Who Bear the Mark of Pain" (Albert Schweitzer)

In Albert Camus's novel *The Fall*, the former judge Jean-Baptiste Clamence ironically describes his own "virtuous benevolence:" We immediately recognize the kind of *Mitleid* Nietzsche criticized as Christian slave morality; the exaltation of oneself by humiliating the other:

> I enjoyed that part of my nature which reacted so appropriately to the widow and orphan that eventually, through exercise, it came to dominate my whole life. For instance, I loved to help blind people cross streets. From as far away as I could see a cane hesitating on the edge of a sidewalk, I would rush forward, sometimes only a second ahead of another charitable hand already outstretched, snatch the blind person from any solicitude but mine, and lead him gently but firmly along the crosswalk among the traffic obstacles toward the refuge of the other sidewalk, where we would separate with a mutual emotion. In the same way, I always enjoyed giving directions in the street, obliging with a light, lending a hand to heavy pushcarts, pushing a stranded car, buying a paper from the Salvation Army lass or flowers from the old peddler, though I knew she stole them from the Montparnasse cemetery. I also liked—and this is harder to say—I liked to give alms. A very Christian friend of mine admitted that one's initial feeling on seeing a beggar approach one's house is unpleasant. Well, with me it was worse: I used to exult ... If I had the luck, certain mornings, to give up my seat in the bus or subway to someone who obviously deserved it, to pick up some object an old lady had dropped and return it to her with a

smile I knew well, or merely to forfeit my taxi to someone in a greater hurry than I, it was a red-letter day.[2]

Clamence revels in his joy that the other's sufferings are not his own; that is why he wants to be as close as possible to them. He cites the example of the people St. Augustine watched in the Roman theaters, wallowing in their own tears. In this instance, the audience is enjoying its own pity. Augustine calls this example of pitying others' suffering, "malevolent compassion" (*malivola benevolentia*).[3] The judge, helping blind people crossing streets, stayed imprisoned within his own imagination. He intended not to overcome the aversion to another's suffering but to rather to intensify it. As Clamence exclaims, "Oh, how he suffers terribly in his distress, I am so glad I am not the dupe!" The act of *Mitleid* toward the blind man helped him to distance himself from his fate and keep his ordered world intact. *Mitleid* became part of his "terror management strategy."

Camus's story, however, does not lead us to an elimination of the very notion of compassion; it rather invites to join the philosopher Emmanuel Housset's fundamental distinction between a "weak" (also in the moral, Nietzschean, sense) and a "strong" version of compassion.

The moment the judge is affected by the fate of a woman, jumping/falling into the river Seine while he is crossing the bridge at night, he is taken into a life-changing event. He now knows what genuine, strong compassion entails—though he does not surrender to the power of what is happening to him.

For even though he heard the woman screams, he decides to continue on his road. That—in his own eyes—unforgivable moment will affect him for the rest of his life, making it impossible to continue his professional life as a judge ironically named "Clamence"[4] (but what's in a name?). The call of strong compassion that he experienced entails that one runs the risk of being changed into another person by participating in someone else's distress.[5] Invaded by the other's suffering presence, one does not stay unaltered, even if one refuses to act upon it.

In strong compassion, this movement of decentering and dispossession is essential. Compassion, therefore, is an ecstatic ontological event that shakes the very ground of our being; it is not an individual virtuous attitude, a moral feature we have or do not have. We cannot stay within ourselves but are turned inside out, sharing physically the other's weal and woe (consider

---

2. Camus, *The Fall*, 20–21.
3. Housset, *L'Intelligence de la Pitié*, 24, referring to Augustine, *Confessiones* 3.3.
4. In French, "clémence" means "leniency."
5. Housset, *L'Intelligence de la Pitié*, 169–70.

the meaning of the New Testament Greek verb σπλαγχνίζομαι [*splagchnizomai*]: "to be moved in the inward parts").[6]

At the end of the novel, Clamence confesses that he sometimes wishes that the young woman would jump a second time from the bridge, so that they "both could be saved." Compassion is not an arbitrary act that you can decide upon; it is a matter of life and death, part of your survival as a moral person.

Aristotle defined compassion as "a painful emotion directed at another person's misfortune or suffering."[7] Compassion is sorrow *for* and *with* the other, or as Augustine puts it in one place, "on behalf of" the other (*City of God* XIV, 9). These classical definitions of the experience of compassion are closer to Camus's narrative than to the concept of rational ethical subjectivity as presupposed by modern moral philosophy: an individual subject separated from his/her world, reflecting on the experience of the other as an object. Shall I *decide* to help the other in her distress or not? What are the *options* and which one shall I *choose*, and on which rational *grounds*? This is an instance of moral experience, rephrased in terms of the ethical laboratory. The modern supposition of a subject-object distinction, once adopted by ethical theory, is a methodological reduction that proved to be quite helpful in the realm of natural science and technology, but turns out to be disastrous when it comes to moral philosophy.[8] Modern ethics, however, introduced also the moral agent as a reflexive self-conscious subject, ontologically separated from others with whom he or she maintains moral relationships. Morality is an act of bridging the gap between two separated moral worlds: the world of the other and the world of the self.

The construction of the modern concept of altruism can illustrate this subject-object dichotomy in ethics. "Altruism," as coined by August Comte in 1851, is built upon the presupposition of the reflexive agency of a morally isolated individual. Altruistic "selflessness" does not presuppose a vulnerable self, assaulted by the distress of others, but is the virtuous acknowledgment of a subject's moral obligation to renounce self-interest, for the sake of society.[9]

---

6. See Annette Merz's contribution in this volume for its etymology.
7. Quoted by Nussbaum, *Upheavals of Thought*, 306.
8. See Wyschogrod, *Saints and Postmodernism*.
9. The word "altruism" (French *altruisme,* from *autrui:* "other people," derived from Latin *alter:* "other") was coined by Auguste Comte, the French founder of positivism, in order to describe the ethical doctrine he supported. In his *Catéchisme Positiviste* (1852) Comte says that altruism, "the definitive formula of human morality, gives a direct sanction exclusively to our instincts of benevolence, the common source of happiness and duty. [Man must serve] humanity, whose we are entirely"; *New World Encyclopedia*.

What manifests itself in the event of compassion, however, reflects the experience of being physically invaded by the other's suffering, without being able to separate exactly what are one's feelings and what are his or hers. There is a commonality of suffering there, "a Fellowship of those who bear the Mark of Pain,"[10] an experience of open personhood that precedes reflection. Crossing the bridge, hearing the woman's scream, and then refusing to run the risk of being transformed, Judge Clamence cannot come to grips with that event in terms of a moral subject taking a rational decision.

Perhaps only a phenomenological approach can come near to an understanding of the experience of compassion. Being human, as phenomenology upholds in its resistance to naturalistic reductionism, is to be understood as being-in-the world ("*In-der-Welt-sein*," Heidegger). We always find ourselves in our pre-reflexive embodiment open and attuned (in a certain "*Stimmung*") to the world. We cannot experience ourselves otherwise than intentionally, addressed by the world's otherness, to which we respond in transcending our selves. Being human is to be "invaded" by the world, and at the same time, to be eccentrically orientated toward otherness.

Strong Compassion: The Decision to Stay

Taking up this line of thinking outlined above, the French phenomenologist Emmanuel Housset holds that the event of compassion proves that our moral selves are always unsettled, taken, even haunted by others. Our identity is deeply affected and marked by alterity. In our utmost inwardness dwells the other. An isolated interiority, the self as an inner castle, is a modern illusion. In ethics, there is no direct perception of the self by the self. The other as a unique, concrete, and irreplaceable person is not a morally intended *object*, but enters my consciousness even before I can say "I."

In the event of compassion this original receptivity manifests itself in the heart of my interiority.[11] Compassion, as the capacity of human beings to receive the suffering or the joy of the other, points at an original commonality that *precedes the distinction between "I" and "Thou."*

This commonality, which also precedes "intersubjectivity," can thus be understood as the emotional common ground between two individuals.

10. "The Fellowship of those who bear the Mark of Pain. Who are the members of this Fellowship? Those who have learned by experience what physical pain and bodily anguish mean, belong together all the world over; they are united by a secret bond"; Schweitzer, *On the Edge*, 173–74.

11. The concept of "altruism" does not capture the experience, but is just an egoism upside down in its presupposition of a privileged ego. See also Housset, *L'intériorité d'Exil*, 317.

In modern philosophy, not only thoughts but also social emotions are presented as reflexive, before they become shared. In his *Theory of Sentiments* (1759), Adam Smith presents sympathy, or as he calls it, "fellow-feeling," as a sentiment of observers who put themselves by a voluntary imaginary act in the place of another person, asking themselves how they would have reacted if the other's circumstances were their own. The phenomenon of compassion, however, reveals the *transitivity* of sensibility. The other is present *in* the self's interiority with his or her otherness.

In Housset's view, pity ("*pitié*") is not an individual moral feeling, but the most fundamental ontological category. Compassion is more a "*Stimmung*" (Heidegger) than an emotion. It is how we are "thrown into life," to use a Heideggerian term once more. The experience of pity precedes our thinking and our feeling; our passivity precedes our reflexivity.[12] Pity is an "original affection," Housset writes, as the French "la pitié est là"[13] expresses the notion that it is there before it comes to mind. The other's distress appeals to us unconditionally; the act of pity is experienced as an obligation even before we make any decision to think, feel, or act compassionately—and have pity. Ethics, therefore, does not start with an isolated thinking person making moral decisions, but with this primordial commonality of one another's suffering or joy.[14]

In this regard, Nietzsche's heavy critique at—what has to be called "weak"—compassion as a "Christian virtue" becomes only understandable in the light of his unmasking of the illusion of modern subjectivity. Nietzsche was right: there is no such thing as a stable rational self that can decide to share—or not—in the sufferings and joys of others. Instead, we are not the master of ourselves when we are affected by the presence of others in our deepest interiority.

The event of strong compassion undermines the idea that there is a substance called "self," which magnifies itself in being there even and also for others. Compassion creates a "we" that precedes the "I." The suffering of the other comes to inhabit one's interiority.

---

12. Housset here follows the basic intuition of Jean-Jacques Rousseau in his *Discourse on Inequality* (1754). Compassion is not an activity, originating in an isolated individual, taking a decision to care for someone; it is an elementary, pre-reflective kind of attention for the other. "It is this compassion . . . that hurries us without reflection to the relief of those who are in distress: it is this which in a state of nature supplies the place of laws, morals and virtues"; Rousseau, *Discourse*, part I.

13. Housset, *Pitié*, 66–67.

14. Housset, *Pitié*, 16.

Perhaps human beings share this experience of commonality with other animals—the warm, indistinctive feeling of belonging to the same herd.[15] Compassion, however, only becomes human when this interiority reveals itself as a responsible self that answers the call of the other. Strong human compassion also withstands the abhorrence that humans share with other animals: the urge to flee the scene of suffering. A compassionate person decides to *join* the distressed in a shared struggle *against* his or her pain.[16]

Paul Ricoeur, in a text written during and after the sickbed of his wife and published posthumously, rightly defines his experience of compassion "not as a moaning-with, as pity, commiseration, figures of regret, it is a struggling-with, an accompanying."[17] In the *decision to stay* and not to flee, a decision often taken pre-reflexively with the body,[18] the "we" of common suffering transforms itself into a responsible "I" taking care of a unique, irreplaceable "Thou." "Moi voici," "here I am," is the place of birth of the ethical self. "It is *you*, and no one else, who should stay with me," the call summons. Suffering binds us together in a primordial commonality, but suffering also individualizes, in making our presence irreplaceable.

Nietzsche then was wrong in suggesting a false alternative between the modern illusion of subjectivity and a postmodern, ethical choice for the power of anonymous instincts. Continuing this line of thought: fellow-feeling only points at a sub-human event—the affective contagion of warm-blooded bodies in a herd. Only the survival of the tribe's selfish genes would be its evolutionary goal. Strong compassion, however, a reality he would not acknowledge, does not abolish the distinctiveness between I and Thou, but—as Emmanuel Levinas continually showed—constitutes a person in his/her moral subjectivity.

Risky Reading: The Parable of the Good Samaritan

The parable of the Good Samaritan (Luke 10:25–38) informed and shaped Christian ethics throughout the ages. The Samaritan is often represented as the neighbor *par excellence*. He is the Christian moral hero, exemplifying virtuous Christian behavior. In this second part of the essay, I will read

15. As elaborated, for example, in the work of the French sociologist Michel Maffesoli. See, among others, his *Le Temps des Tribus*.

16. Rousseau showed to have a sharp phenomenological eye when he defined *pity* (in his *A Dissertation on the Origin and Foundation of the Inequality of Mankind* [1755]) as "an innate repugnance at seeing a fellow-creature suffer."

17. Ricoeur, *Living Up to Death*, 17.

18. We should "depsychologize" compassion, Housset writes in *L'Intériorité de l'Exil*, 320.

the parable of The Good Samaritan (Luke 10:25-38) differently—not as an "example story" ("*Beispielserzählung*")[19] about the virtue of compassionate behavior, but as a narrative which shows how the event of compassion destabilizes fixed moral identities. The parable reads as the story of the deconstruction of ethical subjectivity, the biblical counterpart of Camus's *The Fall*. The two stories differ, not because the Samaritan is a hero and Judge Clamence is not. The difference between the two is that the Samaritan could not resist; he was lured into, and eventually consented in letting himself been overridden by the event of compassion.

In reading the Bible one runs the risk of letting oneself to be altered. In that sense, reading the story of the Good Samaritan can be dangerous for our moral stability. It may create an openness that prepares oneself for being taken by the event of compassion.

We are essentially open to the world, as phenomenology puts it. That means also that we live in and by stories, written and orally. We are always entangled in stories ("*in Geschichten verstrickt*," Wilhelm Schapp).[20] In literary criticism, the so-called reception theory or reader response theory, originating from the work of Hans-Robert Jauss (1921–1997) and Wolfgang Iser (1926–2007), shows how the act of reading is part of our ongoing identity construction. Identities are never fixed; our interiority is never closed. We do not have an interior center. The moment our imagination is captured by something else, we are no longer present, coinciding with ourselves. We are essentially eccentric, as Iser puts it, following Helmut Plessner.

In reading or listening to a story, we are postponing for the time being who we are, and dwell in our imagination with its characters, identify with the roles they are playing, and with what occurs to them. We become, for a moment, participants in their lives. As the story moves on, the reader's imagination cannot dwell in one place. He or she is taken from one point to another, shifting from one "identification" to another. In taking the perspective of the next character, the perspective of the preceding character moves to the background, becoming the subsequent character's horizon. There is no bird's eye perspective in a story. Neither a single perspective can represent a text's meaning or intention, nor can a fixed identity ensure

---

19. As, for example, in Recitative B in Bach's Cantate 164 (*Ihr, die Ihr Euch von Christo Nennet*): "We hear, indeed, what Love itself says:/ Whoever embraces his neighbor with mercy,/ shall receive mercy as his judgment./ However, we heed this not at all!/ Still our neighbor's sighs can be heard!/ He knocks at our heart; it is not opened!/ We observe him, indeed, wringing his hands,/ his eyes, flowing with tears;/ yet our heart resists the urge to love./ The priest and Levite, that walk to one side,/are truly a picture of loveless Christians;/ they behave as if they knew nothing of another's misery,/ they pour neither oil nor wine/ upon their neighbor's wounds."

20. Schapp, *In Geschichten Verstrickt*.

that a story can be fully comprehended. A good text moves, upsets, abhors, and fills us with joy, feelings of intense recognition, or estrangement. All our aesthetic faculties (literally αἴσθησις: "perception from the senses") are touched in the event of reading. Sometimes we end up as someone quite different from who we were before. The act of reading made us into a different person, though we cannot exactly say in what sense we were changed. In the tradition of literary theory, the transformative power of reading has always been acknowledged. Aristotle spoke of *catharsis*, purification or purgation, to describe what might happen in and to the spectator of a tragedy. In medieval Christianity, where tragedies were replaced by passion plays in which the passion of Christ and the saints was performed, one spoke of *compassio*, which then would lead to an *imitatio Christi*.

Many texts may leave their readers indifferent. What makes a text into a transformative text? According to Iser, this only can happen when texts are so organized that their structure leave a "blank" ("*Leerstelle*") for the reader's imaginative play of identification. A good text presumes and allows space for an "implicit reader." The meaning of a text then, in reception theory, is the result of what Iser calls a "passive synthesis," a synthetic activity of the reader, who lets himself or herself be drawn into a reading event which he or she did not control. By the very act of reading, something unforeseeable occurs to the reader.[21] Therefore the essential question in literary hermeneutics is not "what does the story mean?" but: "What happened to the reader after reading it?"

Stories can change people's identity. They can function as an event. How does this happen? It is difficult to say. Stories' meaning are no simple "messages," to be understood and followed like a prescript. The lawyer, after hearing the parable of the Good Samaritan, did not receive clear instructions on how to act, though he received a hint: "Go and do likewise" (Luke 10:37).

The parable of the Good Samaritan is often read as Jesus' illustration of the preceding double love command in the form of a narrative.[22] From Early Christianity onward until the Reformation, this parable has also been interpreted as an allegorical imagination of salvation history (Origen), of the relationship between Jews and Christians (Ambrose), of the relationship between Law and Gospel (Luther), of the grace of Christ (Calvin, who identified the Samaritan with Christ). First comes the moral principle, and then the example story follows. First the ethical discourse, then casuistry. Jesus employed the parable genre, as the New Testament scholar Adolf Jülicher

21. "Durch das was der Leser bewirkt, geschieht ihm auch immer etwas"; Iser, *Der Akt des Lesens*, 44.

22. See Monselewski, *Der Barmherzige Samariter*; and Klemm, *Das Gleichnis vom Barmherziger Samariter*. For a recent overview, see Zimmermann, *Puzzling the Parables*.

wrote, "because he thought that this form was well fit for enlarging the clarity and compelling force of his thoughts."[23]

But perhaps Jesus' choice for the genre of narrative is not to be considered as a pedagogical tool, but as a deliberate paradigm clash, introducing the revolutionary way of doing ethics in the Kingdom of God. Jesus does not go along with the lawyer, who was asking for a discourse in which he, as an ethical subject, could stay unaltered by putting forward the question of who his neighbor is. He did not want to be changed; he only wanted to be informed. The transforming power of Jesus' appeal to him lies in the invitation to submit himself to the story; to let himself be invaded by the story. Seen from this perspective, the double love command is just an abstract condensation of the transforming power of the story, instead of the other way around—the story and illustration of the command. What is Christian ethics else than the enduring readiness to undergo the moral impact of Jesus' narratives?[24]

The Parable as Kingdom Metaphor (Crossan and Funk)

The New Testament scholar John Dominican Crossan writes that the event character of the reign of God is reflected in the language event of the parables.[25] Jesus therefore preached the coming of the Kingdom of God by means of parables which overtake listeners by their subversive power. As soon as you hear "The Kingdom of God is like. . ."—you are taken away from where you are. Crossan considers the Good Samaritan as a "parable of reversal" in

---

23. "(W)eil er fand, wie diese Form vorzüglich geeignet war, die Deutlichkeit und Überzeugungskraft seiner Gedanken zu überhöhen"; Jülicher, *Die Gleichnisreden*, 146.

24. Why did Augustine leave Stoic and eudaemonist philosophy behind? Nicholas Wolterstorff suggests: not because he was convinced by philosophical argument, but because he was reading the Bible intensely. "Augustine's ever deeper immersion in Scripture, from the time of his conversion onward, brought him to the conclusion that our tendency to worry over the physical and mental well-being of family and friends, to weep at funerals for the loss of companionship, and the like is not to be ascribed to our fallenness, but to our created human nature. God made us thus"; Wolterstorff, *Justice*, 199.

25. Crossan, *In Parables*, 21. A parable is "a metaphor of normalcy which intends to create participation in its referent . . . It talks of A so that one can participate in B, or, more accurately, it talks of x so that one can participate in X and so understand the validity of x itself. Its structural pattern is X-in-x"; Crossan, *In Parables*, 15–16. Jesus' parables are metaphors in a fundamental, ontological sense; not an allegorical illustration of a truth from elsewhere. They create a metaphor "in which participation precedes information so the function of the metaphor is to create participation in the metaphor's referent"; Crossan, *In Parables*, 14.

which our common understanding of good and bad literally is revolutionized and turned upside down: the Samaritan, for the Israelite reader a despicable enemy, turns out to be the good guy, the clerical guardians of the moral order on the other hand, the Priest and Levite, are made to look ridiculous. This, obviously, is the way in which God is coming. As Crossan writes, "The hearer struggling with the contradictory dualism Good/Samaritan is actually experiencing in and through this the inbreaking of the Kingdom."[26]

In the "language event" of the parable, the stable moral identity of the reader undergoes a breakdown. In a more (post)modern vocabulary: the ethical subject is deconstructed and unmasked as an illusion. The story, however, ends positively, by showing how the reader can open himself or herself to the event of compassion, in which the presence of the coming God is incarnated in flesh and blood.

In the story, the implicit reader (Iser) is taken, for the duration of the reading, on a fictitious journey from Jerusalem to Jericho. The story in which the reader is going to participate is relatively simple: four characters (victim, priest, Levite, Samaritan), one plot line (the assistance (or lack of assistance) offered to the Samaritan after the robbery), and—depending on whether one decides to also take the framing dialogue between Jesus and the lawyer into the reading[27]—a narrator (Jesus). The poetic structure of the parable is clear and uncomplicated. Following an Aristotelian tradition, it can be divided into five short "episodes" or "unities of thought," distinguishable according to their content and style.[28]

I
A man was going down from Jerusalem to Jericho, and fell into the hands of robbers, who stripped him, beat him, and went away, leaving him half dead.

II
Now by chance a priest was going down that road; and when he saw him, he passed by on the other side.

III
So likewise a Levite, when he came to the place and saw him, passed by on the other side.

---

26. Crossan, *In Parables*, 56.

27. Crossan defends "the thesis . . . that the present context of the Good Samaritan parable in 10:25–29 and 10:37 is not original and therefore cannot be used to interpret the meaning of the parable for Jesus"; Crossan, *In Parables*, 58.

28. See Hedrick, "Poetic Features of the Parable," referring to Aristotle's *Rhetoric* 3.8 and 3.9.

IV

But a Samaritan while traveling came near him; and when he saw him, he was moved with pity. He went to him and bandaged his wounds, having poured oil and wine on them. Then he put him on his own animal, brought him to an inn, and took care of him.

V

The next day he took out two denarii, gave them to the innkeeper, and said, "Take care of him; and when I come back, I will repay you whatever more you spend."

(Luke 10: 25–35, New Revised Standard Version).

Already the size of episode IV indicates that the reader's staging with the Samaritan is expected to be the most intense. There is a parallelism in structure with the previous episodes: The Samaritan also "saw him" (i.e., the victim), but instead of "passing by on the other side" he "was moved with pity" and "went to him."

But before joining the Samaritan's perspective, the readers have to travel. First, they have to share in their imagination the traveler's fate: "a man" (sic), an Everyman on the road and robbed. The victim should earn the reader's sympathy. The reader must be convinced: "This could also have happened to me." For a moment, the reader must pause and *look* at the victim in the ditch before traveling to the next episode.

A person who does not desire to become receptive to the victim first, can never become a Samaritan. This is a first invasion of their imagination by an unexpected alterity, by which readers' presumably stable moral identity is shattered. But subsequently, three other challenges follow. Jauss distinguished several modalities of interaction between readers and the characters with whom they are going to be confronted in the parable.[29] Three of these aspects may be helpful in our case. The victim, stripped and half dead, calls for a *sympathetic* identification. The priest and the Levite, one after the other, enter the reader's sight and reduce him to an *ironic* role taking. As they pass by the victim without turning to him, they provoke double feelings of estrangement on the one hand ("I would have done otherwise!"), but also of recognition on the other hand ("Did I not behave alike then and there?').[30] But time goes by in the reading process, and then the Samaritan enters the scene. Together with a shock ("an enemy!"), the Samaritan's behavior invites the reader to—what Jauss calls—an *admiring* role-taking: "If this is the

---

29. Jauss, *Ästhetische Erfahrung*, 252.

30. Why was it that they walked by? Martin Luther King Jr. showed his strong identificatory reading of the parable with this suggestion: "It's possible these men were afraid." See also Annette Merz, note 37 of her contribution to this volume.

way God's kingdom is present, then I want to be part of it." Participating readers go, during their reading of the parable, through a specter of moral emotions—pity, embarrassment, astonishment, admiration—in which they cannot stick to their cherished moral identity, but through which they are invited to identify with the story's different characters.

Conclusion

The event of compassion, as narrated in the parable of the Good Samaritan, deconstructs the "ethical subject" as the stable center of moral agency. In that story, compassion is not depicted as an individual moral capacity, but as an event that overcomes anyone who does not close him-/herself to the risk of being altered by the joy or the suffering of others. As Robert W. Funk writes, the implicit reader is invited "to join the narrative and live it out." Forget about conventional morality, its rules and principles. Leave that world, well-defined and organized, behind. Let yourself be taken by the event of compassion and see where God brings you, just as the Samaritan did. Join the Kingdom of God![31]

In the parable of the Good Samaritan, compassion is not the merit of a good person, exercising one of the virtues he disposes of as an ethical subject. The good enters the world incarnated in the arch-enemy, a Samaritan, as an unexpected event. As Funk rightly observes, "In the kingdom mercy is always a surprise."[32] Compassion in this parable is a divine experience of contingency, into which readers are drawn—thanks to the "blanks," the "open spaces" the text invites them to occupy. Compassion is not a moral capacity of a stable personality, grounded in itself; it is rather a felicitous handicap of someone unable to keep his or her moral identity intact.

The original Jewish audience must have been shocked by the Samaritan as an image of goodness. But even when in later times he has turned into a "good fellow" anyway, the parable continues to ask for travelling along with all four characters, one after another: victim, indifferent passersby, generous helper. We are never just the person who we think we are. We may easily change into someone we had never thought to be. And that is who we are.

---

31. Funk, *Parables and Presence*, 18.
32. Funk, *Parables and Presence*, 34.

Bibliography

Camus, Albert. *The Fall*. New York: Vintage, 1956.
Caputo, John D. *More Radical Hermeneutics. On Not Knowing Who We Are*. Bloomington: Indiana University Press, 2000.
——— *On Religion*. London: Routledge, 2001.
Crossan, John Dominican. *In Parables. The Challenge of the Historical Jesus*. San Francisco: Harper & Row, 1973.
Hedrick, Charles W. "Poetic Features of the Parable." http://www.newmediabible.org/1goodsam/.
Housset, Emmanuel. *L'Intelligence de la Pitié: Phénomenologie de la Communauté*. Cerf: Paris, 2003.
——— *L'intériorité d'Exil: Le Soi au Risqué de l'Altérité*. Cerf: Paris, 2008.
Funk, Robert W. *Parables and Presence: Forms of the New Testament Tradition*. Philadelphia: Fortress, 1982.
Iser, Wolfgang. *Der Akt des Lesens: Theorie Ästhetischer Wirkung*. Munich: Fink, 1984.
Jauss, Hans Robert. *Ästhetische Erfahrung und Literarische Hermeneutik*. Frankfurt: Suhrkamp, 1977.
Jülicher, Adolf. *Die Gleichnisreden Jesu*. 1910. Repr., Darmstadt: Wissenschaftliche Buchgesellschaft, 1969.
Klemm, Hans Gunther. *Das Gleichnis vom Barmherziger Samariter: Grundzüge der Auslegung im 16/17. Jahrhundert*. Stuttgart: Kohlhammer, 1973.
Maffesoli, Michel. *Le Temps des Tribus: Le Déclin de l'Individualisme dans les Sociétés de Masse*. Paris: Méridiens-Klincksieck, 1988.
Monselewski, Werner. *Der Barmherzige Samariter: Eine Auslegungsgeschichtliche Untersuchung zu Lukas 10, 25–37*. Tübingen: Mohr, 1967.
New World Encyclopedia. "Altruism." http://www.newworldencyclopedia.org/entry/Altruism.
Nussbaum, Martha C. *Upheavals of Thought: The Intelligence of Emotions*. Cambridge: Cambridge University Press, 2003.
Ricoeur, Paul. *Living Up to Death*. Translated by David Pellauer. Chicago: Chicago University Press, 2009.
Rousseau, Jean-Jacques. *Discourse*. Part I. www.constitution.org/jjr/ineq_03.htm.
Schapp, Wilhelm. *In Geschichten Verstrickt: Zum Sein von Ding und Mensch*. Hamburg: Meiner, 1953.
Schweitzer, Albert. *On the Edge of the Primeval Forest*. London: Black, 1924.
Wolterstorff, Nicholas. *Justice: Rights and Wrongs*. Princeton: Princeton University Press, 2008.
Wyschogrod, Edith. *Saints and Postmodernism: Revisioning Moral Philosophy*. Chicago: University of Chicago Press, 1990.
Zimmermann, Ruben. *Puzzling the Parables of Jesus: Methods and Interpretation*. Minneapolis: Fortress, 2015.

Compassion as a Virtue of Love

Pieter Vos

COMPASSION FOR THOSE WHO suffer seems to be a self-evident moral absolute. The conviction that being compassionate belongs to the heart of morality has been part of the history of thought, from antiquity until late modernity. According to Aristotle, what we fear for ourselves excites our compassion when it happens to others.[1] In Buddhism, compassion is the great virtue, and Christian faith presupposes compassion when it commands us to even more demanding charity.[2] In modernity, Rousseau argued that pity or compassion is the mother of all virtues—a natural sentiment that makes any suffering being a fellow creature.[3] Schopenhauer too considered compassion as the motivational force behind morality, the origin of its value, and as holding for our relations with animals as well.[4] According to Nussbaum, compassion is the basic social emotion, which includes a kind of reasoning and involves a move away from egocentric needs toward a concern about the well-being of others, which is necessary to ethics in modern societies.[5]

Yet, in the history of thought, compassion has been a highly contested concept as well. The anti-compassion tradition lists Socrates and Plato, the Stoics, Spinoza, Kant, and it culminated in Nietzsche. According to Socrates and the Stoics, compassion is a moral sentiment unworthy of the dignity of both giver and recipient, based on false beliefs about the value of external goods. To Seneca, compassion or pity (*misericordia*) is "a weakness of the mind."[6] Spinoza considered *commiseratio* or pity as useless, since love

1. Aristotle, *Retorica* II, III, 8, 1386a28.
2. Comte-Sponville, *A Short Treatise*, 116.
3. Rousseau, "Discourse," 160–63.
4. Schopenhauer, *Die Welt als Wille und Vorstellung*, 67. See Comte-Sponville, *A Short Treatise*, 110.
5. Nussbaum, *Upheavals of Thought*, 297–454.
6. Seneca, *De Clementia* 2.4.4: "Et haec vitium animae est."

and generosity should drive us to help our fellow people, not pity.[7] Like the Stoics, Nietzsche argued that compassion multiplies misery: the pain of the one who feels compassion with the sufferer is added to the pain of the sufferer.[8] Moreover, Nietzsche criticized compassion as "disguised egoism" shaped by resentment: "If one does good merely out of pity (*Mitleid*), it is oneself one really does good to."[9] Compassion turns out to be self-deceived egoism of an oppressed self that wants to vent its power where it can, instead of something flowing from authentic motivations of a self-dispossessing self. It is a gratification of egoistic desire, a conservator of misery, and as such a perverted will to power. To the *recipient* compassion brings shame; a damage more significant than the alleviation of other sufferings. Great indebtedness does not make men grateful but vengeful, as Nietzsche puts it.[10] Furthermore, Dostoevsky's "Grand Inquisitor" expresses the possibility of a totalitarian wielding of power which explicitly invokes compassion for suffering humankind as its justification.[11] And Foucault showed how the bureaucratic apparatus of institutionalized compassion is aimed at the disciplining of their patients.[12]

In order to prevent compassion from becoming a naive, idealistic concept, these criticisms must serve as a litmus test in the conceptualization and application of the concept. Hence, the central question of this essay is whether it is possible to think of compassion as not self-serving, as not an expression of power over someone in need. To put it in the words of Bruce K. Ward: Can the mechanism which turns compassion into domination on the one hand and offense that desires revenge on the other hand be broken apart?[13] In trying to find an answer to these questions, I propose to interpret compassion as a virtue of love. I start with Nussbaum's response to the anti-compassion tradition, showing that her response falls short when it comes to Nietzsche's criticism.

---

7. Spinoza, *Ethica* 4.prop. 50: "Commiseratio in homine, qui ex ductu rationis vivit, per se mala, et inutilis est," see prop. 37, prop. 46–47.

8. Nietzsche, *Der Antichrist*, § 7: "Durch das Mitleiden vermehrt und verfielfältigt sich die Einbuße an Kraft noch, die an sich schon das Leiden dem Leben bringt." It is a "*Multiplikator* des Elends."

9. Nietzsche, *The Will to Power*, 199, quoted in Ward, *Redeeming the Enlightenment*, 174.

10. Nietzsche, *Also sprach Zarathustra*, II.3 (Von den Mitleidigen): "Große Verbindlichkeiten machen nicht dankbar, sondern rachsüchtig" (trans. Kaufmann, *Thus Spoke Zarathustra*, 89).

11. Dostoevsky, *The Brothers Karamazov*.

12. Michel Foucault, *The Birth of the Clinic*. See Ward, *Redeeming the Enlightenment*, 161.

13. Ward, *Redeeming the Enlightenment*, 189.

Compassion and the Value of External Goods

Nussbaum has offered one of the most impressive defenses for the political and societal importance of compassion. She not only provides a clear account of the cognitive dimension of compassion (over against Kant), arguing that it involves thoughtful judgments about the sufferings of others,[14] but also defends the concept against the Stoic anti-compassion philosophers and their arguments. These thinkers do not reject compassion for its lack of thoughtful judgment—they accept that compassion involves such judgments, but yet reject these judgments as resting on false beliefs. The crux of this rejection is the affirmation of the fundamental dignity of the human being that cannot be destroyed by any suffering stemming from the loss of external goods.[15] Socrates inaugurated a tradition in which compassion is considered as a moral sentiment unworthy of the dignity of both giver and recipient, based on false beliefs about the value of external goods. The Stoics continued this line of thought, which was, according to Nussbaum, taken over by Spinoza, Kant, and Nietzsche.[16] Since compassion is basically viewed as sympathy with the suffering, the pain, or the sadness of someone who suffers, compassion is based on the false judgment that the fundamental inner virtue, a human being's dignity, is dependent on external goods of life.

Against these objections, Nussbaum argues that a Stoic-inspired conception presupposes a problematic ideal of self-sufficient virtue; i.e., that dependency upon people or things beyond one's control is necessarily a manifestation of weakness and lack of dignity. While being indifferent to the external goods, the Stoic agent resembles a kind of narcissism "in her inability to mourn, her rage of control, her unwillingness to allow that other people may make demands that compromise the equanimity of the self."[17] This ideal conceals a profound fear of contingency. According to Nussbaum, the Stoic fearfully tries to prevent himself from any risk, even at the cost of the value of love.

Nussbaum's positive argument in favor of compassion is based on the acceptance of human vulnerability and the conditions of human existence; i.e., that we are exposed to being seriously damaged in our flourishing by suffering losses that are not the result of our own choices. For there is nothing

---

14. As Nussbaum puts it: "Compassion takes up the onlooker's point of view, making the best judgment the onlooker can make about what is really happening to the person, even when that may differ from the judgment of the person herself"; *Upheavals*, 306.

15. Nussbaum, *Upheavals*, 369–70.

16. Nussbaum, *Upheavals*, 356–58.

17. Nussbaum, *Upheavals*, 373.

wrong with acknowledging that human beings have certain needs to flourish and are vulnerable. This is not to say that the needs of the compassionate are boundless. Compassion is to be directed to fundamental external human needs without which human beings cannot lead human lives, such as water, food, and shelter, and basic freedom of movement, action, expression, and belief, as well as protection from harm and government oppression. If people are devoid of such fundamental needs, it makes sense that we practice compassion. Compassion is both a justified human response to such needs and positively beneficial in its effects in the world. As a social emotion it helps people to cement together in societies and it reduces human suffering by motivating people to make available external goods of food, shelter, health care, and so on, to vulnerable people.[18]

These arguments make perfect sense in response to the Stoic anti-compassion tradition, but Nussbaum's clear and philosophically sophisticated account of compassion is limited as a response to Nietzsche's criticism. Although Nussbaum pays attention to Nietzsche several times,[19] she does not really respond to his claim that compassion is shaped by resentment. Her presupposition is that Nietzsche's critique does not differ very much from the Stoics: "like the Stoics, he is quick to point out that the interest in taking revenge is a product of weakness and lack of power—of that excessive dependence on others and on the goods of the world is the mark of a weak, not of a strong and self-sufficient, human being or society. The compassionate person is as such a weak person."[20] According to Nussbaum, Nietzsche refuses to accept "that human beings need worldly goods in order to function" and "repeatedly asserts the false romantic view that suffering, including basic physical suffering, ennobles and strengthens the spirit," but "his romanticism and his materialism are fundamentally at odds."[21]

However, different from what Nussbaum suggests, Nietzsche's criticism does not only echo the Stoic critique of dependency on external goods and moral weakness. The main problem is that compassion has resentful envy both as its source and as its outcome. Compassion is a conservator of everything miserable, since pity for "the lower and suffering" becomes a "measure of the height of the soul."[22] In effect, this exaltation of compassion not only promotes the weak and weakness, but also functions as a

18. Nussbaum, *Upheavals*, 321, 368–86.
19. Nussbaum, *Upheavals*, 362–63, 367, 372, 383–86.
20. Nussbaum, *Upheavals*, 363.
21. Nussbaum, *Upheavals*, 384–85.
22. Nietzsche, *Der Antichrist*, § 7; Nietzsche, *Writings from the Late Notebooks*, 150, quoted from Ward, *Redeeming the Enlightenment*, 175.

motivation and conservation of envious resentment to those well favored by nature. Resentful envy is a frustrated will to power, and compassion offers it an outlet. Moreover, upon the recipient of compassion it will bring shame, which causes much more damage than other sufferings. For compassion makes the other indebted and great indebtedness does not lead to gratitude but to vengefulness.[23] Nussbaum does not provide us with an adequate response, since her argument is basically restricted to the Stoic anti-compassion tradition and neglects Nietzsche's argument of compassion as resentment and disguised egoism.[24]

How can we respond to Nietzschean criticism more adequately? To start, I will join those accounts of compassion that emphasize the elements of sympathy, love, and even joy for the other as inherent to the virtue of compassion, and continue by asking what love actually means when showing compassion.

Compassion: Sympathy, Joy, and Neighborly Love

In his treatment of the virtue of compassion, the French philosopher André Comte-Sponville acknowledges that compassion may not be very attractive: "[W]e don't like to be the object of compassion, and we don't particularly like to feel compassion either."[25] Yet, compassion is not very different from sympathy, which refers precisely to the Greek origin for the Latin *compassio*. Although in modern usage these words are no longer synonymous, in a certain sense, compassion is a form of sympathy, albeit in a qualified way: "[I]t is sympathy in pain or sadness—in other words, participation in the suffering of others."[26]

Comte-Sponville acknowledges that in this respect compassion only seems to increase the quantity of suffering in the world and in itself is not

23. See for this analysis of Nietzsche and the inadequacy of Nussbaum's response Ward, *Redeeming the Enlightenment*, 173–78.

24. An exception is her remark about the problematic nature of anger and hatred in Augustine: "It was not without reason that Nietzsche stressed the vengeful elements in Christianity. Although it was surely hasty of him to conclude that these elements reveal the essential goal of Christian ethics to be revenge by the weak against the strong, and thus revenge on the very conditions of human life itself, nonetheless there is a disturbing emphasis on anger in Augustine . . .," Nussbaum, *Upheavals*, 548. However, as an argument against Nietzsche this is not sufficient. Moreover, I think her evaluation of Augustine on this point is limited, since Augustine's notion of anger is precisely related to his valuation of external goods as a matter of both compassion and justice. See Wolterstorff, *Justice*, 180–206.

25. Comte-Sponville, *A Short Treatise*, 103.

26. Comte-Sponville, *A Short Treatise*, 105.

effective in taking suffering away. Therefore, he takes up Spinoza's treatment of compassion or pity. As I have already remarked, Spinoza considers compassion that is driven by sadness as useless. It is love and generosity, not pity that should drive us to help our fellow human beings. Contrary to Nietzsche, Spinoza does not aim at a complete *Umwertung aller Werte* ("transvaluation of values"), but rather at learning to practice charity out of love and joy, like the Aristotelian "prudent man" would do it, instead of out of sadness, pity, or duty. Nevertheless, pity or compassion is still better than cruelty or egoism. The different dispositions of joyful love and pitiful compassion even may lead to similar charitable actions.

From this perspective, Comte-Sponville develops a more positive account of compassion; not in terms of pity and sadness, but as an attentive openness, solicitude, patience, and listening. He makes a helpful distinction between *commiseratio*, pity or *Mitleid* on the one hand, and *misericordia* or compassion as a more positive and open attitude on the other hand. In that case it is possible to define compassion as related to joy, rooted in the joy about the other's good fortune. When we rejoice in someone's existence, i.e., when we love that person, we are sad to see him or her suffer. Compassion is a saddened love.[27] A similar conception of *misericordia* in terms of the heart that is directed toward the well-being of the other is already present in Augustine—he even uses the word *compassio* in this respect—defending Cicero's conception of *misericordia* as a true virtue over against the Stoics.[28]

In my view, connecting compassion to joy and love offers a first step to overcome Nietzsche's argument that compassion is rooted in resentment and egoism. Not sadness about unfortunate circumstances as such is the driving force of compassion, but love and joy that unite us with our fellow people. Now, if *love* is decisive in a more positive and open definition of compassion, then the question is: how should we understand love? On the one hand, Comte-Sponville suggests that compassion may be the principal content of *agape* or neighborly love, its truest affect. In that respect, the Buddhist emphasis on compassion is more realistic than Christian neighborly love, since compassion is felt more easily than a truthful charitable impulse. On the other hand, neighborly love surpasses compassion in so far that the

---

27. Comte-Sponville, *A Short Treatise*, 107–8. Note that the distinction between the terms is not absolute. Schopenhauer, for instance, uses the word *Mitleid*, which in this case may be translated as "sympathy" or "compassion", since in his view *Mitleid* is indeed rooted in joy about the other (*Die Welt als Wille und Vorstellung*, 67).

28. Augustine, *De Civitate Dei* 9.5: "Quid est autem misericordia nisi alienae miseriae quaedam in nostro corde compassio." He speaks of mourning with the afflicted in order that they will be liberated from the affliction ("contristari pro adflicto ut liberetur").

latter needs the suffering or misfortune of the other in order to give love, whereas neighborly love does not even need the love of the other in order to give love. Neighborly love is compassion freed from suffering and freed from the ego.[29] In this interpretation, articulated here by a non-Christian philosopher, compassion may be able to counter Nietzschean criticism. Compassion in terms of neighborly love may neither multiply misery— since it does not have suffering but love as its driving force—nor appear to be a disguised egoism, since love does not compete at all.

From this perspective, it is important that the virtue of love be freed from the paradigmatic approach of neighborly love as essentially consisting of "helping the needy," as the Louvain philosopher Paul Moyaert has observed. In this paradigmatic approach, neighborly love is wrongly regarded as an extension of an altruistic disposition: the things we are prepared to do for family, friends, and colleagues, we ought to extend to those outside the immediate circle.[30] This altruistic disposition is not *per se* opposed to self-interest. In the long run we may benefit from the well-being of others. Furthermore, in helping others in need, we often expect results from our willingness to help. We have, for instance, few problems with giving money to the poor if we have the guarantee that it will be put to good use and invested in a worthwhile and efficient way. Contributing to the well-being of the other? Yes, but on the condition that there will be some results. This approach would reaffirm the dialectic of pity, *commiseratio* or *Mitleid* as invoking ingratitude, even hostility and envy in those who receive compassion. Therefore, the conception of a compassionate neighborly love defined as helping those in need falls short.

Essentially, neighborly love may also require giving even when there seems to be no advantage at all. I agree with Moyaert that neighborly love should not be understood from the perspective of "the advantageous effects of helping."[31] Rather, neighborly love is defined by two commandments which make it something absolute for the "giver": "You shall love your neighbor as yourself" (Matthew 22:39) and "you shall love your enemies" (Matthew 5:45). In this sense, neighborly love is an "impossible commandment," because it is without a measure and seemingly against human nature. The commandment speaks not of helping but of *loving* the other. It appears to be irreconcilable with the natural limits of common sense; it asks for exaggerated unselfishness. Nevertheless, the commandment forbids nothing.

---

29. Comte-Sponville, *A Short Treatise*, 116–17, 289.
30. Moyaert, "On Love of Neighbour," 174–75.
31. Moyaert, "On Love of Neighbour," 175.

There is only one way to fail, namely, by not going far enough, since neighborly love even extends to the enemy.[32]

Moyaert points out that the fact that the other is my friend, father, or wife in no way excludes the possibility that in certain circumstances they might likewise become my neighbor. The question is: when does someone become my neighbor? Personal relationships are marked by reciprocity and the interchangeability of the good: what is mine is yours. This reciprocity is interrupted when the other no longer goes along with what I do, say, and desire, and when the other remains indifferent to my way of responding. The most telling example is when a person is no longer someone who knows what he/she is doing, and seems no longer responsible for his/her life and his/her traumatic history. He/she becomes the person about whom we say: he/she cannot help it. Precisely at this point the other becomes the neighbor, becomes a stranger, someone I can no longer understand and with whom I am no longer able to identify. According to Moyaert, neighborly love, on the other hand, is not possible without some process of identification. What touches me is the naked fact that the other is a human being. As Moyaert explains, there is a depersonalizing aspect of neighborly love: the other as neighbor is detached from the frame of meaning provided by personal reactive attitudes, as if the other could be just anyone.[33] This makes clear that neighborly love in principle is not dependent on the response of the other. Neighborly love does not aim for gratitude, since it is also required even when the other is not at all able to respond.

Very importantly, Moyaert points out the meaning of neighborly love as not primarily concerned with helping or giving (with the expectation of gratitude), but with loving. If we interpret compassion in this way, this may counter Nietzsche's argument that compassion is disguised egoism. For neighborly love is in principle not concerned with the results or the effects of charitable actions. As love, it expects nothing in return.

Moyaert explains his view from the traditional works of mercy or charity. In Christianity, it is indeed the works of mercy—seven corporal and seven spiritual works[34]—rather than compassion which function as

32. Moyaert, "On Love of Neighbour," 176.
33. Moyaert, "On Love of Neighbour," 177–80.
34. The seven corporal works of mercy are: to feed the hungry, to give drink to the thirsty, to shelter the stranger, to cloth the naked, to comfort the sick, and to visit the imprisoned, all derived from Matt 25:31–46, and complemented by the seventh work: to bury the dead. Just as the corporal works of mercy are directed toward relieving corporal suffering, the even more important aim of the spiritual works of mercy is to relieve spiritual suffering. The latter works are less known but an important part of the Christian tradition: to instruct the ignorant, to counsel the doubtful, to admonish sinners, to bear wrongs patiently, to forgive offences willingly, to comfort the afflicted,

the paradigm of charity. What is the meaning of these works of mercy? According to Moyaert, burying the dead or clothing another person, for instance, are symbolic activities and not strictly utilitarian. By clothing another I confirm the difference between human persons and animals at the very moment when that difference is on the verge of disappearing. The same holds for burying a dead body. The gravestone signifies the difference at the moment when no visible difference remains. The necessity of reaffirming the separation between human beings and animals, between the sacred and the profane, culture and nature, the symbolic and the utilitarian, is compelling once the other is overwhelmed by natural violence of the vital order: sickness, suffering, hunger and thirst, fragility and death—in short: external goods. By helping people who suffer from these evils and alleviating their needs we remove them from the anonymity of nature and reconfirm their value at the moment when they themselves can no longer assume that value.[35]

But what about the recipient of compassionate neighborly love? Is compassion interpreted in terms of neighborly love still a one-way movement from giver toward receiver, still with the risk of inciting resentment and ingratitude? In order to meet this aspect of Nietzschean criticism, another aspect of neighborly love, which is helpful in thinking through the nature of compassion as a virtue of love, must be elaborated.

No Compassion without Mercy

In a conception of compassion as a one-way movement from giver to recipient the needy one would be excluded from being compassionate himself/herself. Therefore, compassion must be seen as "a work of love even if it can give nothing and is able to do nothing," as the Danish philosopher Søren Kierkegaard puts it in his book on neighborly love.[36] Kierkegaard asks our attention for the fact that all emphasis on charitable donations and gifts may be merciless. In our practices we may not only emphasize the need of the poor but also exclude them from being able to practice neighborly love themselves, since they possess nothing by which they may be generous or charitable. In the name of charity, or mercifulness as Kierkegaard calls it, the poor are mercilessly excluded from being merciful. Therefore,

---

and to pray for the living and the dead.

35. Moyaert, "On Love of Neighbour," 181. See his *De Mateloosheid van het Christendom*, 15–96, for an extensive elaboration of Moyaert's view on neighborly love.

36. Kierkegaard, *Works of Love*, 315–30. Actually, Kierkegaard speaks of mercifulness. I will explain the relationship between compassion and mercy in this section.

Christian discourse should not primarily be about generosity but about the inner quality of love, "then generosity will follow of itself and come to itself accordingly as the individual is capable of it."[37] One can be merciful without having the least thing to give. Using the virtue-ethical language of perfection, Kierkegaard concludes: "This is of great importance, since *being able* to be merciful certainly is a far greater perfection than to have money and then *to be able* to give."[38]

To explain his argument, Kierkegaard retells the story of the Good Samaritan. Suppose that the Good Samaritan would have been a poor man who had nothing at all, no donkey to transport the unfortunate man, nothing to bind him, no money to help him. Then, would he not have been equally as merciful as that merciful Samaritan of which the Bible tells us? Or take the story about the woman who laid two pennies in the temple box (Luke 21:1–4). Christ says about her that she gave more than all the rich people gave. Why? We are inclined to say: because the sacrifice made by the poor widow extends that of the rich person who still has money. But in that case we would still be focused on the *what*. Kierkegaard turns our attention to the *how*. Usually the rich one who gives a huge amount is considered as the one who gives the most, because we think in terms of *what* one gives. Christianity teaches that money in itself is not what counts. Hence, the exhortation is: have mercy; then money can be given.[39]

The gospel teaches us that even the poor can practice neighborly love, even if they have nothing to give or are not able to do anything. For they can still have sympathy for the misery of the other; i.e., be compassionate. Kierkegaard even goes one step further. The poor person can be merciful toward the rich who have money and mercilessly keep it for themselves, or give a stingy gift. The merciful poor can make a stingy gift into a large sum if they mercifully do not upbraid the rich for it, i.e., by forgiving them.[40]

In this argument, Kierkegaard does not only distinguish mercy as a deed of love from the practice of giving material goods, but also points to the meaning of mercy as going beyond mere compassion. Whereas compassion is sympathy for the misery of the other, mercy is basically a quality by which one can endure evil. It is a virtue of forgiveness. Moreover, Kierkegaard turns around the relationship between giver and recipient. It may be the recipient of compassion rather than the giver who will turn out to be the one who is really merciful.

37. Kierkegaard, *Works of Love*, 315.
38. Kierkegaard, *Works of Love*, 317.
39. Kierkegaard, *Works of Love*, 317.
40. Kierkegaard, *Works of Love*, 322–23.

Mercy understood as a virtue of forgiveness is relevant to the Nietzschean problem of resentment and rancor. With Comte-Sponville, mercy can be defined as

> the virtue that triumphs over rancor, over justified hatred (in this respect mercy goes beyond justice), over resentment, over the desire for revenge or punishment; the virtue that forgives not by expunging the wrong—an impossible charge, in any case—but by stilling the grudge we bear against a person who offended or harmed us.[41]

Of course, this does not mean that by being merciful we can erase evil or that the wrong is now considered null and void. Mercy is not opposed to justice, but to resentment, which is a form of hatred. Hence, mercy is different from compassion. Because it is directed to the wrongdoers to whom I probably do not feel any compassion, it is a difficult virtue. The liar and the thief, even the rapist and the torturer are the very ones who ask for my mercy, i.e., for my forgiveness. This seems impossible; but as Comte-Sponville points out, there is some reasonableness in this. Mercy is not based on passion or emotion like compassion, but it is, like prudence, an intellectual virtue. It requires that we understand that the other person is wicked or misguided or ruled by passion or fanaticism. "To forgive is to accept. Not in order to stop fighting, of course, but in order to stop hating."[42] Forgiveness expresses freedom; it is an overabundance of freedom.

I think that this interpretation of mercy makes sense, but I also think that something should be added to explain how mercy is connected to compassion. To get a proper view on this connection, I will again turn to Moyaert. He proposes to define mercy as "patient love."[43] He derives this interpretation from 1 Corinthians 13:4, where Paul says that "love is patient; love is kind; love is not envious or boastful or arrogant. . ." Interpreted as patient love, mercy means to indulge, to endure, to tolerate evil. It is a virtue on the border of active and passive, of doing something and being no longer able to do anything.[44] From this perspective it also becomes clear what loving the enemy may mean. Who is the enemy? The enemy may be a stranger but may also be a member of my family. Moyaert proposes to define the

---

41. Comte-Sponville, *A Small Treatise*, 119.

42. Kierkegaard, *Works of Love*, 122. Also see "Mercy does not nullify this evil will, nor does it give up the fight against it; what mercy does do is refuse to partake of it, to add hatred to hatred, selfishness to selfishness, anger to violence"; Kierkegaard, *Works of Love*, 125.

43. Moyaert, "Barmhartigheid," 61–67.

44. Moyaert, "Barmhartigheid," 64.

enemy as "someone who wants to wrong me."⁴⁵ The love commandment requires that I should not oppose evil, but embrace it. Mercy then comes to mean that we endure the evil in the awareness that not everything can be recognized as good and that the good is sometimes beyond what we are able to realize. In the end, mercy is the virtue of forgiveness, i.e., of acceptance and endurance of what is wrong. In a more general sense, mercy teaches us that our own ability to realize the good is limited. As such, mercy is the virtue we need at the moment in which charitable actions can no longer achieve anything.

Mercy teaches us that all our good works of care and aid, solidarity, and justice, as practiced in or outside institutions of charity and resulting from our compassion and neighborly love, are in the end limited. We should always stay open to the good as something that in the final instance is not in our possession. Moreover, this awareness may prevent compassion from deteriorating into exercising power over someone in need, turning compassion into offense which desires revenge. Only if we practice compassion in a merciful way we keep openness toward the other, as someone who is able to be compassionate, merciful, and loving himself/herself. As Kierkegaard pointed out, the fixed positions of giver and recipient are broken apart as soon as we realize that not only the giver but also the recipient is able to be merciful.

Respect, Self-Dispossession, Belief

The latter argument is promising in relation to the anti-compassion argument that, in helping someone through our compassion, we "transgress grievously against his pride," as Nietzsche puts it;⁴⁶ i.e., the problem that compassion invokes shame and offense from the side of the recipient on the one hand and thereby reveals that resentment may be at the root of compassionate acts on the other hand. Is compassion that is not self-serving possible, beyond the pleasure of control and power over the one to which it is offered?

First, *discerning respect for the other* should always be included in compassion. To explain this, it is helpful to elaborate more on the distinction between compassion and pity. On this issue, Hannah Arendt's distinction is a good starting point. In her view, pity is an abstract concern about the unfortunate in general, and precisely because of its abstract character even proves to be open to cruelty and violence, as Arendt demonstrates. Unlike

---

45. Moyaert, "On Love of Neighbour," 174.
46. Nietzsche, *Thus Spoke Zarathustra*, 89.

pity, compassion comprehends the particular, without any generalization. Whereas pity is abstract, loquacious, and generalizing, compassion is concrete, silent, and specific. It does not reach out farther than what is suffered by one particular person.[47] Comte-Sponville adds some other elements to this distinction: "Pity always entails . . . some degree of contempt, or at least a feeling of superiority on the part of the person who experiences it . . . There is a self-satisfaction in pity that underscores the deficiency of its object."[48] "Pitiful" is a term of depreciation, somewhat similar with "inferior," "pathetic," or "contemptible." In pity, the self can indeed secretly be pleased that it has been spared.[49] Compassion, on the other hand, always entails a measure of respect. Whereas pity comes from the top down, compassion is a horizontal feeling; it realizes equality between giver and receiver by sharing the latter's suffering. There can be no compassion without respect.[50] For compassion is loving without getting paid back, and without respect one ceases to love. This includes the possibility of the reversal of the relationship between giver and recipient, as demonstrated in the way Kierkegaard describes: how one can be merciful even when one has nothing to give. To put it differently: respectful compassion asks for discernment in regard to oneself and the suffering person. Such discerning is not a matter of Nietzschean noble distancing; rather it is a clarity required by a compassion which wants to help through the capacity that imagines oneself as the other.[51]

Second, compassion flows from *self-dispossession and not from self-love*. Compassion out of self-love wants to help because what has happened to others could happen to oneself. Self-dispossessed love means that one is capable of seeing oneself really *as* the other; it is an other-centered intentionality, a manifestation of kenotic love.[52] Almsgiving, taking care of the sick, visiting those in prison, bringing comfort to the distressed, releasing others from their debts to us, protecting the vulnerable, are all visible acts of compassion in the world. But they can be judged to be truly virtuous and

---

47. Arendt, *On Revolution*, 80, quoted by Comte-Sponville, *A Small Treatise*, 114.
48. Comte-Sponville, *A Small Treatise*, 114.
49. Davies, *A Theology of Compassion*, 18, 233–34.
50. Comte-Sponville, *A Small Treatise*, 115.
51. Ward, *Redeeming the Enlightenment*, 188.
52. Davies, *A Theology of Compassion*, 20–21. Davies takes Edith Stein and Etty Hillesum as prime examples of self-dispossessed compassion in which one places oneself at risk for the sake of the other, and contrasts this with the forced dispossession of the Jews in the camps. In this way compassion depends on radical goodness, the assumption of another's suffering as one's own, which makes possible a compassionate re-enactment of the destructive and enforced dispossession suffered by the Jews. See Davies, *A Theology of Compassion*, 16–17.

compassionate only on the grounds of the intentionality at work in them.[53] Other-centered intentionality may include that the self is ready to put itself at risk for the sake of the other, but self-sacrifice in itself is no litmus test of self-dispossessed love of others, since self-sacrifice can also be a matter of self-love.[54] What counts is self-dispossessed love. Theologically, this self-dispossessed act is revealed in "the extreme of human truth," where "we encounter Jesus Christ—the Compassion of God—as the one who goes before and who is already present to us, if unfathomably, in the compassionate act," as Davies puts it.[55]

Finally, compassion *cannot do without belief.* I am not trying to end with an apologetic Christian claim. On the contrary; it is Nietzsche who insists on the inevitable failure of compassion that strives to be humanly self-sufficient. In *Beyond Good and Evil*, he states: "To love humanity *for God's sake*: this has so far been the noblest and remotest sentiment to which mankind has attained . . . That love to mankind . . . is only an *addition* folly and brutishness, that the inclination to this love has first to get its proportion, its delicacy, its grain of salt and sprinkling of ambergris from a higher inclination."[56] According to Nietzsche, this ulterior motive is the highest, although it is at the same time the greatest mistake. We could add Ivan Karamazov's well-known formulation: "There is no virtue [including compassion] if there is no God or immortality."[57] Both agree that the death of God is also the death of compassion. Yet it is Dostoevsky, as Ward points out, who brings in another voice that reverses the relation between God and compassion as presupposed by both Nietzsche and Karamazov, namely Zozima's, who advises a woman "of little faith": "Try to love your neighbors actively and tirelessly. The more you succeed in loving, the more you'll be convinced of the existence of God and the immortality of your soul. And if you reach complete selflessness in the love of your neighbor, then undoubtedly you will believe."[58] If this movement toward God through active love

---

53. Davies, *A Theology of Compassion*, 18.

54. Ward, *Redeeming the Enlightenment*, 188.

55. Davies, *A Theology of Compassion*, 23. See also 232–53 for a theological elaboration of human and divine compassion.

56. Nietzsche, *Jenseits von Gut und Böse*, III, 60: "Den Menschen zu lieben *um Gottes willen*—das war bis jetzt das vornehmste und entlegenste Gefühl, das unter Menschen erreicht worden ist. Daß die Liebe zum Menschen ohne irgendeine heiligende Hinterabsicht eine Dumheit und Tierheid *mehr* ist." Translation: Friedrich Nietzsche, *Beyond Good and Evil*, 42, quoted from Ward, *Redeeming the Enlightenment*, 190.

57. Dostoevsky, *The Brothers Karamazov*, 69, 632, quoted from Ward, *Redeeming the Enlightenment*, 190.

58. Dostoevsky, *The Brothers Karamazov*, 56.

is possible, the consequence is that such love must have real presence in the world already. What counts is to love the person one sees. As Ward concludes, the real difference between Dostoevsky and Nietzsche is less about belief or unbelief in the existence of God than about the reality or unreality of compassionate love.[59] Compassion cannot do without the belief that self-dispossessed love is indeed possible.

Bibliography

Arendt, Hannah. *On Revolution*. New York: Viking, 1963.
Augustine of Hippo. *De Civitate Dei* 9. http://www.thelatinlibrary.com/augustine/civ9.shtml.
Aristotle, *Retorica* 1515. Translated by W. Rhys Roberts as *Rhetoric*. Mineola, NY: Dover, 2004.
Comte-Sponville, André. *A Short Treatise on the Great Virtues: The Uses of Philosophy in Everyday Life*. Translated by Catherine Temerson. London: Vintage, 2002.
Davies, Oliver. *A Theology of Compassion. Metaphysics of Difference and the Renewal of Tradition*. Grand Rapids: Eerdmans, 2001.
Dostoevsky, Fyodor. *The Brothers Karamazov*. Translated by Richard Pevear and Larissa Volokhonsky. New York: Random House, 1991.
Foucault, Michel. *Naissance de la clinique: Une archéologie du regard medical*. Paris: Presses Universitaires de France, 1973. ET: *The Birth of the Clinic: An Archaeology of Medical Perception*. Translated by Alan Sheridan Smith. New York: Pantheon, 1973.
Kierkegaard, Søren. *Works of Love*. Edited and translated by Howard V. Hong and Edna H. Hong, Kierkegaard's Writings 16. Princeton: Princeton University Press, 1995.
Moyaert, Paul. "Barmhartigheid: De deugd van de lankmoedige liefde." In *Voortreffelijk leven: Op zoek naar het juiste midden*, edited by Peter Henk Steenhuis, and Emiel Hakkenes, 60–67. Rotterdam: Lemniscaat, 2009.
———. *De Mateloosheid van het Christendom: Over Naastenliefde, Betekenisincarnatie en Mystieke Liefde*. Nijmegen: SUN, 1998.
———. "On Love of Neighbour." *Ethical Perspectives* 1 (1994) 169–84.
Nietzsche, Friedrich. *Also sprach Zarathustra*. Vol. 2. 1883. Repr., Munich: Hanser, 1954. ET: *Thus Spoke Zarathustra*. Translated by Walter Kaufmann. NewYork: Penguin, 1978.
———. *Beyond Good and Evil*. Translated by Walter Kaufmann. Mineola, NY: Dover, 1997.
———. *Der Antichrist. Fluch auf das Christentum*. Leipzig: Naumann, 1895.
———. *The Will to Power*. Translated by Walter Kaufmann and R. J. Hollingdale. New York: Random House, 1967.
———. *Writings from the Late Notebooks*. Edited by Rüdiger Bittner. Translated by Kate Sturge. Cambridge: Cambridge University Press, 2003.
Nussbaum, Martha. *Upheavals of Thought: The Intelligence of Emotions*. Cambridge: Cambridge University Press, 2001.
Rousseau, Jean-Jacques. *Discours sur l'Origine et les Fondements de l'Inégalité Parmi les Hommes*. ET: "Discourse on the Origin and the Foundations of Inequality among

---

59. Ward, *Redeeming the Enlightenment*, 191–92.

Men." In *The First and Second Discourses and Essay on the Origin of Languages*, by Jean-Jacques Rousseau, edited and translated by Victor Gourevitch, 111–222. New York: Harper & Row, 1986.

Schopenhauer, Arthur. *Die Welt als Wille und Vorstellung*, Volume 4. Zürich: Zürcher, 1977.

Seneca, Lucius Annaeus. *De Clementia* 2. Berlin: de Gruyter, 2016.

Spinoza, Benedict de. *Ethica Ordine Geometrico Demonstrata*. Vol. 4. ET: *The Ethics*. Translated by R. H. M. Elwes. Radford, VA: Wilder, 2007.

Ward, Bruce K. *Redeeming the Enlightenment: Christianity and the Liberal Virtues*. Grand Rapids: Eerdmans, 2010.

Wolterstorff, Nicholas. *Justice: Rights and Wrongs*. Princeton: Princeton University Press, 2008.

Retrieving Compassion

Rethinking the Ethics of Compassion with Levinas and Badiou

Renée van Riessen

Contemporary Perspectives on Compassion

COMPASSION AND EMPATHY ARE words which attract attention in the public debate about a possible new ethics. Several popular writers agree that a new ethics of solidarity is needed—an ethics that would reflect the global situation of humankind and that could give new inspiration for solidarity between people who live in different cultures and different socioeconomic situations. Sometimes, the interwovenness of spirituality and ethics is underlined when compassion is in discussion. This is the case with Karen Armstrong, who launched a model for transforming groups and communities of several backgrounds in the direction of a more compassionate lifestyle: *Twelve Steps to a Compassionate Life*. This was followed by a "Charter of Compassion," which can be signed by city councils and even countries.[1]

Three years after Armstrong's book was published in 2011, the British lifestyle philosopher Roman Krznaric published a book entitled *Empathy. A Handbook for Revolution*, in which (as the title indicates) he announces a revolution of human relationships inspired by the "radical power of empathy."[2]

Although from different backgrounds—Armstrong argues mainly from the perspective of religious studies and the history of religion, whereas Krznaric is one of Britain's leading "popular philosophers"—both books show many similarities. In both cases, the approach is mainly practical (though supported by theoretical insights). Both Armstrong and Krznaric focus on compassion and empathy as an attitude which can be practiced and in which one may become educated and more accomplished through

1. Armstrong, *Twelve Steps*.
2. Krznaric, *Empathy*.

time.³ Both refer to recent biological research of Frans de Waal and others that gives insight into the true character of human nature as related to the behavior of other primates such as bonobos and orangutans. In addition, both give us the same reassuring message about brain and cortex: that aggression is part of the "old brain" that focused human beings (like most animals) on survival, whereas compassion, understood as behaving empathically toward others, is part of the "new brain" that developed later, in the time when primates were forced to cooperate with one another in order to survive. Finally, both also mention the attitude of mammals toward their offspring as a fact that could offer useful insights about the way compassion is anchored in human nature.⁴

Whereas Armstrong and Krznaric emphasize the practical development of a compassionate and empathic attitude to others, philosopher Martha Nussbaum engages in a more theoretical reflection on the phenomenon of compassion. For Nussbaum, compassion is a fundamental ("basic") social emotion: it is the emotion *par excellence* that induces human beings to behave socially. A good example of Nussbaum's argument is found in her explanation of the effect of compassion on social relations by recounting the story of Philoctetes that inspired Sophocles to write the eponymous play.⁵ Nussbaum takes ample time to tell the story of Philoctetes, a good man who was struck by misfortune when he was on his way to Troy to fight on the side of the Greeks. On the island of Lemnos he accidentally trespassed on sacred soil, and was punished with a serpent's bite in his foot. The pain in his foot made him cry out curses which spoiled the religious observances of the other soldiers. Therefore, they decided to leave him alone at Lemnos as a despicable man, without resources apart from his bow and arrows. Ten years later they came to bring him back, having learned that they could not win the war without him. The leaders of the expedition saw Philoctetes as a tool for their purposes, but in Sophocles' play the chorus of soldiers expresses another perspective when they imagine vividly what it is to be like Philoctetes. They protest against the cruelty of the commanders, and express feelings of pity:

> For my part, I pity him—thinking of how, with no living soul
> to care for him, seeing no friendly face, wretched, always alone,

---

3. See also the popular French lifestyle author (and Buddhist monk) Matthieu Ricard, who in 2013 published a hefty volume entitled *Plaidoyer pour l'altruisme*. The book promises to demonstrate that altruism is not an abstract ideal, but an essential dimension of our nature that everyone can cultivate and expand.

4. Krznaric, *Empathy*, 19; Armstrong, *Twelve Steps*.

5. See Nussbaum, "Compassion"; and Nussbaum, *Upheavals of Thought*, 304–5.

he suffers with a fierce affliction, and has no resources to meet his daily needs. How in the world does the poor man survive?[6]

Nussbaum points out that the members of the chorus stand in for the imaginative activity of the audience, "for whom the entire drama is an imaginative act of sympathy." In this way, she considers Philoctetes's story to be the perfect model of the emotion of pity or compassion that lays at the heart of Athenian tragedy.

Indeed, Philoctetes's story is both beautiful and impressive. But why should such an expression of the emotion of compassion or pity in tragedy be important for ethics? Nussbaum gives several answers to this question. *First*, she clarifies that compassion is a central bridge between individual and community, because it is conceived of as our species' way of connecting the concerns of others to our own personal goods. Thus, compassion is a useful emotion that could foster more social behavior. Nussbaum's *second* point is that in several moral theories, compassion is unjustly seen as an irrational force. This claim could lead to a simple dismissal of the emotion on the wrong grounds. Furthermore, the investigation of compassion fits into a larger discussion within social philosophy about the place and value of emotions. Does making room for sentiments like compassion mean that we will base political judgement upon a force that is affective rather than cognitive? Here, Nussbaum shows that Enlightenment thinkers (who at present do not give compassion a central place) could change their attitude and even begin to do so without altering much in the substance of their moral theories. In other words: compassion is not only a basic emotion, but also a kind of reasoning, as it is based on "thought about the well-being of others."[7] But how could one learn such a complex sentiment? To elucidate that, Nussbaum refers to *Émile*, Rousseau's book on education. Rousseau observes that Émile, the boy he was trying to "educate" was unable to interpret gestures of suffering until he became able to imagine the suffering himself. Rousseau concludes that to see the suffering without experiencing the feeling is not to know it. In other words: Émile has to do cognitive work. As Nussbaum argues, "[t]o determine whether Émile has pity, we look for the evidence of a certain sort of thought or imagination in what he says, in what he does."[8] Therefore, Nussbaum sees an important role for literature and theatre, because both can help readers and spectators to experience compassion and to reflect on this emotion. Thus, literature and theatre do

---

6. Sophocles, *Philoctetes*, lines 169–76, quoted from Nussbaum, "Compassion," 27.

7. See Nussbaum, *Upheavals*, 297–454, with a sub-chapter (6, II) on the cognitive structure of compassion.

8. Nussbaum, "Compassion," 38; see also Nussbaum, *Upheavals*, 323.

what philosophy by itself cannot do: they offer a path, a method to become more educated in the complex sentiment of compassion.

Even this too-short overview of contemporary perspectives on compassion and empathy raises several questions. Here, I will mention only two issues that seem to me the most important: one from the perspective of philosophy and the other from the perspective of ethics and philosophy of religion. Both pivot on the question of the good. In the first place, we can ask whether human beings are actually by nature inclined to compassion. This question is prompted by the emphasis Armstrong, Krznaric, and Nussbaum place on compassion as a natural inclination. How should this position be interpreted and, even more important, is education in compassion possible and even "good" *because* it builds on existing inclinations? A second question relates to the premise that the emotion of compassion is useful in social and political contexts. Although this may be taken for granted, one could ask whether this perspective exhausts the subject of compassion and, above all, whether the meaning of compassion is limited by this possible usefulness, as seems to be the case in Martha Nussbaum. In other words, can we conceive of other forms of compassion which are not absorbed by their use in social and political contexts? What is their significance for our understanding of the nature and significance of compassion? In the second part of this article, I will explore this question by looking at Levinas's notion of proximity.

Is Compassion Good Because it is Natural?

This first question has to do with the nature-culture distinction in the phenomenon of compassion. Is compassion a natural phenomenon, and if so, why then should an education in compassion be necessary? In all the approaches mentioned before, compassion is defined primarily as an aspect of natural human behavior. Therefore, the results of neurological and biological research are brought forward by Krznaric, Armstrong, and Nussbaum as a basis for their own choice of an ethics of compassion or empathy. Krznaric, for instance, emphasizes that education in compassion is necessary, because it can help us to reconnect with a real and valuable part of our nature which has faded into the background through the dominant image of what it means to be human, inherited from social Darwinism. Against this image of human being, Krznaric assumes that we need to be educated differently as we have to relearn that empathy and compassion form part of the human nature that we share with other mammals. According to Krznaric, our complex brains are wired both for individualism and empathy, but the individualistic side has been too central in the past three centuries. Therefore, it is time for a change: we should "switch on the empathic brain."[9] Along the same lines, Karen Armstrong points out that education in compassion is crucial because the "old brain" constantly prevents us from successfully developing a more compassionate or empathic attitude. Education in compassion will reinforce the existing natural tendency towards compassionate and empathic behavior.[10] Nussbaum not only presents compassion as a ubiquitous human phenomenon, but also refers to the strong evolutionary evidence that compassion has played a central role in group selection, which particularly pertains to the ethological evidence of its central role in primate species.[11]

From this discussion, it is evident that in our reflections about the desirability of a compassionate life, human nature holds a prominent place. While contemplating whether we should act in a compassionate or empathic way, we not only reflect on the question whether this sort of behavior is appropriate at the given moment, but we are also curious whether (and how far) this type of behavior could be seen as given with human nature as such. Is it "natural" behavior? To what extent is this type of behavior in line with our common ideas about human nature; with the way we are constructed or evaluated; what is *natural* for a human being to perform? What are natural acts and which kinds of acts could be seen as less in line with human nature? In particular, we can conclude that self-understanding, our image of what it is to be human, forms a part of the motivation to advocate empathic and compassionate behavior.

If this is true, or, let us say plausible (seeing the references of Armstrong, Krznaric, and Nussbaum to De Waal's research into the empathy of apes, not to forget De Waals' own conclusions which extend from biology to sociology, and even to ethics), then the theory of human nature formed on the basis of research into the behavior of primates can only be understood in terms of a larger framework that includes certain hypotheses about human behavior. What is natural for human beings? Not, as we were inclined to think, warfare or aggression, nor the competitive behavior that is the outcome of a war of all against all, or a human being acting as a wolf towards another human being (*homo homini lupus*), but rather altruism, compassion, and empathy. This type of behavior, according the argument, is not the result of education, nor the effect of cultural (and thus, counter-natural?) shaping, but should rather be seen as firmly rooted in human nature itself.[12]

---

9. Krznaric, *Empathy*, 32–34.

10. Armstrong, *Twelve Steps*, 9–10.

11. Nussbaum, *Upheavals*, 301; with reference to De Waal (see footnote 12).

12. For more research on this point, see De Waal, *Good Natured*; and De Waal, *The Age of Empathy*.

There thus seems to be a strong argument in defense of an ethics of compassion, in light of the fact that compassion is seen to be exactly in line with nature. And therefore, the whole argument about the natural character of compassion stands in a striking contrast to what Nietzsche cried out in *The Antichrist*: "Pity thwarts the whole law of evolution, which is the law of natural selection."[13] It is clearly with Nietzsche's critique of pity in mind that Armstrong prefers the word "compassion," and announces that she will avoid the word "pity" because it has recently come to have nuances of condescension and superiority toward the sufferer.[14]

Nevertheless, one could ask whether (new) facts about nature in general and about human nature in particular may be the reason to call certain behavior commendable. Also the fact that moral education is possible on the basis of natural inclination—the argument all defenders of compassion refer to—is not in itself a ground for a given moral practice. Morality and nature are definitely interwoven, but this does not mean that they can be reduced to be identical.[15]

Is Compassion Good Because it is a Useful Emotion?

If nature in itself does not offer a ground for arguing that compassionate and empathic behavior is to be preferred above non-compassionate and non-empathic behavior, we have to search for another argument why compassionate behavior is better than being non-compassionate. For instance, one could argue that compassion is preferable because it is a "good" emotion, meaning that it may be useful or profitable. This argumentative strategy is followed by Armstrong, Krznaric, as well as Nussbaum. All three speak highly of the advantageous aspects of a compassionate attitude: compassion has a liberating effect; it broadens the mind and enables us to reach out to others, to be curious about their behavior and way of life. Compassion and empathy are praised for having the effect of an *ekstasis* on the human mind:

13. Nietzsche, *The Antichrist*, 26.
14. Armstrong, *Twelve Steps*, 301.
15. Inspired by Wittgenstein's *On Certainty*, Hermann points to the interwovenness of morality and nature and yet argues that this does not mean that they can be reduced to each other. She also argues that capacity for moral judgement implies feeling in the right (moral) way, and this includes experiencing empathy, having pity for someone who suffers. These are acts that can be learned and that shape us to become participants in moral language-games. Human beings develop moral competence in practice, through interaction with others. But theoretical arguments about the way moral education works can never be the ground of the moral practices we participate in, Hermann, "Man as a Moral Animal."

both offer the possibility of stepping out of one's own mind and looking at the world through the eyes of other people. In our perilously divided world, Armstrong says, engaging in acts of compassion is in our best interest.[16] Empathy deepens personal relationships, and Krznaric sees possibilities of enlarging the empathic circle to include animals and plants, in order to arrive at an attitude of "*biophilia*"—the love for all that lives—which brings to mind Schopenhauer's ethics.[17]

Nussbaum argues that compassion is not a sign of weakness or an irregular emotion, as Kant was inclined to think. On the contrary, it is a *useful* emotion that must be integrated in educational processes. Equally important, compassionate imaging could be a source of inspiration for institutions, as compassion contains "a powerful, if partial, vision of just distribution." Compassion is not only a private "good" emotion, meaning that it is profitable for individuals and their relations to others. It is in the first place a basic social emotion that is useful because it could orient institutions to make this world a better and a more pleasant, peaceful place.[18]

This line of argumentation, according to which compassion is defended and in the same line recommended, because it is an attitude we might need in a divided and competitive world, also gives rise to questions. As in the argument that builds on compassion's naturalness, here too we could ask whether a focus on the useful and profitable effects of compassion perhaps narrows our understanding of compassion in its broadness. In the following section, I will try to clarify this point with the help of phenomenological research into the relation between self and other, referring to the work of Edith Stein and Emmanuel Levinas. Is it possible that emphasizing the usefulness and benefits of compassion has the effects of obscuring another feature of this phenomenon which has to do with our incapacity to understand other persons' motives for their behavior?

Empathy, Nearness, Responsibility

With respect to empathy (in most publications an important aspect of compassion), Husserl student Edith Stein pointed to the fact that it is grounded in humility, because the empathic position is one in which we know that we are not the other. Stein also shows that, in the experience of empathy, there is a difference between the position of the self and the position of the other, which means that empathy could be on the wrong track and should

---

16. Armstrong, *Twelve Steps*, 18; see also 109, 113, 117; and Krznaric, *Empathy*, 166.
17. Krznaric, *Empathy*, 199.
18. Nussbaum, "Compassion," 37; Nussbaum, *Upheavals*, 425–33.

be corrigible. Empathy, Stein argues, is specifically significant ethically, because it can and even has to go through this process of errors and corrections. In other words: empathy does not only claim to directly know or intuit what the other person feels, but it proves to be even more empathic when it expresses this distance between self and other and is able to concede that "I have no idea how you feel."[19]

Stein's remarks on empathy are significant, because they give room to insights about the remaining differences between the empathic self and the other toward whom the empathy is directed. Moreover, they connect the ethical significance of empathy to the degree in which this otherness is expressed in the empathic act itself.

In the philosophy of another Husserl student, Emmanuel Levinas, this difference between self and other is pushed even further toward the notion of a certain "ethical" transcendence of the other. Like Edith Stein, Levinas does not see the other as an alter ego, a replica of the self. The other as a phenomenon, i.e., as he or she "appears" to the self is rather characterized by a certain strangeness and non-familiarity. And it is first and foremost this strangeness that provokes and stimulates responsibility. In his phenomenology of responsibility, Levinas holds that the ethical relation between self and other is inspired by the absence of the possibility of fusion. It is the "alterity" of the other, the strangeness of his or her appearing in an otherwise familiar and orderly world that commands the "self," the "I" to take responsibility for the other.

It is for this reason that Levinas often underlines the asymmetry of the relation between self and other: the other is defined by the fact that he or she is what I am not, being "absolutely other."[20] Responsibility therefore also implies the experience of being *involuntarily* chosen and even elected to do what is necessary to help the other. Compassion as an incentive to responsibility would not so much be an act of the will, flowing from a decision, or a desire to show more understanding or empathy towards another person, but it could also be an invitation or a feeling to be called to go against one's will. Therefore compassion, understood as charitable love or neighborly love, could also imply the experience of being placed in a position in which one simply has no choice, but rather is chosen.

Levinas's phenomenology of responsibility calls for some more attention in this respect, because it is based on a peculiar notion of proximity that both deepens and criticizes the usual conception we have of compassion

---

19. Stein, *On the Problem of Empathy*, 87–89. Therefore, it seems far too optimistic to suggest that most problems in the world could be solved by "more empathy." See Krznaric, *Empathy*, xvi–xxii.

20. Levinas, *Totality and Infinity*, 39.

as the apparently "natural" ability to understand others and to imagine what their feelings are like. In contrast to Armstrong and Nussbaum, who approach compassion and empathy as the ability to know, understand or intuit what the other is feeling, Levinas inspires me to approach compassion from the perspective of proximity. In proximity, the ability to know or understand what the other feels is only secondary compared to features like practically taking care of the other, being engaged in the other's fate, and taking responsibility.[21]

Being connected to responsibility, the phenomenon of nearness or proximity does not necessarily imply empathy or *Einfühlung*. On the contrary, Levinas seems to argue that experiencing responsibility or ethical engagement *precedes* empathy. It rather has its origins in a shared vulnerability, a being exposed as beings of flesh and blood to the same condition. Taking care of the other's needs is realized not in acts of knowing and understanding, but in the immediacy of the sensible: the place where we experience enjoyment as well as frustration.[22] Therefore, proximity as caring for the other does not result in some form of mutual understanding or sharing of feelings. And obviously, compassion as proximity seems to be cut off from empathy as coming close to feelings of friendship, as Levinas's persistent criticism of Buber shows.[23] In proximity, the strangeness of the other person is maintained; it is not cancelled, removed, or nullified by the nearness. Different from empathy and compassion, which can be explained as the ability to draw near to the other by both expressions of feeling or knowing what the other is going through, proximity is beyond the acts of both knowing and understanding. If compassion is connected with proximity as explained by Levinas, it must not be interpreted as an ability to know or understand the other, but rather as a difficult form of love that can even endure the absence of equality and deep differences between the self and the other.

Compassion, Empathy, and the Experience of Difference

In some of the publications mentioned before, compassion is seen as a phenomenon with religious connotations. However, even then, the impact of the religious horizon on compassion is not always very clear, as compassion is also interpreted as an experience or practice that is common to all human beings. Karen Armstrong, for example, sees compassion as the ethical point

---

21. Levinas, *Alterity and Transcendence*, 160–63.
22. Levinas, *Otherwise than Being*, 57.
23. Levinas, *Proper Names*, 25–27.

of departure which all religions have in common. Therefore, she connects the Buddhist notion of *karuna* ("compassion, the desire that all creatures be free of pain") with Confucius's notion of *ren*, which inspires the respect of others, leading to an *ekstasis* that leaves the grasping self behind, and finally with the Golden Rule, which was taught by both Hillel and Jesus.[24] Armstrong draws on diverse religious sources, but eventually aims at a notion of compassion that is free from specific religious content. She concentrates on the work that lies before us as human beings, going from mindfulness, "concern for everybody," "knowledge," and "recognition" to the apotheosis of "loving the enemy." It is this kind of love and "concern for everybody," she assures, that "will serve our best interests better than short-sighted and self-serving politics."[25] Martha Nussbaum, on the other hand, does not even mention the religious roots of the notion of compassion, but carefully confines herself to references from classical and contemporary literary texts.

Also remarkable is the fact that both Nussbaum's and Armstrong's idea of compassion is strongly connected to the attitude of knowing, even to the point where knowledge becomes an essential characteristic of compassion. To mention just one example: an indispensable step in Armstrong's method for arriving at a compassionate life is "to broaden one's *knowledge* about other human beings" (emphasis mine). Armstrong suggests that this could be realized by making the effort to deepen one's knowledge of a certain country or a certain culture. For Nussbaum, equally, compassion is a kind of understanding, which explains her criticism of Enlightenment philosophy for the reason that it regards compassion as an irrational emotion.

Yet, perhaps such a debate on the rational or irrational nature of compassion is misleading. Earlier, I referred to Edith Stein and Emmanuel Levinas, who in their reworking of Husserl's notion of *Einfühlung* called attention to the impact of the *difference* between self and other on our capacity for understanding him or her. In my opinion, an account of what compassion or empathy is should also contain a reference to this difference that seems to escape the dilemma of rationality versus irrationality, or ratio and emotion. The most essential feature of compassion possibly comes to the fore when human beings are able to endure (which does not necessarily mean "to understand") the *difference* between their own selves and the self of another person that remains inaccessible to them, both rationally and emotionally. Then the positive definition of compassion as love of one's neighbor would have to be distinguished from the ability to understand the other and to interpret the other's feelings. Sometimes, Levinas translates

---

24. Armstrong, *Twelve Steps*, 38, 47.
25. Armstrong, *Twelve Steps*, 169.

neighborly love as a return to the fact of the mortality of the other, and to the ethical impossibility of leaving the other alone in this isolation.[26] Perhaps this is a helpful interpretation of compassion, because it allows us to separate it from the bonds of the understandable and the useful. Subsequently, compassion could be defined as bearing the transcendence of the other (that is rooted in his/her mortality). Then, the work of compassion or mercy would be characterized by its capability to go beyond usefulness and to make us forget its possible profit for ourselves or for society. This is how Paul Moyaert defines compassion: by arguing that the core of charitable love must be not in its possible usefulness, but in the ability to be patient with the other and to endure his or her radical otherness.[27] Compassion is not only a "basic social emotion," as Nussbaum argues, but should also be understood as a form of charity which asks for the ability to go beyond what is useful or profitable. For instance, compassion as charity asks for the readiness to be long-suffering, because of the community's powerlessness to restore itself. Charity also has to live through various experiences of distance and difference, as it has to accept, in many circumstances, that "the wound or gap between myself and the neighbour cannot be healed."[28] One is reminded of Kierkegaard, who in *Works of Love* mentions the remembering of the dead as a work of ultimate love and mercy, because is it beyond usefulness and benefit.[29] In the following paragraph, I will reflect on the impact of this experience of difference. What are the implications for an ethics of compassion? What does an ethics of compassion imply when it extends to what is beyond usefulness and understanding?

Levinas and Badiou: Compassion, Fraternity, and the Refusal of Exclusion

In the foregoing, we saw that compassion is sometimes understood as a form of knowledge or understanding, or as a useful social emotion, and that the relation of compassion as an ethical phenomenon with religion is rather superficial (Armstrong) or totally absent (Nussbaum). Perhaps there is a relation between the two. As we have seen, Armstrong sees compassion as the common denominator of various world religions, without religion mattering in any specific sense. Nussbaum, for her part, ignores the

26. Levinas, *Alterity and Transcendence*, 164.
27. Moyaert, "Charitable Love."
28. Moyaert, "Charitable Love," 187.
29. See, for instance, the deliberation on "The Work of Love in Recollecting One Who is Dead," in Kierkegaard, *Works of Love*, 345–59.

contribution of religion to compassion. The explanations that both give of compassion and empathy are characterized by an emphasis on the ability to know, or to have access to the feelings and experiences of the other person, and to use this knowledge for the improvement of the other's situation and eventually the conditions of the social environment and/or the planet earth (Krznaric). But, as we have seen, all authors neglect an aspect of compassion and empathy that comes to the fore in the works of Edith Stein, Emmanuel Levinas, and Søren Kierkegaard. It is an aspect that is explained by Moyaert as the ability for a charitable person to bear the other's transcendence and to endure the strangeness of the other that is given even in situations of what Levinas calls "ethical proximity." Now, we could ask what one should think of this difference in perspective. In what follows, I will try to clarify the difference between the two perspectives on compassion by referring to the difference between ontology and ethics. Here, I will touch upon a discussion that was opened by Alain Badiou, who critically raised questions about the nature and viability of Levinas's ethics, as it distances itself from ontology. I will use Levinas's ethics as a paradigm of an approach to compassion which accounts both for the strangeness and the transcendence of the other. Badiou's debate is clarifying, because it explains the difficult and even problematic position of an ethics that strives to account for the element of strangeness and transcendence hidden in charitable love or neighborly love. Badiou's critical commentary on Levinas leads to refine the question in the following form: What links compassion to neighborly love? What changes will be introduced into our notion of compassion when it is understood as a form of charity, or neighborly love?

In his *Ethics, an Essay on the Understanding of Evil*, Alain Badiou offers a fascinating critique of contemporary ethics, which can also be read as a criticism of contemporary forms of philosophy inspired by compassion or fraternity as the refusal of exclusion.[30] He wonders by what notion of otherness this way of doing philosophy is driven and concludes that it could be characterized as "tourist," in the sense of focusing attention on cultural differences. Many forms of contemporary ethics, Badiou argues, are anxious to prevent and refuse "exclusion." Their ideal is the peaceful coexistence of cultural, religious, and national communities. From his own philosophical point of view that can be characterized as "ontological," Badiou then begins to ask what these differences are supposed to mean. Do they ever become meaningful for thought, or is their function merely to point at the endless multiplicity of humankind? To be sure, it is obvious that differences are everywhere. But in principle the

---

30. Badiou, *Ethics*. Originally published in French as *L'éthique: Essai sur la conscience du mal* (Paris: Hatier 1993).

difference between "me and my cousin" in the city of Lyon would not count more or less than the difference between the Shi'ite community of Iraq and the cowboys of Texas (the example is from Badiou).

From this perspective, Badiou develops a criticism of the *culturalist* foundation of contemporary ethics: this form of ethics seeks its point of departure in "a tourist's fascination for the diversity of morals, customs and beliefs," whereas "genuine thought" would rather distance itself from the "tourist" perspective. Genuine thought implies the recognition and affirmation of the enormous set of differences given in reality. These differences simply are "what there is," whereas truth is inclined to cast off such differences and make them insignificant. Therefore, still according to Badiou, the "recognition of the other" and the ethics that strives for such recognition contain no truth: it fails to shed a new light on the given situation in which differences exist.

Badiou's argument could be interpreted as a critique of Levinas's ethics, and as an attempt to indicate where Levinas fails to express a truth when he anchors ethics in infinite otherness.[31] A closer look, however, shows that this is only one side of Badiou's commentary on Levinas. Carefully read, these paragraphs from Badiou's *Ethics* make another distinction more plausible, i.e., the one between an ethics of the other that cannot but refer to religion as its last horizon of meaning (as Levinas does), and a more general ethics of otherness that stays within the human being and therefore *refuses* such reference to the religious. Badiou explains the difference between the two forms of ethics of otherness with reference to their respective framing of the notion of finiteness. With Levinas, the idea of Otherness is carried by a principle of alterity that transcends mere finite experience, and which is therefore called "Altogether-Other." According to Badiou, this expression "Altogether-Other" is "most obviously the ethical name for God," and therefore he claims that the notion of Altogether-Otherness must be presupposed in any finite devotion to the non-identical. In short: "There can be no ethics without God the ineffable." In other words: Levinas would remind us that every effort to turn ethics into the principle of thought is "essentially religious." This is the main reason why Badiou considers Levinas's philosophy to be "no longer Greek," which is another expression to say that Levinas's line of thought no longer belongs to the sphere of philosophy. It is a "philosophy annulled by theology, itself no longer a theology . . . but, precisely, an ethics." In summary, Levinas must be regarded as the philosopher who made visible that ethics, as soon as

---

31. For a thoughtful analysis of Badiou's interpretation of Levinas, see Strhan, *Levinas: Subjectivity, Education*.

it is distanced from its Greek usage (i.e., from its subordination to the theoretical), becomes a category of "pious discourse."[32]

Badiou then continues to point out that contemporary ethics most of the time proceeds differently from Levinas. It takes over some aspects of Levinas's ethics of the infinitely other, while *suppressing* the religious character of the ethics of otherness. The result is an ethics in which difference as such is glorified, and respect for differences and the ethics of human rights are beginning to define an identity in which, paradoxically, there is no room for any real difference. Here the celebrated other is presented as acceptable only if he/she is a *good* other, which means: if he/she is the same as us. Badiou, ironically says: "Respect for differences of course! As long as the different be like us: parliamentary-democratic, pro free-market economics, in favour of freedom of opinion, feminism, the environment. . ."[33]

In our discussion on compassion, its usefulness and supposed relation to rationality, this commentary on Levinas is helpful, because it sheds new light on the relation between Levinas's ethics of Otherness and the ethics of compassion as proposed by Nussbaum and Armstrong. Unlike Badiou, who himself proposes to follow an a-religious system of thought (there is no God), I would like to suggest the following line of thought: what if there is truth in Levinas's notion of an ethics that comes before ontology and therefore (in order to be able to understand itself as distinct from Greek ontology) has to listen to more than one source, that is to say, both to religious and philosophical sources?[34]

In my view, Badiou's most valuable suggestion is that ethics as such presupposes a form of (religious) otherness which attempts not only to respect or tolerate, but also to live and to bear deep differences. If an ethics of compassion is possible at all, then it would need a more explicit expression of its religious presuppositions. This will possibly lead to the discovery of *more* differences, because religions not only have similarities, but also differ profoundly from each other. Recognition, and what is more, *bearing* the otherness and transcendence of the other,[35] presupposes the notion of infinite otherness, which could be interpreted as a religious notion.

---

32. Badiou, *Ethics*, 22–23.

33. Badiou, *Ethics*, 24. To prove the point, Badiou suggests considering the obsessive resentment expressed by partisans of ethics (and, we could add, "compassion" or "empathy") regarding anything that resembles Islamic fundamentalism.

34. Levinas, *Humanisme*, 89–90. For an interpretation, see my *Man as a Place of God*, 372–78, and footnote 33.

35. See the earlier-mentioned notion of compassion as bearing the transcendence of the other in Moyaert.

This approach opens up a new perspective on the meaning of Levinas's notion of the Infinite, and on the relation between religion and ethics as well. To mention Kierkegaard's *Works of Love* again: How could neighborly love and compassion be possible without the notion of a love that both *precedes* and *transcends* the human and finite possibilities of loving one's neighbor? Or, more in the line of Levinas: How could the other be perceived as "infinitely other" without reference, be it in the form of a trace, to an infinite otherness (or "*illeïté*," as a name for God) which commands us to one another?

As I pointed out before, proximity is a central feature in Levinas's perspective on compassion, and it works in two ways. In the first place, it helps to articulate in which human experience the ethical encounter is rooted. But at the same time, proximity is the phenomenon that makes the word "God" understandable and even concrete. After all, speaking of God—referring to God—is more than a question of belief versus rationality. Levinas was perfectly aware of the problematic place of the word "God" with its religious connotations in the area of philosophy. For this reason, he made use of the expression "divine comedy" to refer to the ethical intrigue that surpasses understanding and therefore could be a trace of this word for the infinite which no longer has a place in philosophy.[36] Experiences, such as responsibility which comes *before* freedom, or preparedness to take the place of another person, give insight into the way in which the word "God" can acquire new meaning beyond the realm of knowing.[37]

For Levinas, this is the really new—and possibly decisive—moment in modern philosophy: the discovery that humanness is not *knowledge* about God, but rather the place where God works, where "God lives."[38] Thus, compassion and mercy can be understood as concrete phenomena of God's presence and thus as phenomena where the human being is fully human and at the same time rises above mere humanity.

Following this line of thought, I come to the conclusion (a provisional conclusion) that compassion should not exclusively be understood as a form of empathy or *Einfühlung*, or as a way to come near to the other through understanding. Instead, it should be seen as the ability to engage with others despite their strangeness and incomprehensibility. Compassion, understood

---

36. "Divine comedy," see Levinas, *Of God Who Comes to Mind*, 65–70.

37. "The face is the locus of the word of God," Levinas, *Alterity and Transcendence*, 104.

38. Thus Levinas in an interview with Christoph von Wolzogen, published in the German translation of *Humanisme de l'autre homme*. The need for phenomenological concreteness in the use of the word "God" is a constant theme in Levinas's work; Levinas, *Humanismus des Anderen Menschen*, 139–40.

as mercy or charity is not a form of knowledge, but first and foremost a strange and even difficult form of love. Therefore, compassion is in itself neither natural nor merely useful, but rather exceeds such frameworks of interpretation. Understood as a form of love, compassion is special, because it refers to a love that both precedes and transcends human possibilities of loving one's neighbor. The human being is rightly "more than human" here. Therefore an attempt to understand the phenomenon of compassion could be a reason to invoke other sources, religious sources for instance, and to speak (and listen to) different languages, as places where "extremes meet."[39]

Bibliography

Armstrong, Karen. *Twelve Steps to a Compassionate Life*. New York: Anchor, 2011.
Badiou, Alain. *Ethics: An Essay on the Understanding of Evil*. Translated by Peter Hallward. London: Verso, 2001.
De Waal, Frans. *The Age of Empathy: Nature's Lessons for a Kinder Society*. London: Souvenir, 2010.
———. *Good Natured: The Origins of Right and Wrong in Humans and Other Animals*. Cambridge, MA: Harvard University Press, 1996.
Derrida, Jacques. "Violence and Metaphysics. An Essay on the Thought of Emmanuel Levinas." In *Writing and Difference*, translated by Alan Bass, 97–192. London: Routledge, 2001.
Hermann, Julia. "Man as a Moral Animal: Moral Language-Games, Certainty, and the Emotions." In *Language, Ethics and Animal Life. Wittgenstein and Beyond*, edited by M. Burley, and N. Hämäläinen, 111–23. London: Bloomsbury, 2012.
Kierkegaard, Søren. *Works of Love*. Kierkegaard's Writings 16. Princeton: Princeton University Press, 1995.
Krznaric, Roman. *Empathy: A Handbook for Revolution*. London: Rider, 2014.
Levinas, Emmanuel. *Alterity and Transcendence*. Translated by Michael B. Smith. London: Athlone, 1999.
———. *Humanisme de l'Autre Homme*. Montpellier: Fata Morgana, 1972.

39. See the end of "Violence and Metaphysics," Derrida's early but still thought-provoking article on Levinas, in *Writing and Difference*. The final words of this text are: "Jewgreek is greekjew. Extremes meet"; a quotation from James Joyce's *Ulysses*. In Derrida's text the "Jewish" refers to a language that reaches out for the ethical as well as for the infinite, whereas "greek" refers to philosophical language that has a preference for the ontological. In Badiou's *Ethics*, the same division returns with the use of the words "ontological" (for "greek", or "philosophical") and "ethical" (for "Jewish") as a form of pious discourse. Badiou's appraisal of Levinas as the philosopher who showed that ethics is only possible with a reference to some form of religious or "pious" discourse is perfectly in line with Derrida's interpretation of Levinas. In criticizing Levinas, both Derrida and Badiou make visible that there is a deeper problem at stake, which has to do with the relation of ethics to ontology, or, to put it more polemically, with the impossibility to give ethics a place within a purely philosophical ontology. This problem has been put on the agenda by Martin Heidegger and since then has never left contemporary philosophy.

———. *Humanismus des Anderen Menschen*. Hamburg: Felix Meiner, 1989.

———. *Of God Who Comes to Mind*. Translated by Bettina Bergo. Stanford, CA: Stanford University Press, 1998.

———. *Otherwise than Being: Or Beyond Essence*. Pittsburgh: Duquesne University Press 1998.

———. *Proper Names*. Stanford, CA: Stanford University Press, 1996.

———. *Totality and Infinity: An Essay on Exteriority*. Pittsburgh: Duquesne University Press, 1969.

Moyaert, Paul. "Charitable Love: Bearing the Other's Transcendence." *European Journal for Philosophy of Religion* 8 (2016) 183–200.

Nietzsche, Friedrich. *The Antichrist*. Translated by H. L. Mencken. Tucson: Sharp, 1999.

Nussbaum, Martha. "Compassion, the Basic Social Emotion." *Social Philosophy and Policy* 13 (1996) 27–57.

———. *Upheavals of Thought. The Intelligence of Emotions*. Cambridge: Cambridge University Press, 2001.

Ricard, Matthieu. *Plaidoyer pour l'Altruisme: La Force de la Bienveillance*. Paris: NiL, 2013.

Stein, Edith. *On the Problem of Empathy*. Vol. 3 of *The Collected Works of Edith Stein*. Washington, DC: ICS, 1989.

Strhan, Anna. *Levinas, Subjectivity, Education. Towards an Ethics of Radical Responsibility*. Oxford: Wiley-Blackwell, 2012.

Van Riessen, Renée D. N. *Man as a Place of God. Levinas's Hermeneutics of Kenosis*. Dordrecht: Springer, 2007.

Ways of Teaching Compassion in the Synoptic Gospels

Annette Merz

Compassion is a topic that attracts plenty of attention nowadays, socially as well as academically. I intend to contribute to this discussion from the perspective of my own field, namely, New Testament.[1] In the first paragraph I shall go into the historical embedment of the discourse on "compassion" in the New Testament in Hellenistic Judaism and its distinctiveness from classical thought. I briefly mention the most important Greek words describing this concept, as well as their meaning. After that, I shall discuss key aspects of compassion in the synoptic gospels in two paragraphs, dedicated to Mark, and to Matthew and Luke respectively.[2] Whereas often the parable of the compassionate Samaritan is regarded as the main gospel tradition to be discussed in this regard, I strive to discern different ways of teaching compassion in the synoptics and different ways of theological reasoning connected to this teaching. I hope to demonstrate that the synoptic gospels can be regarded as a "manual of compassion" with several quite distinct chapters.

---

1. A first version of this essay was delivered in Dutch as an academic speech at the *Dies Natalis* of the Protestant Theological University, in Amsterdam, on December 6, 2016. I thank all colleagues who responded with helpful comments and suggestions and especially Ria Smit who translated the Dutch version into English and improved the reworked version.

2. The traditional Jewish language of compassion that is dealt with in this essay is nearly completely absent in the gospel of John and Johannine literature. It is beyond the scope of this article to discuss the reasons for this.

Compassion in the Literature of Second Temple Judaism and Classical Antiquity

In its speaking about divine and human compassion, the New Testament is deeply rooted in the traditions of Israel and expands on the language usage of Judaism of the Hellenistic age. It has been shown in recent scholarship that one can identify an increase in reflection on emotions in general, and on compassion in particular, in the literature of Hellenistic Judaism.[3] Proverbs 17:5 allows an informative comparison between a Hebrew proverb and its amplification in the Septuagint. The Hebrew version consists of a parallelism:

> Those who mock the poor insult their Maker (e.g. God the creator); those who are glad at calamity (of another) will not go unpunished.

Here, *Schadenfreude* (malicious pleasure), one of the evil opponents of compassion, is exposed. In the Septuagint translation of this verse, we see a characteristic addition:

> He that laughs at the poor provokes him that made him; and he that rejoices at the destruction of another shall not be held guiltless, but he that has compassion shall find mercy (ὁ δὲ ἐπισπλαγχνιζόμενος ἐλεηθήσεται).

In this passage, we encounter terms and theological notions which are also omnipresent in the gospels. Firstly, the obvious eschatologization should be noted: the retaliation that would meet up with the mocker *in this life* in the Hebrew Bible is transferred to the future judgment where God will judge all persons according to their deeds.[4] When Jesus proclaims in the Sermon on the Mount according to Matthew: "Blessed are the merciful, for they will receive mercy (μακάριοι οἱ ἐλεήμονες, ὅτι αὐτοὶ ἐλεηθήσονται)", he uses exactly the same theological reasoning (see beneath). If we look more closely at the vocabulary, we observe that the addition in Proverbs

---

3. See Giese, "Compassion for the Lowly in Septuagint Proverbs," for the selected example. For a more detailed view and overview of research on compassion in antiquity, Mirguet, "Emotional Responses," and the responses of Pearce (858–62), Lateiner (863–8), and Konstan (869–72) in the same volume. A full treatment of the topic is provided by the yet unpublished work of Mirguet, *An Early History of Compassion*. I am very grateful to the author for providing me with a pdf copy of her comprehensive and insightful study.

4. As usual, the passive forms are to be understood as *passiva divina*. Using the passive voice avoids the direct naming of God as the causal agent; this in adherence to the commandment not to abuse the name of God.

17:5 LXX uses words of roots that belong to the most frequently used in the writings of Hellenistic Judaism when dealing with compassion. These include the verb σπλαγχνίζομαι, with the accompanying noun σπλάγχνα, and the verb ἐλεέω, of which the root appears in several derivations, such as in ἔλεος, ἐλεημοσύνη, ἐλεήμων. The top three are complemented by the root οἰκτ- (οἰκτίρω, οἰκτιρμός, οἰκτίρμων).[5]

Let us dwell for a moment on σπλαγχνίζομαι / σπλάγχνα.[6] In Classical Greek, σπλάγχνα depicts the inner organs, in the first place those of sacrificial animals, but also those of human beings. The active verbs σπλαγχνεύω and σπλαγχνίζω then mean "eating of the inner organs on the occasion of a sacrifice." In authors such as Aristophanes, Sophocles, and Aeschylus, we find the idea of the σπλάγχνα as the seat of the passions: wrath, pain, fear, and love are sensed in the inner organs. But an association of σπλάγχνα with *commiseration* can only be found in Greek—apart from only one exception in Chrysippus[7]—in the Judeo-Hellenistic literature and later on in Christian writings. And there it appears abundantly. As an explanation for this, Françoise Mirguet pointed out a narrowing in the meaning of σπλάγχνα in some Judeo-Hellenistic writings. There, the σπλάγχνα are the seat of a specific emotion, namely, the love for a child by a parent, felt inside the parent's innermost, specifically in situations of pain and danger. One can also detect Hebrew influence here, where רֶחֶם designates the womb and רַחֲמִים the inner organs. רַחֲמִים became a fixed metaphor, mainly in the psalms and the prophets, for the mercy of God, and the verb רחם pi./ *richam*, "showing compassion, " is also mostly used with God as a subject. On the other hand, the Greek root σπλαγχ- is used for both human and godly compassion. James 5:11, for example, states, in line with the Old Testament use, of the *kyrios*: πολύσπλαγχνός ἐστιν ὁ κύριος καὶ οἰκτίρμων, "The Lord is compassionate and merciful." The verb σπλαγχνίζομαι finally is used in the Septuagint and the gospels with relation to human beings, as we already saw above (Prov 17:5 LXX), and will investigate in more detail later. It describes being moved by compassion as a strong bodily reaction.

Before we completely shift our attention to the early Christian writings, brief reflection on the Old Testament image of the merciful God and

---

5. (ἐπι)σπλαγχνίζομαι (to feel pity, to be moved by compassion) / σπλάγχνα (the innermost, heart; love); ἐλεέω (to be merciful); ἔλεος (compassion, mercy); ἐλεημοσύνη (pity, mercy; charity, alms); ἐλεήμων (pitiful, merciful, compassionate); οἰκτίρω (to pity, have compassion); οἰκτιρμός (compassion); οἰκτίρμων (merciful).

6. See for the following Mirguet, "Compassion in the Making."

7. Fragment 904 in Chrysippe, *Œuvre Philosophique*; this corresponds to fragment 902 in Von Arnim, Stoicorum Veterum Fragmenta, 249, cited by Mirguet, "Compassion in the Making," § 5, with footnote 2.

its relation to classical thinking is called for.[8] The fact that the God of Israel is merciful, concerned about the people, full of compassion with their suffering, and even merciful with regard to their sins, is a notion alien to classical antiquity. In Homer, the gods may indeed occasionally show mercy, but compassion certainly is no consistent feature of the gods and not something that human beings can call upon. In the Greek tragedies, the gods present themselves as merciless spectators of human suffering and pain. And among ancient philosophers, compassion as an attribute of gods is not even an option. David Konstan mentions three reasons for this in his important book *Pity Transformed*.[9] Firstly, under the influential definition of Aristotle, mercy (ἔλεος) can only be experienced by people who are similar in nature to the suffering person.[10] Compassion can only be experienced by those who identify with the unfortunate person, who can imagine that they themselves or their loved ones could be subjected to similar misery. The gods, on the other hand, are not susceptible to catastrophe. Secondly, it does not fit in with the philosophical ideas about gods as being in principle not susceptible to feelings. A (pseudo-) Platonic letter formulates the prevailing conviction as follows: "The divine rests beyond pleasure and pain."[11] Thirdly, especially the Stoics emphasized that in juridical and administrative contexts justice may not be thwarted by compassion. While *human beings* were not supposed to give in to impulses of compassion, "[h]ow could one ascribe so corrupting a passion to the immortal gods?"[12]

This brings us to another significant difference between classical Greek notions of compassion and the Judeo-Christian conviction. To Aristotle, an important condition for feeling ἔλεος was that the suffering was undeserved. In the LXX and the New Testament, on the other hand, ἔλεος, according to Danker, can be defined as "kindness or concern expressed for someone in need," where the need does not *necessarily* have to be undeserved.[13] More than that, we shall later see that the need is often explicitly mapped with human guilt.

---

8. For a deeper understanding of the OT conception of Gods mercy, see Spieckermann, "Barmherzig und gnädig ist der Herr"; Dozeman, "Inner-Biblical Interpretation"; Clark, "The Word 'Hesed'"; Franz, *Der barmherzige und gnädige Gott*.

9. Konstan, *Pity Transformed*, 105–24.

10. Aristotle, *Retorica* 2.8.

11. πόρρω γὰρ ἡδονῆς ἵδρυται καὶ λύπης τὸ θεῖον (Ep. 3.315c), translation from Konstan, *Pity Transformed*, 112.

12. Konstan, *Pity Transformed*, 113.

13. Danker, *A Greek-English Lexicon*, s.v. ἔλεος.

David Konstan mentions that since imperial times, the concepts ἔλεος and *misericordia/clementia* also featured outside of Judeo-Christian circles as positive characteristics of gods and rulers. There is no consensus among scholars of antiquity about how one could explain this. Did people lose their trust in the righteousness of gods and rules, and did they therefore appeal to their compassion? Was this an understandable reaction over against the Stoics and their reservation toward emotions, a reaction that brought to the fore the value of compassion once again? Or is it a sign of increasing Jewish and later Christian influence on the ideas of late antiquity?[14] At any rate, it is clear that the early Christian usage has its roots in a key religious conviction of Israel, an interpretation with very old documentation that experienced a revival within various Jewish movements during the first century.

Jesus as a Model of Compassionate Action in the Gospel of Mark

The gospel of Mark is a good starting point for our research into the New Testament, because the topic of compassion has a single clear focus here. The evangelists Matthew and Luke took over this focus virtually unchanged, but supplemented it in various ways, which leads to a more multicolored image in them. Mark is monothematic; all his explicit references to compassion are related to miracles of Jesus.[15] He presents Jesus as a miracle worker and teacher, focused on healing bodily harm and ending physical suffering caused by illness, social and religious exclusion, and hunger.[16] In what follows, I shall sketch the main contours of the image of the compassionate Jesus and his message according to Mark in four steps.

---

14. See Konstan, *Pity Transformed*, 117–20; and Mirguet, *An Early History*, chapter 5 ("In dialogue with the Empire").

15. The explicit references to compassion are related to healings by Jesus (1:41; 5:19; 9:22; 10:47–48) and to his teaching and subsequent feeding (6:34; 8:2). Four times the verb σπλαγχνίζομαι is used by the narrator (1:41; 6:34) and by characters (8:2 [Jesus referring to himself]; 9:22 [the father of the boy with epilepsy asking Jesus to have pity]), three times the verb ἐλεέω is employed by characters (5:19 [Jesus, talking about Gods mercy]; 10:47–48 [Bartimaeus, asking the son of David to have mercy]). In the following I will depart from these explicit references to compassion, which have the effect of characterizing Jesus as a compassionate healer and teacher, but will in one case include a text that shows a remarkable absence of this character trait (e.g., Mark 7:24–30).

16. According to my opinion, the best book on this topic has not been written by an exegete or a theologian, but by an American neurologist and Episcopalian Christian. In *Compassion as a Subversive Activity*, David Urion writes about his daily care for children with severe neurological disorders and in an impressive way brings these reports of his experiences into discussion with the narratives of healings in the gospel of Mark.

The Kingdom Comes Through Deeds of Compassion

In the gospel of Mark, Jesus' deeds of compassion are features of the coming of the kingdom of God in the here and now. That can be deduced from the first programmatic chapter of his gospel (1:1–45). Here, Mark shows who Jesus is, what his message is, and how he brings this message to the people. Through the baptism and temptation we see who Jesus is, namely, the one gifted with the spirit of God, the beloved "Son of God," the lord over Satan, wild animals, and angels. Mark 1:14–15 sums up his task and the core of his message as follows: Jesus is prophet of the good news of God. He proclaims the coming of the eschaton, the anticipated last days: "The time is fulfilled, and the Kingdom of God has come near; repent, and believe in the good news." Subsequently, we see how Jesus brings this core message to the people: he invites four fishermen to follow him and to share in his task as "fishers of people" (1:16–20). He proclaims his message in the synagogue, which leaves everyone astounded and which provokes a first dramatic test of strength with the powers of evil in the form of an unclean spirit (1:21–28).

The report of Jesus' "new teaching—with authority" (1:22, 27) and of his authority to command unclean spirits spreads superfast, and, still on the same day, he first heals the mother-in-law of Simon in Capernaum, then "all who were sick or possessed with demons," many "who were sick with various diseases," and he casts out many demons (1:29–34). The next day, he departs with the disciples to teach in the synagogues all over Galilee and cast out demons (1:35–39). This first phase of Jesus' appearances ends in 1:40–45 with the healing of a leper, where the role of compassion in the healing process is identified for the first time: the sick person asks for help, Jesus is moved with pity[17] and heals him. We shall look at this text in more detail later, but now we first deal with the broader lines. Jesus' actions are characterized by ἐξουσία, authority, which has two dimensions: verbal authority (teaching) and deeds of authority (healings and other actions that express a prophetic self-awareness). In the context of Jewish eschatological expectations, these two dimensions belong together. According to the prophet Isaiah, it is a feature of the time of salvation that the sick people will be healed and that the good news will

---

17. Here, one has to remark that the text in Mark 1:41 is not completely undisputed. The modern critical editions read, in accordance with the majority of manuscripts, "he was moved with pity (σπλαγχνισθείς)." Four manuscripts of the Western text tradition, the *Codex Bezae Cantabrigiensis* and three Old-Latin witnesses, however, read "he was filled with anger," probably to obtain harmonization with the negatively tinged actions of Jesus in v. 43. The swing from compassion (v. 41) to a stern warning (v. 43) can, however, be explained well from Jesus' movements and the sick person(s) in the context: Jesus is increasingly being followed by crowds of sick people and being discovered in the secret places to which he had withdrawn himself (1:32–34; 35–37, 45; 2:1–2).

be proclaimed to the poor (Isaiah 26:19; 29:18; 35:5-6; 42:18; 61:1). One can also find this tradition in the Dead Sea Scrolls (4Q 521)[18] and in Luke and Matthew, who take over a Jesus logion from the Saying Source that explicitly makes this link, namely, the response to the question by John the Baptist (QLk 7:18-23).[19] The two dimensions of Jesus' authority are reflected in the fact that in the gospel of Mark strong expressions of compassion are linked to the healings by Jesus (in 1:41; 5:19; 9:22; 10:47-48), but also once to his teaching. In Mark 6:34, we read:

> [34] As he went ashore, he saw a great crowd; and he had compassion for them, because they were like sheep without a shepherd; and he began to teach them many things.

The compassion is also extended beyond that, namely, to the lack of food: after the teaching, there follows a first miraculous feeding. In Mark 8:2, Jesus' compassion is even linked directly to the hunger of the crowd. From the symbolic twelve and seven baskets of left-over broken pieces taken up afterwards it becomes clear who those are that gather around the table in the desert: at the first feeding, this is the eschatological, renewed Israel, and at the second one, the believers from all nations.[20]

I summarize: The kingdom of God becomes present in the gospel of Mark in the here and now, where people feel the closeness of God through teaching, healing, and an over-abundant communal meal. Compassion is the motive behind Jesus' actions of proclaiming, healing, and inviting people to the table.

---

18. "For he will honor the pious upon the throne of an eternal kingdom, freeing prisoners, giving sight to the blind, straightening out the twis[ted] . . . And for[e]ver shall I cling [to those who h]ope, and in his mercy . . . And the Lord will perform marvelous acts, such as have not existed, just as he sa[id, for] he will heal the badly wounded and will make the dead live; he will proclaim good news to the poor and [. . .] he will lead the [. . .] and enrich the hungry" (4Q 521, fragment 2, 7-12); cited from García Martínez and Tigchelaar, *The Dead Sea Scrolls*.

19. QLk 7:18-23: [22]And he answered them: "Go and tell John what you have seen and heard: the blind receive their sight, the lame walk, the lepers are cleansed, the deaf hear, the dead are raised, the poor have good news brought to them. [23]And blessed is anyone who takes no offense at me." See also the the Q-logion: "But if it is by the finger of God that I cast out the demons, then the kingdom of God has come to you" (QLk 11:20), which explicitly links the proclamation of the kingdom of God to the exorcisms.

20. A thorough analysis of Jesus' meals as a symbol of the kingdom is provided by Smit, *Fellowship and Food in the Kingdom*.

Being Moved Reciprocally as a Feature of Compassion

Let us look more closely at the relational aspect of the encounter between Jesus and the needy, and the role of compassion in this.

> [40] A leper came to him begging him, and kneeling he said to him, "If you choose, you can make me clean." [41] Moved with pity, Jesus stretched out his hand and touched him, and said to him, "I do choose. Be made clean!" [42] Immediately the leprosy left him, and he was made clean (Mark 1:40–42).

The healing of the leper in Mark 1:40–45 is in many respects a classical synoptic miracle narrative, but it is particularly characterized by the reciprocal reaching out, compared to the standard model. The sick person comes to Jesus and expresses his trust in the authority of the miracle worker; Jesus is moved with pity and touches the leper; he subsequently confirms that he indeed wishes to take away the ailment, gives an order ("be made clean"), and the miracle happens. Because we are dealing with a leper, whom one should not touch under any circumstances, the order of the actions is crucial here. The man comes so close to Jesus as it is allowed by his illness. Bodily contact is impossible, but he "comes in" to Jesus with his expression of trust: "If you choose, you can make me clean." He begs him to take away the barrier that separates him from normal people. Jesus allows himself to be moved by the man's need and his trust; he feels compassion. The direct result of this is that he makes physical contact and with that breaks down the invisible wall of separation existing between the untouchable and all non-lepers. The word that works miracles simply confirms that which has already happened in the reciprocal reaching out and in the touching through trust. In other miracle narratives, Jesus puts this into words by his statements: "Your faith has saved you," or: "Everything is possible for those who trust/have faith."

On the basis of Mark 1:45, compassion can therefore be described as reciprocal opening up in trust. Two narratives illustrate how important it is when this does not happen, or not happens directly: Mark 6:1–6 and Mark 7:24–30, which mirror each other, because they show that both parties have to be open for a miracle to happen.

Mark 6:1–6 tells that Jesus' teaching in the synagogue of Nazareth was met with disbelief (6:6: ἀπιστία). The people were not susceptible to the teaching and the powerful deeds from a former fellow villager. And therefore, we read in Mark 6:5, he could not do a single miracle there.

Not much later, things almost went wrong on Jesus' side as well (Mark 7:24–30). A Greek-speaking women came to him; a woman from Syrophoenician origin from the city of Tyre; a non-Jew who is still prepared to put aside her fear for the unknown and to fall before the feet of a Jewish miracle worker for the sake of healing her daughter. But at first Jesus does not let her experience any compassion; on the contrary, he treats her terribly and makes the distance between them so wide that it may seem unsurpassable.[21] She, who begs for the healing of her daughter, has to hear that he cannot throw his bread, which is destined for Jewish children, to the dogs. In this narrative, the woman is the heroine of the compassion, because she shows understanding for his rejection. Having been called a dog, she actually shows her human imagination and shrewdness. She replies to Jesus by taking over the image of the dog used by Jesus but changing the picture in such a way that it shows a world in which she does justice to both of them. He may still call her daughter a "dog," so be it, if only she can get some crumbs falling from the table. In fact, she calls him to task regarding the compassion that people can feel for all fellow creatures and regarding the abundance of gifts that God has bestowed on him. There is absolutely no shortage of bread. One only has to prepare space at the table. Jesus expresses his admiration for her reply and does no longer refuse to take up her little daughter in the circle of those for whom he feels compassion, and brings about healing. With this, a fundamental breakthrough has been achieved; the future community of heathens has in anticipation been written into the charter of foundation of faith. It certainly then is no coincidence that Jesus, after his encounter with the Syrophoenician woman, performs a second feeding on the other side of the lake of Galilee, in the area of the Decapolis, for 4000 people, and that this time, not twelve, but seven baskets of bread were left over.

Boundaries of Compassion Extended by Inclusion of the Stigmatized

With his descriptions of compassion and overcoming obstacles to empathy, the evangelist Mark shows himself as a psychologically sensitive author and a sociologist *avant la lettre*. Lepers form a strongly stigmatized group; they elicit disgust and the fear of infection. The Syrophoenician woman is doubly inferior in the eyes of a Jewish man: as a heathen and as a woman. Furthermore, she is viewed with extra bitter jealousy as a representative of the rich *Herrenklasse* in the city that exploited the Jewish rural population

---

21. Still one of the best interpretations of this narrative: Theissen, *Lokalkolorit und Zeitgeschichte*, 62-84; ET: *The Gospels in Context*, 60-80. Theissen shows specifically that the expression of the bread of the (Jewish) children that is being thrown to the dogs (heathens) concurs with the socioeconomic reality: the Jewish villages in the area of Tyre were the bread basket of the Hellenistic metropolis. In times of famine the urban dwellers bought everything and the producers were left hungry.

and took away their last pieces of bread, so that the Jewish children indeed very often went hungry. Finally, the possessed person in Mark 5, who lives in cave tombs and is tormented by demons and provoked to self-mutilation—demons having the name of the foreign occupiers ("legions")—is alienated from all human contact. Jesus shows his involvement specifically in the suffering of these marginalized people. The effect of this is an appeal on readers of all times to realize their own boundaries of compassion and involvement, and move them. David Urion is a prime witness to this effect of the gospel stories on him as a neurologist and devoted member of an Episcopalian community. In several examples, he writes about severely sick children who are marginalized in the Christian communal life because their illnesses are experienced as strange or repulsive, or because their vulnerability is so obvious that the people in the community cannot deal with it; and he writes about the miracles of inclusion that sometimes happen. But he also points out the global dimension—quite rightly so, because the justice of the kingdom of God does not know a policy of own-country-first:

> Every day, we offer less than the crumbs under our table to a world that is suffering. HIV/AIDS may be a treatable illness in the developed world, but in Africa, Asia, and the Caribbean it kills huge numbers of people daily. These people are our brothers and sisters. Every day, millions suffer from malaria, and thousands die ... In the moment of our baptism, we made a promise that we would resist all the forces of darkness, we would struggle against all the forces that corrupt and destroy the creatures of God. We cannot walk away from those promises lightly ... However we try to evade the question, the Syrophoenician woman sits there waiting for us, with her child possessed by a demon.[22]

All compassionate deeds of Jesus in the gospel of Mark are focused on restoring damaged communities or creating community. He touches the leper before the priest, the guardian of the boundaries defined by the laws of purity of the group, has declared him clean. He eats with the tax collectors and sinners before they had officially atoned and compares this with his healings by saying that the healthy do not need a physician (Mark 2:17). Matthew and Luke emphasize this aspect of Jesus' compassionate interventions even stronger. Matthew also identifies it as an act of compassion, by having Jesus quoting Hosea 6:6 as defense for sharing the table with sinners: "I desire mercy, not sacrifice" (Matt 9:13).

With David Urion, Jesus' programmatic solidarity with the weak can be described as a subversive political strategy: compassion as an antidote against

---

22. Urion, *Compassion as a Subversive Activity*, 117–18.

the usual divide and rule. Because, in the moment of compassion, shared human vulnerability is stronger than anything that can separate people.

Human Compassion as Transcendental Power

And where does God fit into this picture? Since the evangelist ascribes all deeds and expressions of compassion to Jesus, God's compassion almost disappears in the gospel of Mark. Mark 5:19 is the only significant exception. Jesus sends the healed man of Gerasenes back to his home with the order: "Go home to your friends, and tell them how much the Lord has done for you, and what mercy he has shown you." The formerly possessed man obeys, but with a significant change: he proclaims in the Decapolis what Jesus had done for him (5:20). This shows how the evangelist views the relationship between God and Jesus. They are not identical, but Jesus mediates the compassion of God, and where Jesus' deeds are proclaimed the God of Israel is glorified.[23]

Mark 5:19–20 points out a key theoretical and theological insight: it is always a matter of interpretation to whom we ascribe a compassionate act by ourselves or others. Is it our own genetically determined ability, required through socialization, to assist the Other through shared human self-interest? Or is it a transcendental power, in Judeo-Christian terms: the compassion of God that is working; a power that rises beyond human limitations? Could it be that those who know they are related to a transcendental source of power have more power available? Conclusive objective answers to such questions cannot be given by scientific experiments, at least not at the moment. In these matters, each person has to be his or her own experiential expert.

I conclude: To the evangelist Mark, the compassion of the Messiah is part of his connection with God and proof of the dawning of the eschatological reality (the kingdom of God) in the here and now. It is striking that Jesus' compassion is brought to the attention of the reader through explicit mentioning or through a clear narrative element in those cases where one can expect strong religious or cultural resistance against it (in the cases of the leper, the person in the graves possessed by the legions, the daughter of the Syrophoenician woman who was compared with dogs). The resultant appeal brought to the readers is indirect; they are summoned by the example of Jesus to move the boundaries of their own compassion. A direct appeal to the readers to be compassionate is missing in the gospel of Mark. That changes when we inquire into compassion in the gospels of Matthew

---

23. Marcus, *Mark 1–8*, 354.

and Luke, because with these evangelists compassion is an important topic in Jesus' teachings.

Jesus' Teaching of Compassion in the Gospels of Matthew and Luke

Whereas Mark mainly makes an *indirect* appeal to the reader regarding Jesus' deeds of compassion, an indirect appeal to *imitatio Christi*, Jesus often appeals *directly* to his audience to show compassion in the gospels of Matthew and Luke.[24] "Be merciful, just as your Father is merciful" (Luke 6:36)—thus reads the summary of a series of commandments to generosity and love, even to the enemy, in the Sermon on the Plain.[25] In the Sermon on the Mount, the merciful are blessed (Matt 5:7), and giving alms is encouraged in Matthew 6:1–4;[26] the Greek word ἐλεημοσύνη used here means compassion in general and giving alms in particular.[27] Specific emphasis is placed here on the warning that this traditional act of compassion should not be used for self-promotion. This type of direct admonition has close parallels in Jewish literature of the Second Temple Period and the Rabbinic Period. The appeal to compassion is theologically motivated in various ways. The three most important lines of thought here are:

1. Compassion is *imitatio Dei*.
2. Compassion is the core of the Torah.
3. Compassion, in its two forms of readiness to forgive and generosity to the needy, leads to salvation in judgment.

---

24. In my view, it is possible to treat Luke and Matthew together in this section, as the main lines of the discourse on compassion converge to a great extent, presumably reaching back to the teachings of the Historical Jesus. I do not assume that there are no differences, though. See the following footnotes on literature with a special focus on Luke and Matthew. I will not deal with questions regarding the Historical Jesus in this essay, but I certainly agree with Snodgrass's view that compassion is one of the central aspects of his actions and his message, rooted in the experience of the eschatological fulfilment of Isaianic promises; see Snodgrass, "The Gospel of Jesus."

25. There are several studies on compassion in Luke that go into more detail than is possible here. See espesically Van Staden, "Compassion—The Essence of Life"; Gerber, "Les emplois d' ἔλεος en Luc-Actes"; Riemersma, "Barmhartigheid."

26. A detailed study on compassion in Matthew is provided by Weren, "Broederschap en Barmhartigheid."

27. The admonition to give alms is also part of Jesus' teaching in the gospel of Luke; see Luke 11:41 and 12:33. On ἐλεημοσύνη, see Heiligenthal, "Werke der Barmherzigkeit."

These theological lines of thought can be illustrated by means of many texts from the New Testament and Jewish literature. I will restrict myself to the most effective way to promote compassion in the Jesus tradition, which is through the great parables of Jesus. The parables share with Mark's miracle stories the fact that a more indirect appeal is made to readers; that one is more tempted than summoned to take up a compassionate attitude.[28]

Compassion as Imitatio Dei

In Luke, the discourse on compassion is framed by the many references to God's compassion in Israel's history and its recent culmination in the events leading to the birth of the Messiah[29] and Jesus' programmatic admonition: "Be merciful, just as your Father is merciful" (Luke 6:36). The most well-known illustration of this principle is, of course, to be found in the story of the stranded adventurer from Luke 15:11–32, whose father was filled with compassion even before his son could express his confession of guilt (Luke 15:20). The reader remains with the brother who still does not find it so easy to share in the joy of the father. The open end of the story allows any reader to carry out the required learning process (of adopting the compassion modelled by the father) at his or her own pace. But this is not a story concept distinctive of Luke. The laborer who started working early in the morning in Matthew 20:1–16 is faced with an appeal to his capability for compassion, too. When the generous landowner says to him: "Or is your eye evil because I am generous?" (v. 15, Lexham English Bible), he uses, with the expression "evil eye," a well-known metaphor for jealousy or miserliness. Father and employer are without doubt metaphors for God, whose compassion with sinners and deprived people in general should be pursued. In the meantime, empirical research has confirmed what Jesus knows intuitively, namely, that there are few matters that stand more in the way of compassion with a needy person than the worry of not having or not getting enough oneself. Therefore, the fact that these parabolic traditions emphasize that those who give or grant should not be needy themselves, is important. The father says to his son: "all that is mine is yours" (Luke 15:31); the landowner pays the agreed-upon daily wage (Matt 20:2, 13–14) and the children at the table are not hungry when the dogs get the crumbs (Mark 7:28).[30]

---

28. Due to space restrictions, I cannot provide a full exegetical treatment here. I will strictly concentrate on matters related to the topic of compassion and need to be very selective even there.

29. See Luke 1:50, 54–55, 58, 72, 78.

30. In the latter case, we do not explicitly deal with *imitatio Dei / Christi*; superficially

Compassion as Core of the Torah

The fact that showing compassion is a way to fulfil the love command and thereby a (or the) core precept of the Mosaic law is not a Christian invention, but a theological conviction visible in many Judeo-Hellenistic texts (including New Testament traditions) as Françoise Mirguet has shown. She convincingly brought this development into relation with the problem of the adaptation of Jewish identity in the non-Jewish world.[31] It can be conceived, however, that by the first century CE, those traditions had become common in Jewish communities in Palestine as well. Whereas Luke is our main witness for this tendency, it can also be found in the special material of Matthew (see Matt 23:23).

The most distinguishing parable that defines compassion as an expression of love for one's fellow human beings and as the core of the Torah is that of the compassionate Samaritan (Luke 10:30–36), which Jesus relates as a response to the question: "Who is my neighbor?," after love for God and the neighbor have been determined as the core of God's law (Luke 10:25–29).[32] "Which of these three ... was a neighbor to the man who fell into the hands of the robbers?," Jesus finally asks. "The one who showed [literally: did] him mercy" (Luke 10:37), the lawyer answered and he is summoned, as we all are, to do "likewise."[33]

In a renowned experiment in the social sciences, which researched the influence of situational variables on actions, students of theology were sent away, after a short briefing, to a film shooting under the assumption that they

---

seen, it might even be the opposite: the Messiah is prompted to take note of an everyday example. To those who look with the eyes of faith and take the Jewish tradition into account, this example shows the goodness of the Creator, and compassionate children acting according to the will of the heavenly Father.

31. Mirguet, *An Early History*, 255: "On the one hand, pity and compassion, established through translation as a divine attribute, have become, by association, a distinctive flavor of Jewish identity. Jewish ancestors are reshaped into paragons of pity; likewise, pity is retrojected into the Torah. On the other hand, as mentioned above, compassion is also strongly associated with a spontaneous drive that human beings naturally possess. Urging pity and compassion to all creatively adapts Jewish identity to a new cultural context, harmonizing it with the perceived ideals of the broader human community. Compassion makes the self a 'citizen of the world' at the same time as it fulfills the Jewish law. More affective than love, compassion is also more reliant on bonds—and more likely, therefore, to form new ones."

32. I thankfully adopt the title "compassionate Samaritan" from Robbins, "The Sensory-Aesthetic Texture."

33. ποιέω ἔλεος μετά is a translation of the Hebrew phrase עשה חסד עם (e.g., Gen 19:19; 20:13; 21:23), in the LXX used in Jud 1:24; 8:35; 1 Kgs 15:6; 20:8; 2 Kgs 3:8; 9:1, 7; 10:2, Ruth 1:8; 1 Chr 19:2; 2 Chr 24:22.

would have to talk about the parable of the Good Samaritan. On their way, they encountered a clearly needy person, placed there by the researchers. There was one variable which had a significant influence on the willingness to give assistance: time pressure. Those who had much time to get to the film set were statistically more prepared to give assistance. Under time pressure, assistance was given less often. There were always a few students who gave help, and even under ideal circumstances not all of them gave help.[34]

Jesus does not tell in his parable why the priest and the Levite went by without giving assistance. This openness is rhetorically effective, because it stimulates the (self-critical) reader to ask: "Which solution would I myself be inclined to choose?"[35] Jesus gives a reason why the Samaritan did indeed give assistance: "he was moved with pity"; he felt compassion (10:33). In the discussion following on the parable, the *feeling* of compassion (ἐσπλαγχνίσθη, 10:33), which led to action, is then summarized as *compassionate action* (ὁ ποιήσας τὸ ἔλεος μετ' αὐτοῦ, 10:37), which fulfils the law.[36] But, as the described experiment and everyday experience teach us, it is not enough to *know and to agree* that compassionate action is necessary—one should in the first instance be able to allow this feeling, and to

---

34. See Zimbardo, *The Lucifer Effect*, 316–17.

35. In the literature, an intense discussion has been going on in the last decades about the question of why the priest and the Levite went by. Often, scholars adhere to the hypothesis that it was their interpretation of the laws of purity that held them back; see, for example, Derret, *Law in the New Testament*, 208–27. In Borg, *Conflict*, this idea is expanded into the fundamental contrast of compassion over against holiness/purity as key religious ideas in Jesus and the Pharisees respectively—a concept worthy of further critical discussion. An opposing position is forcefully stated by Levine, *Short Stories by Jesus*, 71–106. She points out that interpretation of the parable is often guided by an obsessive concentration on the priest and the Levite as representatives of Judaism as a religion that focuses xenophobically and fanatically on the laws of purity at the cost of compassion.

36. The "opus internum" (feeling compassion) and the "opus externum" (doing compassion) are part of a series of steps related several times in Luke, and which has been called a "movement of mercy" ("*beweging van barmhartigheid*") by De Haas: consisting of seeing, feeling compassion, moving toward the needy and providing help. See De Haas, *Jezus, de Barmhartige*, 57, cited from Riemersma, "Barmhartigheid," 5. Riemersma himself offers the interpretation that because Luke 10:37 is the only instance where ποιέω ἔλεος is used with reference to a human character in Luke and has the definite article with it, the author intents to say that the Samaritan is acting as God here ("Barmhartigheid," 14–16). I think that this interpretation slightly overstates the case, for two reasons: firstly, the love command had already been reshaped into compassion in pre-Christian Judeo-Hellenistic texts, as especially Mirguet has shown (see *An Early History*, chap. 4.4–5). Secondly, with Luke 6:36 as a guiding principle, *all* human compassionate behavior must be regarded as *imitatio Dei*. The main point in Luke 10:37 is that fulfilment of the love command that summarizes the law is done through compassion, and this is what all human beings are supposed to do (see also Luke 16:29–31).

allow oneself to become the medium of action, in the crucial moment. The above-mentioned social science experiment has shown one important variable which could be influential in whether or not one will allow feelings of compassion: being under time and performance pressure. Most people will probably recognize this just too well. Other reasons are easily imaginable.[37] If we want to be honest with ourselves, we have to acknowledge the fact that failing, in spite of all our good intentions, is the rule rather than the exception. Therefore, the third theological pillar in Jesus' call for compassion, which puts human dependence on forgiveness at the heart of matters, is immensely important.

Compassion as Leading to Salvation in Judgment

Compassion, which can lead to salvation in the last judgment (or, in case of its absence, to damnation), is clearly developed along two lines: as compassion with the needy and as goodwill and forgiveness toward fellow human beings who fail or become guilty. This second aspect is expressed very clearly in the parable of the two slaves in Matthew 18 by the king who, himself, had forgiven the debt, having been moved by pity (σπλαγχνισθείς in 18:27): "Should you not have had mercy on your fellow slave, as I had mercy on you?" (18:33: οὐκ ἔδει καὶ σὲ ἐλεῆσαι τὸν σύνδουλόν σου, ὡς κἀγὼ σὲ ἠλέησα). The message of this grim story—no mercy for the merciless—needs to be complemented by logia of Jesus that stress the positive side of the process—blessed are the merciful who will receive mercy—which aims at healing relations between human beings and between human beings and God, damaged by guilt.[38] The positive effect of these teachings lies in the discernment and individual appropriation of human fallibility. Sociopsychological research has proven that being able to admit mistakes and ask for forgiveness is a crucial factor in preventing conditions that suffocate compassion.[39] The pivotal role in the gospels of giving and receiving forgiveness

---

37. Levine, *Short Stories*, 94, mentions the suspicion of Martin Luther King Jr.: "It's possible these men were afraid"—an interpretation that is plausible and impressive and which testifies of King's great capacity for compassion!

38. See, for example, Mark 11:25; Luke 11:3–4/Matt 6:12, 14–15; Matt 5:23–24; Luke 17:3–4/Matt 18:21–22. Newman, "The Quality of Mercy," shows that in the rabbinic tradition the duty to forgive is rooted in two major theological convictions: that Jews have to emulate the merciful God (*imitatio Dei*) and be truthful to the special covenantal relationship established between this God and Israel.

39. Forty-five years ago, the social psychologist Philip Zimbardo headed the renowned Stanford Prison Experiment in which normal students changed into sadistic prison guards. Since then, Zimbardo has researched the circumstances that stimulate

as expressions of compassion and as conditions for not being condemned oneself is significant from this psychological perspective.

The parable in Luke 16 of the rich man and Lazarus who sits covered with sores at the gate of his house, focuses the attention on the lack of solidarity and compassion with the poor as a reason for condemnation. The rich man does not show any compassion with the hunger of Lazarus. But after they both died, when he is tormented in hell, and when Lazarus is sitting by Abraham's side, he called out to Abraham to have mercy on him by sending Lazarus to cool his tongue in the flames of the hell (16:24: "Father Abraham, have mercy on me / πάτερ Ἀβραάμ, ἐλέησόν με)." Abraham does not react to this, and as a response to the request that he sends Lazarus as an envoy back to earth to convert the still living brothers of the rich man, he receives the following answer: "They have Moses and the prophets; they should listen to them" (Luke 16:27–31). According to Jesus, anyone can acknowledge compassion with the needy as the core of the scriptures (see above); whoever does not listen to that deserves condemnation. A parallel tradition with similar content in the gospel of Matthew is the great vision of the judgment in Matthew 25:31–46. Here, an extra layer of Christ mysticism is added to the notion that what has been done to the weakest of humankind has been done to the Son of God, a variation of the above-cited Jewish conviction that the creator is offended when one of the creatures is injured.

Nowadays, parables such as the eventually merciless king in Matthew 18 and the story of Lazarus in Luke 16, of course, cause great indignation. Because, whereas we in the best of circumstances are still prepared to receive admonitions about our own vulnerability and fallibility, the merciless judge sketched here looks more like a monstrous product of infinitely stretched-out human vengeance than like the merciful God. On the other hand: how merciless can some people be, sometimes even without identifiable reasons? And how terrible are the circumstances in which people who become victims and perpetrators are sometimes trapped? One can understand the desire for eternal punishment and suitable deterrence. Furthermore, it is

---

the merciless handling of fellow human beings in experimental contexts, but has also done research into real excesses of violence, such as those that occurred in Abu Ghraib. During the past few years, Zimbardo also concentrated on detecting strategies that specifically help to offer resistance against social systems and circumstances that suffocate compassion. In *The Lucifer Effect*, 444–89 Zimbardo describes ten strategies, some of which form, in my opinion, secular versions of attitudes central to the Judeo-Christian discourses on compassion. This is certainly true for Zimbardo's first strategy of encouraging admission of mistakes and asking for forgiveness, which reduce "the need to justify or rationalize our mistakes and thereby to continue to give support to bad or immoral actions. Confession of error undercuts the motivation to reduce cognitive dissonance; dissonance evaporates when a reality check occurs," 452.

important to realize that the attempt to deter people by means of gruesome scenarios of punishment is actually meant to encourage people to repent so that they eventually do not end up in the situation depicted in such bold colors. To a certain extent, insights from social psychology can enlighten the psychological usefulness of biblical judgment scenes.[40]

Concluding Reflections

Exegetically, one of the interesting outcomes of this short overview of synoptic traditions on compassion is the preeminence of narrative and imaginative material over direct exhortative traditions. In Mark, there is no appeal to being compassionate from the mouth of Jesus at all. What speaks forcefully to the reader are Mark's examples of Jesus being compassionate and mediating God's compassion in his actions that bring forth the new inclusive community of the kingdom: in healing, teaching, and feeding. In Matthew and Luke, some of the traditional Jewish admonitions to act compassionately are reproduced in the teachings of Jesus, and a special focus on compassion as a characteristic of God can be seen especially in Luke. But again, what have the most profound effect on the reader are stories, parables of Jesus that visualize compassionate behavior or the opposite—merciless conduct. Obviously, what those stories provide for the readers are possibilities to identify with the characters, villains, and heroes, and with their actions and destinies as a way to get in contact with their own feelings and possible (re-)actions with regard to situations that

---

40. Here, especially the third and seventh of Zimbardo's strategies (see previous note) are relevant. Zimbardo points out how important it is that individuals consciously accept responsibility for their actions, and that they view their own actions from a perspective that includes the past and the future: "By developing a balanced time perspective in which past, present, and future can be called into action depending on the situation and task at hand, you will be in a better position to act responsibly and wisely than when your time perspective is biased toward reliance on only one or two time frames. Situational power is weakened when past and future combine to contain the excesses of the present," Zimbardo, *The Lucifer Effect*, 455. Once again, these insights annunciate secular versions of central biblical truths. The eschatological perspective in its two forms, namely, as expectation of the kingdom of God on earth and as individual judgment, may certainly contribute to responsible action in the here and now. It puts this action into perspective of a future that matters and holds individuals responsible for their deeds. And with regard to being rooted in a past that can serve as a corrective, the following can briefly be said: Jesus' example, through his compassionate acts that are at the center of the Gospel's narratives, his explicit teachings of compassion, and the meta-story—which displays the conviction that in Christ God became human and was sharing in the suffering of the world, with the aim of eventually overcoming it—are forceful reminders for anyone who is rooted in this tradition.

require a compassionate response. Theologically important is the centrality of reciprocity and interchangeability of positions in those traditions if we contemplate them in a synopsis. When it comes to compassion, all human beings are needy and all can become exemplary providers, and even God, the ultimate source of mercy, is, from a deeply mystical perspective, dependent on and a receiver of human compassion. Jesus is, of course, the hero of compassion in the gospels, but even he once needed the compassionate response of the Syrophoenician woman to overcome his temporary narrow-mindedness and embrace the perspective of God, who feeds all. God comes to rule through human acts of compassion, and in each needy person that is or is not taken care of the eternal judge can be encountered. Human beings are called to imitate the merciful God in ordinary scenarios: a forgiving father and even children who feed dogs can become appropriate images of God's compassion. In the narrative tradition regarding compassion in the gospels, the borders between transcendence and immanence are blurred to a remarkable degree.

Bibliography

Aristotle. *Rhetorica* 1515. ET: *Rhetoric*. Translated by W. Rhys Roberts. Mineola, NY: Dover, 2004.

Arnim, Hans Friedrich August von. *Stoicorum Veterum Fragmenta*. Vol. 2. Leipzig: Teubner, 1903–1905.

Borg, Marcus J. *Conflict, Holiness, and Politics in the Teachings of Jesus*. New York: Mellen, 1998.

Chrysippe, of Soli. *Œuvre Philosophique*. Vol. 2. Translated and annotated by R. Dufour. Paris: Les Belles Lettres, 2004.

Clark, Gordon R. *The Word "Hesed" in the Hebrew Bible*. Journal for the Study of the Old Testament Supplement Series 157. Sheffield: Sheffield Academic, 1993.

Danker, Frederick W. ἔλεος. In *Greek-English Lexicon of the New Testament and Other Early Christian Literature*, by Walter Bauer. 3rd ed. Chicago: University of Chicago Press, 2000.

De Haas, V. *Jezus, de Barmhartige, onze Broeder*. Barmhartigheid en Broederschap. Congregatiereeks 1996–2002 3. Tilburg: Barmhartigheid en Broederschap Generaal Bestuur Fraters CMM, 2000.

Derret, J. Duncan M. *Law in the New Testament*. Eugene, OR: Wipf and Stock, 1970.

Dozeman, Thomas B. "Inner-Biblical Interpretation of YAHWEH's Gracious and Compassionate Character." *Journal of Biblical Literature* 108 (1989) 207–23.

Franz, Matthias. *Der barmherzige und gnädige Gott: Die Gnadenrede vom Sinai (Exodus 34,6–7) und ihre Parallelen im Alten Testament und seiner Umwelt*. Beiträge zur Wissenschaft vom Alten (und Neuen) Testament 20. Stuttgart: Kohlhammer, 2003.

García Martínez, Florentino, and Eibert J. C. Tigchelaar. *The Dead Sea Scrolls*. Vol. 2. Study ed. Leiden: Brill, 1998.

Gerber, Daniel. "Les emplois d' ἔλεος en Luc-Actes." In *"Car C'Est L'Amour Qui me Plait, Non Le Sacrifice...:" Recherches sur Osée 6:6 et Son Interprétation Juive et Chrétienne*, edited by Eberhard Bons, 81–95. Journal for the Study of the Old Testament Supplement Series 88. Leiden: Brill, 2004.

Giese, Ronald L., Jr. "Compassion for the Lowly in Septuagint Proverbs." *Journal for the Study of the Pseudepigrapha* 11 (1993) 109–17.

Heiligenthal, Roman. "Werke der Barmherzigkeit oder Almosen?: Zur Bedeutung von ἐλεημοσύνη." *Novum Testamentum* 25 (1983) 289–301.

Konstan, David. *Pity Transformed*. London: Bloomsbury, 2001.

———. "The Varieties of Pity." *Journal of Biblical Literature* 133 (2014) 869–72.

Lateiner, Donald. "Pain and Pity in Two Postbiblical Responses to Joseph's Power in Genesis." *Journal of Biblical Literature* 133 (2014) 863–68.

Levine, Amy-Jill. *Short Stories by Jesus. The Enigmatic Parables of a Controversial Rabbi*. New York: HarperCollins, 2014.

Marcus, Joel. *Mark 1-8*. Anchor Yale Bible 27. New Haven: Yale University Press, 2000.

Mirguet, Françoise. "Compassion in the Making: Lexicographic Explorations in Judeo-Hellenistic Literature." *Center for Hellenic Studies Research Bulletin* 1 (2013). http://www.chs-fellows.org/2013/07/08/compassion-in-the-making-lexicographic-explorations-in-judeo-hellenistic-literature/#_ftn2.

———. *An Early History of Compassion: Emotion and Imagination in Hellenistic Judaism*. Cambridge: Cambridge University Press, forthcoming.

———. "Emotional Responses to the Pain of Others in Josephus's Rewritten Scriptures and the Testament of Zebulun: Between Power and Vulnerability." *Journal of Biblical Literature* 133 (2014) 838–57.

Newman, Louis E. "The Quality of Mercy: On the Duty to Forgive in the Judaic Tradition." *Journal of Religious Ethics* 15 (1987) 155–72.

Pearce, Sarah Judith. "Pity and Emotion in Josephus's Reading of Joseph." *Journal of Biblical Literature* 133 (2014) 858–62.

Riemersma, Nico. "'Barmhartigheid' in Lucas-Handelingen: Een Bijbels-Theologische Studie." 2016. http://www.nicoriemersma.nl/storage/blog/Barmhartigheid_in_Lucas-Handelingen._Een_bijbels-theologische_studie.pdf.

Robbins, Vernon K. "The Sensory-Aesthetic Texture of the Compassionate Samaritan Parable in Luke 10." In *Literary Encounters with the Reign of God*, edited by Sharon H. Ringe, and H. C. Paul Kim, 247–64. New York: T. & T. Clark, 2004.

Smit, Peter-Ben. *Fellowship and Food in the Kingdom: Eschatological Meals and Scenes of Utopian Abundance in the New Testament*. Wissenschaftliche Untersuchungen zum Neuen Testament 2/234. Tübingen: Mohr/Siebeck, 2008.

Snodgrass, Klyne. "The Gospel of Jesus." In *The Written Gospel*, edited by Markus Bockmuehl and Donald A. Hagner, 31–44. Cambridge: Cambridge University Press, 2005.

Spieckermann, Hermann. "Barmherzig und gnädig ist der Herr..." *Zeitschrift für die Alttestamentliche Wissenschaft* 102 (1990) 1–18.

Theissen, Gerd. *Lokalkolorit und Zeitgeschichte in den Evangelien*. Freiburg, Switzerland: Universitätsverlag, 1989, ²1992. ET: *The Gospels in Context: Social and Political History in the Synoptic Tradition*. Translated by Linda M. Maloney. Minneapolis: Fortress, 1991.

Urion, David K. *Compassion as a Subversive Activity: Illness, Community, and the Gospel of Mark*. Cambridge, MA: Cowley, 2006.

Van Staden, Piet. *Compassion—The Essence of Life. A Social-Scientific Study of the Religious Symbolic Universe Reflected in the Ideology/Theology of Luke*. HTS Supplement 4. Pretoria: HTS, 1991. http://hdl.handle.net/2263/50092.

Weren, Wim J. C. "Broederschap en Barmhartigheid in Mattheus. Een Tekstsemantische Studie." In *Broeder Jehosjoea*, edited by Dick Akerboom et al., 249–65. Kampen: Kok, 1994.

Zimbardo, Philip. *The Lucifer Effect: How Good People Turn Evil*. New York: Random House, 2007.

Compassion of and with Christ in the Late Medieval Spirituality of the Bloodied Pen and Paint Brush

Len Hansen

As ALL DISCOURSES ON important theological concepts, that on the concept of compassion has a centuries-long history. In its own way, this conference, too, now forms part of that history. Themes addressed in the contributions to this book also remind us of how understandings of compassion have developed and how they have differed over time and still differ. This essay wants to contribute to the discussion by revisiting compassion as it was understood and, therefore, depicted and described in the Late Middle Ages in Western Christianity. Examples of written and visual expressions of the Passion of Christ will be used as point of departure. However, these expressions have in common that they are representative of the abundance of extremely violent and gruesome images from that time. The images and texts referred to in this essay will not only show how compassion was understood, but also why it was depicted in the ways it was and, broader, how it reflected and informed the spirituality of the time.

The Bloodied Paintbrush—Late Medieval Depictions of the Passion

When speaking of the Late Middle Ages, I am referring to the period from 1300 to 1500 (fourteenth and fifteenth CE). This era followed the so-called High or Scholastic Middle Ages (1100 to 1300) and preceded the era of the Early Renaissance. In terms of art, this forms part of the Gothic era (divided into Early (1150 to 1250), High (1250 to 1375), and International Gothic

(1375 to 1450) periods), which spread from France to the rest of Northern Europe. The Gothic era in turn was preceded by the Romanesque Era and, again, by the era of Early Renaissance art.

For many contemporary eyes and ears, the accounts and depictions of the Passion of Christ in the Late Middle Ages is understandably shocking—whether in visual art (in what became known as *Andachtsbilder*, or devotional images, in the form of paintings belonging to the rich or the crude woodcuts of the poor,[1] to altarpieces and manuscript illuminations), in literature (from private devotional literature to liturgical literature), but also in the performing arts (in drama and song). Below follow a few examples of these art forms, which will set the scene for investigating the possible reasons behind these depictions and descriptions, and their links to late medieval understandings of compassion.

During the 15th annual German Historical Institute Lecture in Washington, DC, in 2001, renowned feminist medieval scholar Caroline Walker Bynum spoke on "Violent Imagery in Late Medieval Piety." Walker Bynum refers to the unsettling images one encounters in many sightseeing tours of many European cathedrals or art museums, which shows "twisted crucifixes bearing a dead and tortured God, the *transi* tombs that display carvings of the elite of Europe, nude and gnawed by worms, [and] . . . vast altarpieces telling of grisly and prolonged executions of the culture's martyred heroes and heroines, the saints."[2]

From the many depictions of the crucifixion, the deposition from the cross, the lamentation (at the foot of the cross), and the *Imago Pietatis* (the dead Christ at the grave), it is clear that this was not the time of "sweet-faced Madonnas with chubby babies, cozy scenes of domestic life of God's family" or "saccharine-sweet plaster figurine[s]."[3] These made way for disturbing depictions of real, truly flesh-*and*-blood human beings,[4] the stuff of nightmares.[5] It was indeed the time of a parade of "severed body parts, monstrous claws, torn hunks of flesh . . . [and] streams of bright red blood"![6] These are artistic expressions form the fourteenth-, fifteenth-, and some from the very early sixteenth-century art (history does not lend itself to precise cut-off dates).

1. O'Kane, "Picturing 'The Man of Sorrows,'" 69.
2. Walker Bynum, "Violent Imagery," 3.
3. Walker Bynum, "Violent Imagery," 3.
4. "[I]n the words of Amadeus of Lausanne . . . 'groans, sobs, sighs, sorrow, grief, agony, distress of heart, fires, a death more cruel than death'"; Neff, "The Pain of Compassio," 254.
5. Neff, "The Pain of Compassio," 254.
6. Walker Bynum, "Violent Imagery," 3.

Probably the most famous of these grisly images is the crucifixion scene on the Isenheim Altarpiece by Matthias Grünewald, who was born just two decades before the end of our era, but who clearly shows late medieval artistic roots. This work of art depicts "the tattered, discolored, tormented body of the savior"[7] with blood streaming from his feet and hands appearing as claws of *rigor mortis* [figure 1].[8]

Figure 1

In another painting, Lorenzo Monaco (ca. 1370 to ca. 1425) in 1402 depicted Christ as the Man of Sorrows, with his mother and St. John [figure 2].[9]

Christ is surrounded by the instruments of his torture and execution (the so-called *arma Christi*). The knife represents Christ's circumcision; three nails in the left corner above, the violation of his hands and feet,[10] and a single head to the left stands for mocking, beating, and humiliation. The Man of Sorrows (based on the so-called Suffering Servant of Isaiah 53) and the *arma Christi* were among the most popular late medieval art themes and represent some of the most grisly examples thereof.

Figure 2

7. Morgan, *Visual Piety*, 63.

8. Matthias Grünewald, *Detail from the Isenheim Altarpiece*, 1516. Online at: https://uploads4.wikiart.org/images/matthias-gr%C3%BCnewald/the-crucifixion-detail-from-the-isenheim-altarpiece.jpg. All images in this essay are available in the public domain and have been obtained from www.wikiart.org or https://en.wikipedia.org.

9. Lorenzo Monaco, *Christ as the man of Sorrows with the Virgin, St. John, and the Instruments of the Passion*, 1404. Galleria dell' Accademia, Florence, Italy. Online at: https://en.wikipedia.org/wiki/Arma_Christi#/media/File:Don_Lorenzo_Monaco_014.jpg.

10. Note instead of four nails—one each for each hand and foot—the intensified pain suggested by driving a single nail (*clavo uno*) through both feet in the then "new mode of portraying Christ . . . the intensified pathos associated with the three-nailed iconography, [which] could discomfit unaccustomed viewers"; Lipton, "The Sweet Lean of His Head," 1184–85.

Figure 3

Master Francke's 1430 painting [figure 3][11] shows a tall angel holding up the ashen body of the suffering Christ, whose eyes are open, still alive, if only just. Christ is clearly in pain and weak—he can barely grasp the scourge in his right hand. Two more angels in front hold the *arma Christi*; their wings are black, representing mourning. Note the detail on the cross in the background—the veins in the wood, the nails jutting out, as if Christ's hands has just been torn from them.

Yet another striking image is today found, not far from here, in Utrecht's Catherine Convent. It shows another fifteenth-century painting, Geertgen's Man of Sorrows [figure 4].[12]

As was often the case, Christ is standing in the grave, holding the cross, blood splattered all over his body. He is again surrounded by angels and the *arma Christi*—this time including the scouring column in the right-hand corner.

Compare also Hans Memling's (ca. 1433–1494) painting from the same century—this time depicting a very life-like Christ and his mother. They are again surrounded by the *arma Christi* in the background [figure 5].[13]

Figure 4

11. Master Francke, *Man of Sorrows with* Arma Christi *and Angels*, 1430. Online at: https://en.wikipedia.org/wiki/Master_Francke#/media/File:Meister_Francke_004.jpg.

12. Geerten tot Sint Jans, *Man of Sorrows*, ca. 1495. Museum Catharijneconvent, Utrecht. Online at: https://en.wikipedia.org/wiki/Man_of_Sorrows_(Geertgen_tot_Sint_Jans)#/media/File:Geertgen_tot_Sint_Jans_-_Man_of_Sorrows_-_WGA08517.jpg.

13. Hans Memling, *The Man of Sorrows in the arms of the Virgin*, ca. 1430.

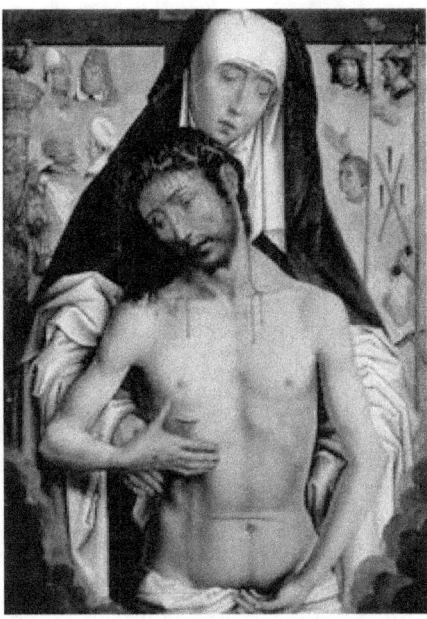

Figure 5

Note the shocking contrast between the Christ figure's pale skin and the crimson streams of blood flowing from Christ's side compared with the trickling of blood from somewhere behind his ears.

In an anonymous fifteenth-century Man of Sorrows [figure 6],[14] an emaciated Christ (note the clearly visible ribs) is covered with a profusion of scourging marks and droplets of blood—also a favorite way of depicting the dying Christ at the time.

The Bloodied Pen—Late Medieval Descriptions of the Passion

With regard to literature,[15] the narratives of Christ's passion are no less violent. Although all medieval devotional writings on the Passion derive from the gospels' accounts, Thomas Bestul mentions the extent to which they do differ. In many cases, in the later Middle Ages, one finds it "increasingly common to find narratives that go far beyond the gospel

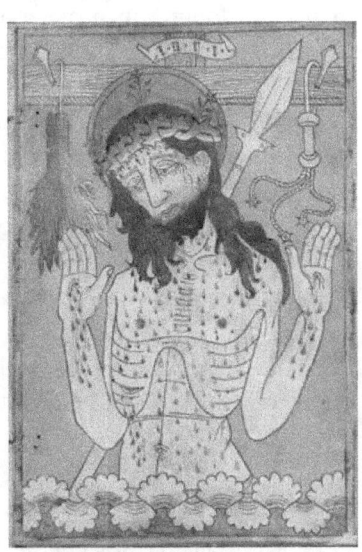

Figure 6

Capilla Real de Granada, Granada, Spain. Online at: https://en.wikipedia.org/wiki/Arma_Christi#/media/File:Hans_Memling_-_The_Man_of_Sorrows_in_the_arms_of_the_Virgin_-_Google_Art_Project.jpg.

14. Unknown Artist, German woodcut with hand-colouring, 1465-70. Art Institute of Chicago. Online at: https://en.wikipedia.org/wiki/Man_of_Sorrows#/media/File:Man_of_Sorrows_-_Google_Art_Project.jpg.

15. With literature, I include liturgical texts and dramatic texts, even if these may strictly speaking also qualify as "depictions."

record by including details that have no warrant in the biblical text."[16] One especially grisly example in many late medieval Passion treatises is the addition to the story of Christ's arrest in Gethsemane where "Christ's hands were tied so tightly that blood burst from his fingernails."[17] Since the Bible offers very little detail on the act of crucifixion itself, details such as these were simply added—such as the stretching out of the body of Christ on the cross before it is fastened to it with nails. Apparently, the latter was needed because the holes for the nails on the cross were made beforehand so the arms of Christ had to be forcibly stretched out "as the skin of a drum" (as per Bonaventure) in order to reach these holes. Having nailed Christ to the cross, tells the thirteenth-century *Dialogue of the Blessed Mary and Anselm about the Passion of the Lord*, the cross was dropped into a prepared hole in the ground. The impact of the cross hitting the ground would then have resulted in Christ's hands, muscles, and veins being torn asunder.[18]

Medieval authors did not see anything wrong with these embellishments and found much material to base them on the Hebrew Bible. Did Christ himself not state (in Luke 24:44) "that everything written about me in the law of Moses, the prophets, and the psalms, must be fulfilled"? And, following the age-old typological method of interpretation, late medieval authors on the Passion did exactly that, of which scholars such as Bestul and Viladesau give several examples.

One well-known application of the Old Testament was of the words "they have numbered my bones—Ps. 22:17."[19] It is thus understandable that so many paintings of the crucified Christ clearly shows him emaciated, his ribcage and ribs clearly visible (compare our example of the Man of Sorrows in Figure 6 above). Actually, some texts expressly mention the fact that Christ's ribs could be counted! Another often-found reference is that

---

16. Bestul, *Texts of the Passion*, 26.

17. Bestul, *Texts of the Passion*, 27.

18. Viladesau, *The Beauty of the Cross*, 199. With such obsessive focus on the wounds of Christ, it is not surprising that one of the popular devotions that originated in late medieval times was that of the Five Wounds of Christ (hands, feet, and side). Many prayers honoring the wounds of Christ were composed. According to a tradition of the time, there were all in all 5,466 wounds across the body of Christ and it was told that the German mystic Gertrude of Helfta (1256 to ca. 1302) recited a daily prayer in honor of these 5,644 wounds. In southern Germany, in the fourteenth century, fifteen *Our Fathers* were also recited each day, amounting to 5,475 in the course of the year, honoring and approximating the 5,644 wounds. A special mass, the Golden Mass, also existed in memory of the wounds of Christ and a special feast in honor of the wounds also spread from Germany across many parts of Europe from the fourteenth century onward; Williams, *The Five Wounds of Jesus*.

19. Viladesau, *The Beauty of the Cross*, 115.

the flagellation of Christ was so intense that to "the present day" the blood stains remain on the flagellation column. In Peter Comestor's twelfth-century *Historia scholastica*, an authoritative late medieval historical account of Passion, "the thorns drew gore from his [Christ's] head; there was already gore on his back as a result of the scourging; and the bloody sweat from the Garden touched the other parts of his body; so that not only his back, hands, feet, and sides but also his clothing, were covered with blood."[20]

Jacobus de Voragine's thirteenth-century *Legenda aurea* (the Golden Legend) became the standard hagiographical collection of the Late Middle Ages, describing not only the lives of the saints, but also the Passion itself. This work was enormously influential in other devotional descriptions and depictions of the crucifixion. One interesting instance comes from the pen of a woman, the Carthusian prioress Marguerite d'Oingt (early fourteenth century). She compares the crucifixion with (bloody) childbirth, exclaiming: "Ah, Sweet Lord Jesus Christ, who has seen a woman give birth thus! And when the hour of birth came, they placed You on the bed of the Cross. And it is not astonishing your veins ruptured, as you gave birth in one single day to the whole world!"[21]

As will be seen later, the so-called affective spirituality, especially as promoted by the Franciscans of the time, was fundamental to the intense interest in the Passion and the growth in bloody descriptions thereof. In the thirteenth century, one of the greatest Franciscan writers, Bonaventure (1221–1274), wrote two treatises on the Passion, namely *Lignum Vitae* and the *Vitis Mystica*, or "Tractatus de Passione Domini." According to Bestul, *Lignum Vitae* is a "well-stocked storehouse of the earlier commonplaces of the Passion,"[22] such as an account of how "Christ is hurled to the ground, and pushed, pulled, and stretched by his tormentors."[23] In Bonaventure's account, as the Man of Sorrows in Isaiah 1:6, Christ is covered in blood from head to foot, and the extent of his wounds makes him resemble a leper covered with open sores (drawing on Isa 53:4) (again compare Figure 6 above for a similar effect produced in painting). Bonaventure thus often affords "attention to the physical details of Christ's suffering, bleeding body, deformed by pain and injury, an attention verging upon obsession."[24]

In the *Vitis Mystica*, an extended metaphor of the vine is used to show how, as the vine is pruned, Christ first suffered the pain of circumcision, and

---

20. Translated and quoted in Bestul, *Texts of the Passion*, 31.
21. Translated and quoted in Neff, "The Pain of Compassio," 269.
22. Bestul, *Texts of the Passion*, 43.
23. Bestul, *Texts of the Passion*, 44.
24. Bestul, *Texts of the Passion*, 44.

that later his body on the cross is similar to the gnarled trunk of a vine. Where Christ in the gospels only wore a crimson cloak, in Bonaventure's account his whole body, albeit now almost drained of blood, is crimson from the blood from his wounds.[25] A later grim example of an elaboration on Bonaventure's Passion narrative is when "the clothing stuck to Christ's body is pulled off so cruelly [after his scouring] that gobbets of flesh are torn away with it"! (52)[26]

Finally, in late medieval drama, too, one finds increasing references to the violence suffered by Christ. According to Robinson, the so-called mystery plays shared the "sensational realism" of other religious arts of the time.[27] As such, these immensely popular fourteenth- to sixteenth-century spectacles were often overflowing with blood and gore. These plays transformed public spaces, such as marketplaces, town squares, and sites of pilgrimage.[28] According to Jennifer Trafton, especially noticeable was that these plays followed for the most part the gospels' Passion narratives, "with a remarkable exception: their expanded characterization of the villains and tormenters. No opportunity was missed to heap insult, humiliation, or torture upon the silent, patient Christ. The Crucifixion itself was drawn out in excruciating detail—beyond even the Gospel accounts."[29]

To end this section, it must be remembered that violent imagery and literature in the Late Middle Ages were not limited to representations of the Passion.[30] One may ask, however, why was it so prevalent in the latter

---

25. See also the description of the scourging of Christ in the so-called *Meditationes Vitae Christi*, from the early fourteenth century, which stands clearly in the Bonaventuran tradition: "The flower of all flesh and of all human nature is covered with bruises and cuts. The royal blood flows all about, from all parts of his body. Again and again, repeatedly, closer and closer, it is done, bruise upon bruise, and cut upon cut, until not only the torturers but also the spectators are tired; then he is ordered untied"; translated and quoted in Bestul, *Texts of the Passion*, 49.

26. These images and narratives are not only found in personal devotional literature, but also in the (especially Easter) liturgy. See, for example, Robbins's 1939 study "The 'Arma Christi' Rolls" of the liturgical use of an *Arma Christi* poem during Holy Week in late medieval England. Bestul, *Texts of the Passion*, 28, refers to the use of the Isaiahan Man of Sorrows imagery during Holy Week, and Walker Bynum, "Violent Imagery," 12, refers to "an instance of dramatic enhancement of the Easter liturgy with a wooden Christ complete with bleeding wound in his side—the blood flowing at just the right moment from a hidden bladder filled with animal blood!"

27. Robinson, "The Late Medieval Cult," 508.

28. Merback, "Living Image of Pity," 165.

29. Trafton, "The Ageless Drama of the Passion," no page number.

30. For the general frequency of violence in medieval literature, see Tracy's 2012 work *Torture and Brutality*. Also see, for example, Bale's quote from Prudentius's *Psychomachia*, a late-Latin text that visualized the battles between the virtues and the vices and that would have been known to all medieval schoolboys. Here is how this text describes Soberness smashing the lips of Indulgence with a rock: "[T]he teeth within

representations, especially since its extent and extreme nature was seemingly absent before this time? For this one has to look, both for theoretical and theological reasons, at the important role that compassion played in this whole phenomenon.

From the Violence of the Passion of Christ to Late Medieval Affective Spirituality

One way of understanding the late medieval obsession with the violence of the Passion is offered by Anthony Bale's views on the interconnectedness of affective piety, violence, memory, and the Passion in the Middle Ages. According to Bale, "by emphasizing the subjective nature of their religious experience and the humanity of Christ, medieval people demand that we acknowledge their feelings."[31] Today this is often called the "affective spirituality" of the time, "spectacular [in its] performances of religious empathy, sensation and suffering."[32] This was not only found in the extreme in the lives of ascetics, mystics, and extremist groups such as the flagellants, but also (albeit to a lesser degree) in the lives of ordinary faithful.

Late medieval religion used the body in the quest for practical and religious experience, and the medieval body "offered an agency in which sensations such as pain, violence against one's self, terror, eroticism, enclosure and fear were actively welcomed into one's life."[33] And, they were welcomed for a reason. Bale agrees with philosopher Jesse Prinz that, more than mere "aesthetic" description, the affective spirituality of the time was similar to so-called constructive sentimentalism, where one is morally educated according to one's emotional disposition—e.g., where the emotion of disgust confirms a moral disposition of intolerance. No wonder, says Bale, did mystical texts exhort the reader/listener toward "'felings & stiringes' through the visions of Christ's Passion with 'the innere eye of thi soule.'"[34]

Furthermore, medieval people did not see books and pictures as something separate from themselves—either from their minds or bodies. Thus,

---

are loosened, the gullet cut, and the mangled tongue fills it with bloody fragments; her gorge rises at the strange meal; gulping down the pulped bone she spews up again the lumps she has swallowed"; translated and quoted in Bale, *Feeling Persecuted*, 34.

31. Bale, *Feeling Persecuted*, 20.

32. Bale, *Feeling Persecuted*, 18.

33. Bale, *Feeling Persecuted*, 18. See Morgan, *Visual Piety*, 61: "Later medieval piety and its instrument, the devotional image, seized on the body as the medium for identifying oneself with Christ."

34. Bale, *The Jew in the Medieval Book*, 21.

"books, altarpieces, rosaries, chaplets, diagrams, jewelry, amulets—were not remote from the viewer but a stimulus to affective responses, touching the viewer, as one might be touched in love or violence; like Christ's body and blood in the Eucharistic wafer, devotional objects could be so close that they could move into the viewer, reader or user."[35]

This was true of reading and of hearing, but especially of seeing, what Morgan calls "the piety of looking."[36] According to Jill Bennet, this seeing creates an "emphatic vision" and "[v]iewing, on this account is not restricted to retinal impression and interpretations; the engagement of the senses implies a transformative process through which the properties of images are transferred to the viewer. In effect one becomes the image through an encounter with it."[37]

This kind of seeing in turn creates a special kind of memory, says Viladesau;[38] one grounded in the salvation events of the past, but which orientates the viewer toward the future. Bale gives examples of late medieval writers on memory and rhetoric who knew of these powers of emotions. According to the thirteenth-century Dominican aesthetic theorist John of Genoa, for example, sentimental and violent images should be used "so that the mystery of the incarnation and the examples of the saints be more active in our memory through being daily presented to our eyes" and "to excite feelings [*affectum*][sic] of devotion, these being aroused more effectively by things seen than by things heard."[39] Similarly, Italian grammarian Boncompango da Signa (thirteenth century) and the Englishman Thomas Brandwardine (fourteenth century) produced theories on ways to practice and aid memory that flowed from "fearful images of violence replete with conflict, spilt blood, rent limbs, 'foulness,' harlotry and grotesquery."[40] Da Signa would affirm "that offensive acts and unexpected events cling more fervently to the memory."[41]

Thus, it is precisely that "the memory of image was persuasive and dramatic because it was violent."[42] And it is therefore not surprising that

---

35. Bale, *The Jew in the Medieval Book*, 21.
36. Morgan, *Visual Piety*, 60.
37. Bennet, "Stigmata and Sense Memory," 6.
38. Viladesau, *The Beauty of the Cross*, 124.
39. Bale, *Feeling Persecuted*, 21. Or, as William Durandus quotes Gregory in defense of sacred images: "When the forms of external objects are drawn into the heart, they are as it were painted there, because the thoughts of them are their images"; quoted by Morgan, *Visual Piety*, 61.
40. Bale, *Feeling Persecuted*, 35.
41. Bestul, *Texts of the Passion*, 37.
42. Enders, *The Medieval Theater of Cruelty*, 66.

Bale concludes that, even though the Middle Ages was a very violent time, the violence in religious imagery had less to do with the latter than with "personal, pious, moral and intellectual education."[43] Not only writers in the Late Middle Ages knew this, but also artists. Their focus was less on *what* was depicted than "on responses to the work of art (that is, what one 'does' in front of it, or with it), and on the development of new states of consciousness through the use of works of art."[44] So, where does compassion fit into this view of violence-induced affective piety? This is discussed in the following section.

From Theology to Affective Spirituality to the Compassion of and with Christ

The power of perception, imagination, and emotions was no less unfamiliar to medieval theologians than it was to medieval artists. According to Lipton,

> medieval theologians from Pseudo-Dionysius through Abbot Suger, Hugh and Richard of Saint-Victor, Aquinas, Bonaventure, and beyond accorded precisely this initiatory role to visual perception, envisioning an ascending hierarchy that passed from sight, through imagination, to intellect or understanding.[45]

However, the late medieval obsession with the Passion of Christ and the bloody and violent depictions and descriptions of it did, of course, not develop in a theological vacuum. The Passion narratives and associated developments in other forms of art derive from a very long tradition of Christian texts on the Passion that saw the latter as the central event in human history. These texts include the gospels, but also the liturgy, apocryphal gospels (not surprisingly, especially the so-called *Gospel of Nicodemus*), as well as a wide variety of historical and exegetical texts (e.g., by Augustine, Jerome, Gregory the Great, the Venerable Bede, etc.).[46] According to Bestul, the obsession with the Suffering Christ, the dying Christ of the Late Middle Ages, so far

---

43. Bale, *Feeling Persceuted*, 37.

44. Marrow, "Symbol and Meaning," 151.

45. Lipton, "The Sweet Lean of His Head," 1179. One may also compare Bale's reference in *The Jew in the Medieval Book*, 25, to the importance of the experience of emotion, particularly fear, in Aristotelian philosophy as rediscovered during in the High Middle Ages, which unfortunately fall outside of the boundaries of this essay.

46. For an interesting development across the centuries, see Madigan's chapter on the interpretation of Peter Lombard (and to a lesser extent, Bonaventure) of Hillary of Poitiers (sixth century) in *The Passions of Christ*.

removed from the triumphant, resurrected Christ of earlier times[47] had its theological roots two centuries earlier in the "profound changes in western theology and spirituality that are memorably expressed in the writings of Anselm of Canterbury in the late eleventh century."[48] Anselm's question of *"Cur Deus homo?"* and the protracted theological debates that followed in the wake of it has been described as an "Anselmian transformation" in both theological outlook and devotional practice.

The nature of the so-called transformation was a fresh interpretation of the Incarnation that led to a new understanding of the importance of Christ's propitiatory sacrifice of himself as a human being on behalf of the whole human race. This, in turn, lead to a heightened emphasis on Christ's suffering humanity and an intense interest in all aspects of Christ's life in human flesh; an interest which, by extension, included the Virgin Mary as his mother. [49]

Not only Anselm, but also other great scholastic theologians, such as Abelard, Peter Lombard and Alexander of Hales, gave "significance to the human appropriation of salvation [in which] [t]he passion inspires us to love, faith, compassion and imitation."[50]

The "humanization"[51] of both art and devotion was, according to Walker Bynum, part of "a new understanding of the human person as inseparable from the body. The soul, in other words, was incomplete without the body."[52] Furthermore, this was accompanied by new emphases on individual spiritual growth, the role of private meditation in it and the consciousness of the extent of God's love that made spiritual growth possible—of course, affective spirituality emphasized the love for Christ in his human form, an intense consciousness of his suffering, as well as a longing for union with him. Such spiritual innovations originated in the traditional Benedictine monasticism of the eleventh century (of which John Fécamp—and Anselm himself—was part).[53] It gained momentum in the new vigor of the new monastic orders

---

47. See Morgan, *Visual Piety*, 60; and Viladesau, *The Beauty of the Cross*, 111.

48. Bestul, *Texts of the Passion*, 35.

49. One example of the suffering of Mary that was depicted and described quite literally occurred with reference to the prophecy of the high priest Simeon during the biblical account of the Presentation in the Temple (Luke 2:35) that "a sword will pierce your [Mary's] own soul too." According to Marrow in "Symbol and Meaning," 151, texts of the eleventh century already referred to the *gladius compassionis* (the sword of compassion) and by the thirteenth century this sword became a conventional artistic symbol of the Virgin's compassion or sorrow, depicting her as being pierced by (up to seven) swords, as the Virgin of Seven Sorrows.

50. Viladesau, *The Beauty of the Cross*, 92.

51. Viladesau, *The Beauty of the Cross*, 88.

52. Quoted in Morgan, *Visual Piety*, 62–63.

53. See Anselm's statement that the more one emphasizes Christ's "fatigue, hunger,

of the twelfth century—particularly among the Cistercians (with its great proponents Bernard of Clairvaux and Aelred of Rievaulx).

However, it reached its high point in the Franciscan spirituality of the thirteenth and fourteenth centuries (see Bonaventure above). In line with the mendicancy of the Franciscans, this devotion left the cloister to become part of the spiritual practices of the laity. According to Viladesau (*The Beauty of the Cross*), it was the Franciscan friars who concluded that the best way to lead ordinary people to real contrition was to excite compassion and remorse and doing so by placing before their minds—and eyes, by way of art, "Bible of the Simple" (Gregory the Great)—the flesh of the Savior on the cross.[54]

It has already been mentioned that within the context of late medieval affective spirituality, emotions—such as those provoked by the depictions and descriptions of violence—were clearly understood as being formative for spiritual growth and moral education. One of the primary emotions to evoke was compassion. On the one hand, it was to evoke compassion *with* the suffering Christ. However, on the other hand, it was to intensify the consciousness *of* the extent of the compassion of the crucified Christ with sinful humanity that was to be experienced, but also to be imitated. What follows below are some of the many examples of how, in this way, the faithful were guided toward experiencing and imitating compassion across the variety of art forms referred to above.

First of all, the "bloodied" pages and canvasses of late medieval Passion accounts wished to provoke an emotional response in the form of understanding and appreciating the enormity of Christ's suffering and thus his compassion with humanity so that one may comprehend the enormity of one's sin and culpability to Christ's suffering. In this regard, Gertrude Schiller comments with reference to the many depictions of the *arma Christi* that "[t]he spectator . . . is supposed to recognize that his [sic] own sins are connected with the sufferings of Christ," that there is a "correspondence between human sin and the Passion of Christ [implying] that individual sins caused specific sufferings."[55]

Likewise, with regard to the popular depictions of the Man of Sorrows, Schiller comments on the emotions these elicit—intimacy, *compassion*, exhortation, and intercession—by showing "Christ who has mercy on mankind

---

thirst, beatings, and crucifixion and death between thieves . . . the greater is the love and generosity that he has shown toward us . . . For it was fitting that just as death entered the human race through the disobedience of a human being, so too life should be restored by the obedience of a human being . . . [which] demonstrate[s] the indescribable beauty that belongs to our redemption."

54. See Lipton, "The Sweet Lean of His Head," 1172.
55. Schiller, *Iconography of Christian Art*, 191.

[and who] himself implores mercy: 'Have done now.'"⁵⁶ Martin O'Kane calls this at the same time a religiosity of ecstasy and love, as well as one of blame and self-reproach.⁵⁷ The Man of Sorrows, specifically, "was an aching revelation of one's own guilt and encouraged a blaming of oneself and a call to repentance."⁵⁸ Van Os refers to a miniature in a famous thirteenth-century Franciscan prayer book containing prayers attributed to Bernard of Clairvaux, which depicts the Man of Sorrows, and in which one prayer also makes this connection: "O how intensely thou embraced me, good Jesu, when the blood went forth from thy heart, water [went forth] from thy side and the soul [went forth] from thy body. Most sweet youth, what hast thou done that thou shouldst suffer so? Surely I too am the cause of thy sorrow."⁵⁹

Bestul shows the same dynamic at work in the late medieval liturgy of Holy Week.⁶⁰ In the so-called *improperia* or reproaches during the Good Friday service, Christ addresses the people who are the cause of his death and asks, "What more should I have done for thee that I have not done?" In the mystery plays, such reproaches were often found in the monologues of Christ as he addressed the spectators. And it was apparently highly effective, as Robinson reports, quoting a late fourteenth-century preacher telling how men and women during such a play "ben movyd to compassion and devocioun wepynge bitere teris" ["been moved to compassion and devotion weeping bitter tears"—LH].⁶¹

Bale also quotes an anonymous Augustinian commentator from the late fourteenth century on a depiction of the Passion, which shows the link between seeing and feeling compassion: "He is shown to us crucified, wounded, beaten and crowned with thorns ... And the vision causes the heart to tremble, the soul is wounded, the mind is touched, [and] the spirit feels compassion..."⁶² And, in a Belgian *Meditation* from the mid to late twelfth century, one reads the following words attributed to Christ on the cross, touching

---

56. Schiller, *Iconography of Christian Art*, 198; my emphasis.
57. O'Kane, "Picturing 'The man of Sorrows,'" 75.
58. O'Kane, "Picturing 'The man of Sorrows,'" 75.
59. Van Os, "The Discovery of an Early Man of Sorrows," 74–75.
60. Bestul, *Texts of the Passion*, 29.
61. Robinson, "The Late Medieval Cult," 508. The late thirteenth century was also the time of the introduction of the Adoration of the Cross and the introduction of the Stabat Mater into the Easter liturgy, which, amongst others includes the words: "Holy mother, do this: Affix the wound of the Crucified deeply into my heart ... Make me bear his wounds ... Make me able to feel the power of sorrow ... Make me truly weep with you. Sorrow along with the crucified ... To stand beside the cross with you. To freely share with you in your lament is what I desire"; see Viladesau, *The Beauty of the Cross*, 133.
62. Bale, *Feeling Persecuted*, 30.

on both Christ's pity and the culpability of humankind to his suffering: "See that my feet have been fixed by the nail of pity thus, so that I can in no way flee you, because pity holds me entirely bound; nor will I flee you as you merit on account of your sins, because my hands are pierced with nails."

One of the most widely-read devotional works of the late Middle Ages, Ludolph of Saxony's fourteenth-century *Vita Christi*, expressly instructs its readers that meditation on the Passion of Christ should move them to tearful compassion.[63] Rupert of Deutz, in an explanation of the efficacy of images, similarly states: "While we externally image forth [Christ's] death through the likeness of the cross, we [are kindled] inwardly to love of him."[64]

In his *Little Book of Truth* (ca. 1327), Dominican mystic Heinrich Suso expresses the spirituality of imaging Christ in the life of the believer in the following way: "A detached person must remove from himself the form of the creature, become formed after Christ, and super-formed in divinity." Interestingly, Morgan notes that the Middle High German verb for "to form" that Suso uses is *bilden,* the noun from which was *bilde* or image. The link to the image was explicit in Suso's conception of the mystical union with God stressed in a devotional piety informed by the cult of the *Andachtsbild* or devotional image. Morgan also refers to one of Suso's disciples, a Dominican nun from a convent in Ulm, who depicted Suso's explanations in his *Little Book* in a collection of sketches showing how the "soul returned from death to emulate the self-denial of Christ and become conformed, in Suso's words, 'to the image of the Son of God.'"[65]

Yet, the expectation was not only that the viewer/listener/spectator should experience compassion with Christ and realize the greatness of his/her sins. One was not only expected to imitate Christ in the sense that "the viewer's identification with Christ is to become a kind of *com-passio,* a suffering with him,"[66] but also to be led into sharing Christ's compassion in acts of practical charity toward the poor and suffering.[67] The idea of imitating Christ is plentiful in the writings of both the Dominicans and the Franciscans of the Late Middle Ages.[68] One of the great examples of such imitation of Christ was, of course, Francis of Assisi, but also other saints.

---

63. "Compassionate [sic] our Lord, for he is bearing all this torment for you; shed abundant tears and wash reverently away with them the spittle with which those profane wretches have besmeared his face. For who, hearing or considering this in his mind ... could refrain himself from tears?"; quoted in Marrow, "Symbol and Meaning," 154.

64. In Lipton, "The Sweet Lean of His Head," 1179.

65. Morgan, *Visual Piety*, 61.

66. Renna, "The Jews in The Golden Legend," 140.

67. Viladesau, *The Beauty of the Cross*, 122.

68. It was the Franciscan "obsession with the Passion of Christ" that led, amongst

Finally, not only Francis and the other saints served as examples of conformity to the compassion of Christ. Indeed, the primary example was that of Mary the Mother of Christ and again her Christ compassion was often reflected in Mary by way of emotionally-charged Passion depictions. As such, Neff states that "[i]n compassion, Mary suffers pain, even faints away death-like on Calvary [the popular so-called Swoon of the Virgin at the foot of the cross—LH], because she shares Christ's Passion; this literally is her *compassion*."[69] Neff illustrates this with reference to Rogier van der Weyden's "perfectly choreographed" image of the Deposition from the Cross, "where the pallor and limp pose of the Virgin exactly repeat those of Christ in death" [figure 7].[70]

Figure 7

---

other things, to one of the most famous Easter devotions, the practice of the *via crucis* (the fourteen stations of the cross); see Morgan, *Visual Piety*, 63; Homan, "Devotional Themes," 335. The deposition from the cross and the entombment of Christ was in fact the origins of a new genre of religious art in thirteenth-century Northern Europe, the *pietà*; Viladesau, *The Beauty of the Cross*, 115.

69. Neff, "The Pain of Compassio," 255.

70. Neff, "The Pain of Compassio," 255. Rogier van der Weyden, *The Deposition from the Cross*, ca. 1435. Museo del Prado. Online at: https://en.wikipedia.org/wiki/Rogier_van_der_Weyden.

Conclusion—The Dark Underbelly of Late Medieval Compassion with Christ

In this essay, depictions and descriptions of the Passion of Christ were used to show how Christian compassion was understood in the Late Middle Ages, but also how art, in its various forms, served as vehicle for expressing but also teaching this compassion. It was also explained how this Christ's Passion and compassion featured in the so-called affective spirituality of the time and how it was also linked with the broader theological discourse on the humanity of Christ since the High Middle Ages. That the artistic expressions of the Passion of Christ were manifold and widely distributed and accessible to medieval Christians is clear, as is the fact that it was highly effective in provoking intended emotional responses.

Compassion was one of these responses, a consciousness of humanity's sinfulness another. However, neither the picture of the bloodied paintbrush nor the story of the bloodied pen will be complete without reference to their dark underbelly. Space does not allow any detailed treatment of this, save to mention—as many studies of the time has shown—that the shocking depictions of the Passion was also a reflection and served (intentionally or not) to stimulate severe and violent anti-Semitism against medieval European Jews. They, the descendants of the Jews of the biblical narrative[71] were often seen and treated as the tormentors of Christ and treated with equal brutality by medieval Christians. Thus, in a highly ironic reversal, the spirituality of the bloodied pen and paintbrush—so much part of late medieval affective piety—turned the "Man of Sorrows" from a "living god of reconciliation" to "an atavistic icon of bloody persecution"[72] and a theology of love (of and for Christ) into a theology of hate.[73] But that is a story for another day.

---

71. This terrible effect of the violent images and stories in late medieval religious art is not only noted by Walker Bynum ("Violent Imagery"), Lipton ("The Sweet Lean of His Head"), Jordan ("The Last Tormentor of Christ"), Renna ("The Jews in The Golden Legend"), Marrow ("'Circumdederunt me canes multi'"), and Van Os ("The Discovery of an Early Man of Sorrows"), but also forms the focus of many essays and books on the topic. See, for example, Bale, *The Jew in the Medieval Book*; *Feeling Persecuted*; Frassetto, *Christian Attitudes to Jews*.

72. Van Os, "The Discovery of an Early Man of Sorrows," 75.

73. Ocker, "Ritual murder," 153.

Bibliography

Bale, Anthony. *The Jew in the Medieval Book: English Antisemitisms, 1350–1500.* Cambridge Studies in Medieval Literature. Cambridge: Cambridge University Press, 2006.

Bale, Anthony. *Feeling Persecuted: Christians, Jews and Images of Violence in the Middle Ages.* London: Reaktion, 2010.

Bennet, Jill. "Stigmata and Sense Memory: St. Francis and the Affective Image." *Art History* 24 (2001) 1–16.

Bestul, Thomas. *Texts of the Passion: Latin Devotional Literature and Medieval Society.* Philadelphia: University of Pennsylvania Press, 1996.

Enders, Jody. *The Medieval Theater of Cruelty: Rhetoric, Memory, Violence.* Ithaca, NY: Cornell University Press, 1999.

Frassetto, Michael, ed. *Christian Attitudes toward the Jews in the Middle Ages.* Routledge Medieval Casebooks 37. New York: Routledge, 2007.

Homan, Richard L. "Devotional Themes in the Violence and Humor of the 'Play of the Sacrament.'" *Comparative Drama* 20 (1986–1987) 327–40.

Jordan, William C. "The Last Tormentor of Christ: An Image of the Jew in Ancient and Medieval Exegesis, Art, and Drama." *Jewish Quarterly Review* (NS) 78 (1987) 21–47.

Lipton, Sarah. "'The Sweet Lean of His Head': Writing about Looking at the Crucifix in the High Middle." *Speculum* 80 (2005) 1172–1208.

Marrow, James. "'Circumdederunt Me Canes Multi.' Christ's Tormentors in Northern European Art of the Late Middle Ages and Early Renaissance." *Art Bulletin* 59 (1977) 167–81.

———. "Symbol and Meaning in Northern European Art of the Late Middle Ages and the Early Renaissance." *Simiolus: Netherlands Quarterly for the History of Art* 16 (1986) 150–69.

Merback, Mitchell. "The Living Image of Pity: Mimetic Violence, Peace-Keeping and Salvific Spectacle in the Flagellant Processions of the Later Middle Ages." In *Images of Medieval Sanctity: Essays in Honour of Gary Dickson*, edited by Debra Higgs Strickland, 135–80. Leiden: Brill, 2007.

Madigan, Kevin. *The Passions of Christ in High Medieval Thought.* Oxford: Oxford University Press, 2007.

Morgan, David. *Visual Piety: A History and Theory of Popular Religious Images.* Berkeley: University of California Press, 1998.

Neff, Amy. 1998. "The Pain of Compassio. Mary's Labor at the Foot of the Cross." *Art Bulletin* 80 (1998) 254–73.

Ocker, Christopher. "Ritual Murder and the Subjectivity of Christ: A Choice in Medieval Christianity?" *Harvard Theological Review* 91 (1998) 153–92.

O'Kane, Martin. "Picturing 'The Man of Sorrows': The Passion-Filled Afterlives of a Biblical Icon." *Religion and the Arts* 9 (2005) 62–100.

Renna, Thomas. "The Jews in The Golden Legend." In *Christian Attitudes to Jews in the Middle Ages*, edited by Michael Frassetto, 137–50. Routledge Medieval Casebooks 37. New York: Routledge, 2007.

Robbins, Russell. "The 'Arma Christi' Rolls." *Modern Language Review* 34 (1939) 415–21.

Robinson, James W. "The Late Medieval Cult of Jesus and the Mystery Plays." *Publications of Modern Language Association* 80 (1965) 508–14.

Schiller, Gertrude. *Iconography of Christian Art*. Vol. 2. Translated by Janet Seligman. London: Humphries, 1972.

Strickland, Debra H. 2007. *Images of Medieval Sanctity. Essays in Honour of Gary Dickson*. Leiden: Brill, 2007.

Tracy, Larissa. *Torture and Brutality in Medieval Literature: Negotiations of National Identity*. Cambridge: Brewer, 2012.

Trafton, Jennifer. "The Ageless Drama of the Passion." *Christianity Today*, 2008. http://www.christianitytoday.com/history/2008/august/ageless-drama-of-passion.html.

Van Os, Henk W. "The Discovery of an Early Man of Sorrows on a Dominican Triptych." *Journal of the Warburg and Courtauld Institutes* 41 (1978) 65–75.

Viladesau, Richard. *The Beauty of the Cross: The Passion of Christ in Theology and the Arts—From the Catacombs to the Eve of the Renaissance*. Oxford: Oxford University Press, 2006.

Walker Bynum, Caroline. "Violent Imagery in Late Medieval Piety." *German Historical Institute Bulletin* 30 (2002) 3–36.

Williams, David. *The Five Wounds of Jesus*. Leominster, MA: Gracewing, 2004.

Enacting Compassion

Justice as/and Compassion?
On the Good Samaritan and Political Theology

Dirk J. Smit

On the Good Samaritan

WHEN WE WERE STUDENTS during the 1970s, some of us—white, Afrikaans-speaking, Reformed theological students on our way to the ministry in racially divided Reformed churches—were deeply concerned about the injustice of the apartheid system and ideology and challenged by questions on how to respond to the apartheid realities in church and society. Many of us felt challenged by the issues that Reinhold Niebuhr already raised in *Moral Man and Immoral Society* (1932): the question whether it is possible, and if indeed, how to make any meaningful difference in the face of systematic and structural injustice. Can care and compassion make any difference when confronted by structure and system, can love contribute meaningfully when faced by regulation, power, and law—whether social, political, or economic law—and religiously justified as natural and divine?

Some of us were therefore intrigued by expositions of the parable of the Good Samaritan in Luke 10:25–37, which argued that an even more responsible reaction by the Samaritan would perhaps have been something completely different from the spontaneous and self-sacrificing compassionate love that one finds in the biblical account, which after all benefited only one victim, but left the road as dangerous as it had been before. Should the Samaritan not (also, or even: rather) have approached the local government, influenced public opinion, if necessary organized protest and public support? Would the better response not have been to employ and strengthen a police force, secure the lonely road, build hospitals to care for victims, raise taxes to help fund all these public services, create jobs for the poor, curb unemployment, improve education, better integrate the robbers into community life and society?[1]

Often these suggestions would become so attractive and convincing that the Samaritan's personal morality pictured and praised in the parable— go and do likewise, become a neighbor to others in distress—came to be regarded as meaningless and useless, as part of the problem rather than the solution. Acts of compassion could only contribute to make things worse, serve to extend the injustice and cover up the systemic violence.

Needed therefore, rather than love, was law, according to such readings of the parable. Or better, the story was now retold to show that law itself *is* love in action. The law is moral and intended to be moral—to improve quality of life for human beings, protect the weak and vulnerable, stop the wicked, ensure diverse and complex forms of love, including security of expectations and therefore social trust, the feeling of security and of being protected, equality for all irrespective of background or status, guarantees of personal freedoms; in short, allowing future travelers to move safely and without fear between Jerusalem and Jericho.

Could it be that globalization today leads many to similar conclusions, because many feel faced with similar realities and experiences? After all, many people struggle against what they experience and describe as the many new forms of exclusion caused and accelerated by globalization, even calling it new forms of apartheid? Many cry out against the structural inequalities, the "great divide" and the "great escape"—so dramatically visible in global wealth and health? Many point to what they see as injustice and willful destruction of human life and the ecology? Many wonder how to react meaningfully and debate what is at stake for their personal integrity, but also for the witness of the ecumenical church and for responsible social, political, and economic responses to global developments? Not surprisingly, many again feel convinced that more regulation is needed and that international law should counter the injustice and destruction. For them, law *is* the form of love needed today; justice *is* the form compassion should take.

On Justice as Compassion?

It is easy to see why this conviction, that law is a form of love, that justice is the face of compassion, has often been particularly attractive to members of the Reformed community and tradition in South Africa. The law already fulfilled such a constructive and life-giving and life-affirming role for John

---

1. Jansen, *Barmhartige Samaritaan*; Jens, *Der barmherzige Samariter*; Mazamisa, *Beatific Comradeship*.

Calvin—ranging from creation to covenant to commandments to the gospel, according to John Hesselink's authoritative *Calvin's Concept of the Law*. It is against this broader theological background that Calvin could describe the Christian life as *iustitiae amor*, as love of justice, and explain the ten commandments by not merely seeing what is forbidden but much rather—in often remarkable fashion—searching for the positive and life-affirming intentions behind each commandment; since indeed, for Calvin law is love in action, justice is the face of compassion. It was indeed Calvin's so-called social ethics that inspired many of us at the time to see the temptations of the apartheid ideology.[2]

It is therefore also not surprising that in both traditions of Reformed theology that deeply influenced South African Reformed theology during the twentieth century, including the theology of apartheid and the theology of the struggle against apartheid, namely the respective histories of reception of Abraham Kuyper and Karl Barth, albeit in fundamentally different ways, the law was also seen positively as the face or outer form of God's grace and gospel, of love and compassion.[3] More recent writings on Reformed faith, the two kingdoms, and natural law reflect the same spirit.[4] In particular, the work of two well-known Reformed thinkers, important for South African discourses today, reflects the same positive and constructive views of law, namely a long tradition of publications by the German systematic theologian Michael Welker[5] and several works by the North American philosopher Nicholas Wolterstorff.[6]

In South Africa itself, the popular and influential theologian and activist Allan Boesak—also from the Reformed tradition and in a long-standing personal friendship with Wolterstorff with deep mutual appreciation—was probably the paradigmatic example of this approach, over several decades, publicly calling for justice in many ways, attacking the apartheid state as

2. See my "Iets dat diepgaander is."

3. See, for example, Botman, "'Dutch' and Reformed and 'Black' and Reformed."

4. See, for example, VanDrunen, "The Natural Law and Liberal Traditions." For the strong historical bond between the developing Reformed self-understanding and notions of law, justice and rights, also see Strohm, *Ethik im frühen Calvinismus*; Witte, *The Reformation of Rights*.

5. Welker has been interested in the positive relation between gospel and law for his whole academic career. For recent statements, see his "Justice—Mercy—Worship" and "The Power of Mercy."

6. Wolterstorff told the story—in his autobiographical *Journey toward Justice*—how his own interest in issues of justice only gradually developed, amongst others as a result of his experiences in apartheid South Africa, with the failure of Reformed churches and theology to respond to what should have been such obvious social and economic injustices and violations of human rights.

illegitimate (even initiating and leading a controversial national day of prayer for the fall of the apartheid government), organizing political resistance (which included playing a leading role in the formation of the powerful United Democratic Front), being active under popular slogans like "no peace without justice" and "no education without liberation," and in general, according to his own later autobiographical account, being unable to make up his mind between being a church leader and a political activist. He has always been deeply interested in power—but power for the sake of justice. It is therefore not surprising that even his most recent work is still focused on questions of justice, albeit now on a larger, more global scale.[7]

At the same time, of course, not all Reformed thinkers share these convictions while obviously not all thinkers—including theologians—with such a high regard for law and justice come from Reformed background.[8]

Looking back, it seems almost self-evident why an interest in politics, questions of justice and law, and the role of power—public, structural, systemic, and institutional—dominated much of the struggle discourses against apartheid. The relation between church and state was at the heart of the struggle in church and theology, and at the heart of those debates was the conviction that only political power could change the laws and therefore the realities and experiences of justice and injustice. For many, the struggle was not primarily one of morality, ethics, love, and compassion; in fact, ideals of reconciliation and forgiveness were often seen as personal virtues focused on interpersonal relationships only and therefore regarded with deep skepsis and even rejected out of hand, for example, in the case of the influential *Kairos Document*; but the struggle was rather about questions of structure and power, of law and justice. Love was to be seen in law; compassion had to show the face of justice.

It is therefore not surprising that the struggle found its culmination in 1994 with the radical transformation of South Africa into a liberal democracy, with a Constitution including a bill of rights serving as social contract, the separation of powers protected by the Constitution, the rule of law, free and fair elections between multiple political parties based on law, and the legal protection of human rights, civil rights, and civil liberties. For many, this

---

7. For an autobiographical account of his life between church and politics, see Boesak, *Running with Horses*; for a recent statement of his views on justice in the globalizing world, see his *Kairos, Crisis, and Global Apartheid*.

8. In *Gerechtigkeit und Recht*, in a section on "Gerechtigkeit und Liebe," Huber therefore uses two well-known Reformed theologians as illustrations of thinkers who do not succeed in seeing justice as compassion, namely, Reinhold Niebuhr and Emil Brunner; see Huber, *Gerechtigkeit und Recht*. He uses the Lutheran theologian Wolfhart Pannenberg as illustration of justice as love. One could also add himself in, for example, "Recht im Horizont der Liebe."

became the fulfilment of the promises and dreams of the struggle against the injustices of apartheid. For many, the Constitution therefore finally provides the answer to the questions of the years before on how to respond, as individuals, but also as churches and as society.

The Constitution, as our social contract with one another, defines us as citizens in a new liberal democracy, in a new nation-state based on the rule of law, guaranteeing our equality and protecting our individual freedoms to pursue our common values, drawn as shared lessons from our painful past and described in our Constitution's preamble, values to which we now jointly commit ourselves. All apartheid laws will gradually be removed and all new laws will have to reflect the social contract of the Constitution—some leading constitutional judges and legal experts even describe those constitutional values as *ubuntu* values, common human values—and it will therefore in future be the task of the Constitutional Court to assure that this is indeed the case; in theological terms one could perhaps say its task is to ensure that our laws truly embody our mutual love for one another, that our compassion for one another becomes visible in justice.[9]

Again, if aspects of globalization indeed today—often inspired by such dreams of unlimited progress, personal success, and individual flourishing—challenge us with new forms of injustice and new experiences of exclusion, marginalization, and apartheid, can we then dream similar dreams and put our hope in similar promises as those of the apartheid struggle? Is it imaginable that law—in the form of international and global legal institutions, arrangements, treaties, and powers, including international courts—will eventually protect humanity, overcome inequality, uproot poverty, safeguard the ecology, end the destruction of natural resources, make universal *ubuntu* possible, produce human flourishing, lead to justice as compassion on a global scale?

On Justice and Compassion?

To consider only one intriguing example of a critical response to these questions, one may remember the skeptical argument of the sociologist Zygmunt Bauman in his lectures published as *Does Ethics have a Chance in a World of Consumers?* Law alone is for him not sufficient to help us face the challenges of our globalizing world since more is needed, namely ethics; yet he seems doubtful whether such ethics still stands a chance in our world of consumers.

---

9. See, for example, Makgoro, "Ubuntu and the Law in South Africa."

Even if it is today empirically demonstrable that and how altruism is integral to our human evolution,[10] it still remains obvious too that in our complex, globalizing world we most certainly have difficulties imagining and practicing adequate forms of altruism and compassion toward one another, sufficient to deal with our ever-changing challenges. It is therefore not surprising that Terry Eagleton describes our moral dilemmas today with the phrase *Trouble with Strangers*.[11] Living with the neighbor is indeed in our globalizing world today for many people in many places a threatening and terrifying experience.[12] To claim that law is insufficient to deal with our challenges and that we need something more, like altruism and compassion, is one thing, but to understand what that compassion would and could entail, to imagine the necessary practical implementation, and to find the necessary motivation are all still completely different challenges.

One practical illustration from debates in South Africa during these days could perhaps demonstrate this insufficiency of the law, namely the question concerning appropriate ways to respond to what seems like growing racism in society. Recent times are marked by many incidents of crude racism—on social media and in public life. In an attempt to respond, government considers using the legal instruments at its disposal, by making racism illegal, defining all possible forms of racism, and prescribing judicial penalties. Even if this may be necessary and helpful to a certain extent, regarding extreme forms of racism, it is obvious that this will not really go the root of the phenomenon, and in some ways it may even worsen the situation. Other forms of action are clearly needed, since the roots of the problem, even if racism is also structural and systematic, are clearly to be found in the hearts and minds of people, and they have ultimately to be addressed and transformed in different ways and by other actors and agencies—but how, and by whom? Racism can certainly be declared illegal, at least in some specified forms, but the nonracialism (professed in the Constitution) can clearly not be commanded, ordered, regulated, legalized—so how *is* it to be attained in a deeply racist society with racist histories and memories and racist legacies and structures?

The question whether law is sufficient for a humane society, whether law indeed embodies and guarantees love, or whether love should not be seen as something different and more, whether it is not better to think in terms of justice *and* compassion rather than only justice *as* compassion, has accordingly occupied many of us during the years of apartheid.

---

10. See, for example, some classical collections, by Sober and Wilson, *Unto Others*; Post et al., *Altruism*; Coplan and Goldie, *Empathy*; Nowak and Coakley, *Evolution, Games, and God*.

11. Eagleton, *Trouble with Strangers*.

12. Žižek et al., *The Neighbor*.

In fact, more traditional readings of the parable of the Good Samaritan—secondly—inspired such self-critical questions. After all, was the thrust of the examples in the parable of those who walked past the victim and who failed to respond to his need not precisely to suggest that they were motivated by respect for and obedience to the law? Was the fact that they were respectively a priest and Levite not a clue that it was precisely a failure of the law to make them into neighbors? Was the compassion of the Samaritan not directly contrasted with the obedience to "law and order" on their part? Do they not play their social roles according to the law, while the Samaritan breaks the rules and ignores the prescriptions, for the sake of the victim in need? Therefore, even if their laws were also the embodiment of love, was the parable not intended as a reminder that there are moments and situations in which the law does not provide solutions, but in fact helps to create and worsen the crises?[13]

Once again, Calvin already shared this position. In his exposition of the Ten Commandments, for example, he repeatedly showed how it is possible for us to use the law in order to protect us from the deepest intention of the law. We deny others justice by hiding behind "a semblance of justice" (8th commandment, *Inst.* II/8.45), we grow rich by injustice "by means lawful and unlawful" (8th commandment, *Inst.* II/8.46), we "limit our love to our own connections" and we can of course do that by using the law (*Inst.* II/8.55), so that, appealing to the parable of the Good Samaritan, Calvin could claim "I say that the whole human race, without exception, are to be embraced with one feeling of charity; that here there is no distinction of Greek or Barbarian, worthy or unworthy, friend or foe, since all are to be viewed not in themselves, but in God. If we turn from this view, there is no wonder that we entangle ourselves in error"[14]—yet is this not precisely what we can so easily do by using the instruments of our laws?

In legal thought, one of the most influential statements of this critical question came from the German legal scholar and former Minister of Justice during the Weimar Republic, Gustav Radbruch. It became known as the Radbruch thesis and his development of this thesis has often been described by some as the most important legal contribution of the twentieth century.[15] In short, it claims that law itself can be judged to be unjust. Positive law is no guarantee that justice is being done. Something may be legal but illegitimate. We may be faced with "unrichtiges Recht." The law itself should therefore be judged, against the law of justice—but what is that? How does

---

13. See Frits de Lange's contribution to this volume, "The Event of Compassion."
14. References from Calvin, *Calvin's Institutes*.
15. Radbruch, "Gesetzliches Unrecht und übergesetzliches Recht."

this happen? When, and by whom? With whose authority? In whose name? This implies, at least in principle, that "law and order," the existing legal situation, should not have a final say, since there is a norm, a measure, against which to measure the measure—but where? Could this perhaps be love, compassion—but how? And why?

On Justice and Compassion, Yes—But With Whom?

In South Africa, this problem received a classical statement by the renowned poet and playwright Adam Small in his poem called "What abou' de lô?"[16] It opens with the powerful words (in the Kaapse Afrikaans which he deliberately used during the early years of the struggle):

> *Diana was 'n wit nôi/Martin was 'n bryn boy//dey fell in love// sê Diana se mense/ ... sê Martin se mense/ ... /sê almal die mense/what abou' de lô//sê Martin sê Diana watte lô/God's lô/ man's lô/devil's lô/watte lô.*[17]

This question, namely against whose law their actions were measured, is then movingly developed in the rest of the poem.[18]

But are these critical questions also applicable to potential limitations of the laws of nation-states, to political liberalism, even to the South African Constitution? Many of those voices arguing for a new political theology seem to claim that these critical questions indeed apply to political laws. Of course, they differ widely among themselves. The crucial point is that—in the words of Nicholas Wolterstorff—political theology is not theology, but a form of political thought.[19] It is an attempt to understand the foundations of contemporary politics (and the economy, and therefore the nature of our globalizing world) in terms of more than law, namely in terms of ultimate concerns and convictions that make society and world, our common life together, possible and plausible. How do we envisage the world—including ourselves and our place in it, together with others? How to we see life together? How do we understand ourselves and others? What do we really believe? And if we do not believe, then how do we see "life after faith"?[20]

16. Small, *Kitaar my Kruis*.
17. These are just a few excerpts, roughly translated: Diana was a white girl/ Martin was a brown guy/ they fell in love// Diana's family said ... Martin's family said ... everybody said/ what about the law// Martin said Diana said which law/ God's law/ human law/ devil's law which law.
18. See my "'Whose Law?'"
19. Wolterstorff, *The Mighty and the Almighty*.
20. Kitcher, *Life After Faith*.

One example could suffice as representative of the logic of such recent political theology, namely the wide-ranging and intriguing interdisciplinary work of Paul W. Kahn, Professor of Law and the Humanities and Director of the Center for Human Rights at Yale Law School. In 2011 he published a fascinating small study, imitating the original work on political theology by the controversial German legal scholar Carl Schmitt.[21] He also called his work *Political Theology* and he also gave the subtitle *Four New Chapters on the Concept of Sovereignty*—only the "new" was new. In this book he asked "[E]ven of just laws, we can and do ask, 'Whose laws are they?' Is this not the question that Europeans ask of the output of Brussels? Is it not the same question Americans ask of international law?"[22] *Political Theology* is, however, only the culmination of a project that began a long time before, already since Kahn's earlier work called *Law and Love. The Trials of King Lear*, in which he used Shakespeare's *King Lear* to demonstrate that "law" should always be understood within the wider context of culture—precisely the same spirit in which Radbruch also worked in Germany. Kahn attempted to show that in the Judeo-Christian tradition law could always be understood from two perspectives; on the one hand, as protection against chaos and violence and, on the other hand, itself as a form of violence, to be overcome by communities beyond law, communities of love. He reads the tragic conflicts of *King Lear* as demonstration of the incommensurability of these two perspectives, with the result that love often pays a costly price for the claims and power of political law.[23]

Kahn applied these convictions then explicitly in his study called *Putting Liberalism in its Place*.[24] For him, liberalism can only play its political role once one understands the broader context and background, which, however, is not always the case, according to him. This broader background, he explains, is that the self-understanding of the nation-state always presupposes a form of sovereignty, in the case of the United States, a popular sovereignty, namely faith in and commitment to "We the People," the imagined community of the revolutionary moment when the nation was born. Simply put, the nation-state rests on imagination, on a constructed world of meaning, he often says, on what the people "believe" about themselves, on the community which the people "love," and for which they are willing to sacrifice, if necessary their own lives, and for which they are also willing to

21. For an instructive overview of the wide-ranging and complex impact of Schmitt's recent influence in the United States, see Francis Schüssler Fiorenza's essay "Prospects for Political Theology."

22. Kahn, *Political Theology*, 141.

23. Kahn, *Law and Love*.

24. Kahn, *Putting Liberalism in Its Place*.

kill the enemy wanting to kill them.[25] Putting liberalism in its place means for him to challenge people to see and acknowledge these forms of faith and love on which the liberal state with its laws ultimately depends. Liberalism is blind to its own nature and therefore to the faith, love, and identity that really holds it together—and makes it willing and able to act internationally and globally in ways that seem to deeply contradict its own rule of law. The categories on which liberalism ultimately rests are not reason and interest—as itself mistakenly believes—but love, according to Kahn. The real question is therefore whom we love, as a nation—and whom not.

In his follow-up study called *Out of Eden. Adam and Eve and the Problem of Evil*, Kahn continued this project.[26] Liberalism acknowledges the claims of reason on the one hand, regarded as so-called universal values, and the pressures of self-interest and desire on the other hand, regarded as the individual's search for happiness and flourishing, but fails to recognize a third and extremely important factor of identity and motivation, namely the faculty of the will.[27] Some would argue that globalization is undermining this "faith, love and will" of the nation-state by promoting real universalism (the universalism already mistakenly claimed by the citizens of the nation-state, based on their so-called universal values and laws), but Kahn is not convinced, and points to the radical decentralization and localism characterizing our global world, with martyrs and sacrifices and languages of enemies and foes, all the key terms already used by Carl Schmitt in his political theology.[28] Modernity, modern theory, liberalism all fail to grasp evil, because it measures behavior against the standards of reason and

---

25. This is for Kahn the key issue—this willingness to sacrifice. Without that the nation-state does not exist, because then it has no sovereignty. It is not the rule of law that most fundamentally characterizes liberal democracies, as many people may think, but the faith and the love and the hope and the imagination—the notions of sanctity and transcendence, which make the willingness to kill and be killed possible, he argues. Ultimately, the truth is that liberalism is not based on a social contract (between actual citizens), but on (the willingness to) sacrifice.

26 These two books together developed a political theology in order to fulfil the role that liberalism alone is unable to play, according to him. He presented this as the political theology of modernity, which Clifford Geertz already famously called for; see Kahn, *Out of Eden*.

27. In *Out of Eden*, Kahn appealed again and again to what he calls the two foundational myths of the Judeo-Christian tradition, in Gen 1 and 2 respectively, to argue that will is fundamental to the modern liberal state, as seen in the concept of popular sovereignty.

28. The real theme of this second book is evil, particularly political evil, but Kahn wants to show how closely (personal, but also political) evil is linked to love and to our will. In fact, for him evil is pathology of the will, evil is love gone wrong, evil is misdirected transcendence, false sacralization, the result of loss of faith or misdirection of faith.

therefore seeks psychological, sociological, and educational explanations and solutions. It fails to see the role of the will and love in evil.

In a later work called *Sacred Violence. Torture, Terror, and Sovereignty*, Kahn further developed some of these themes. Modernity (and liberalism) is much more fundamentally based on violence than most people understand. The violent will underlying the nation-state and liberal democracy is only revealed when nations are faced with threat, today in many ways the threats of terror and therefore the questions of torture. For many people, the threat of torture may suddenly reveal that their liberal rejection of the possibility of torture was not really based on universal values, as they might have thought, but rather on their mistaken belief that torture was no longer necessary, since everyone plays according to the same rules. As soon as terror threatens their imagined existence—the community of their faith, love, hope, and will—they are therefore willing to reconsider the possibility of torture.[29]

Against this background, *Political Theology* is then published in 2011.[30] Many today find Schmitt's two canonical claims, namely "sovereign is he who decides on the exception" and "all significant concepts of the modern theory of the state are secularized theological concepts" as puzzling as they are shocking, he says. These claims seem to be completely inconsistent with modern beliefs about the rule of law, separation of powers, and judicial review. Yet, he argues, puzzling as they may seem on first impression, most American readers may just have an intuition that Schmitt is pointing to some aspects of the contemporary American situation that are difficult to understand within the terms of contemporary political theory—in other words, only in terms of law, without something else, something more, and it is for this something more that he hopes to argue a case in his own version of political theology.[31] Americans will only understand themselves and their practices if they do not only look at law, but also ask other questions about themselves, about what they believe, what they do, and why.[32]

---

29. "Although we may have lost the capacity to speak of evil," Kahn says, "the persistence of evil may be the most pressing problem faced by contemporary Western thought"; *Out of Eden*, 10.

30. See also Kahn's lecture "A Political Theology for a Civil Religion."

31. In four chapters, Kahn points to the role of civil religion, of citizen sacrifice, of the sacred, and of the religious concept of the covenant supporting the popular understanding of the constitution, rather than merely a legally binding social contract. "Political theology," he says, "begins where law ends."

32. "Liberal theory puts contract at the origins of the political community; political theology puts sacrifice at the point of origin . . . Both contract and sacrifice are ideas of freedom. The former gives us our idea of the rule of law, the latter our idea of popular sovereignty. On this difference turns not only the distinction of political theory from political theology, but also our understanding of ourselves and of our relationship to

"Political theology," Kahn says, "rests on faith, not argument, and on sacrifice, not contract. It rests on Kant's third question: in what can we hope? Theory has no capacity to speak the sacred . . . The danger is that it will reduce politics to justice. It is like trying to theorize love."[33] Indeed, for him, having put liberalism in its place, political life is ultimately not about law and justice, but about faith, love, and hope, about questions of identity, belonging, and will, about experiences of sacredness and willingness to sacrifice, about knowing who we are because we know where we belong, whose we are, what we believe, and in whom we trust. In this sense, for Kahn, law needs love, but love is always in danger of becoming evil. Once again, love in this sense—compassion, care—is not about incidental acts of solidarity, empathy, and charity in specific moments, but rather about being aware of and giving account of the objects of our shared desires, recognizing and acknowledging what we ultimately believe in, treasure, pursue, care for, and are willing to sacrifice for, if anything at all.

Kahn is continuously distancing himself critically from his mentor Hannah Arendt, in several of these books, primarily because she does not understand the importance of love, which then leads to other misunderstandings as well, according to him; for example, the fact that she misreads evil when she speaks about its banality. Arendt, too, like liberal theory, according to him, "turned from the existential to the social and the historical" in her attempt to understand Eichmann and to understand evil. She also looked for rational and psychological causes, and found it in Eichmann's thoughtlessness, in the fact that he could not think properly. Kahn disagrees. For him, Eichmann mouthed clichés, yes, "but they are about sacrifice." Eichmann wanted "to follow the rule of law" because he believed—he believed the lawmaker, Hitler, and he believed the clichés of patriotism, he dedicated himself wholly to the idea and to the dignity that would come from his disregard of his own personal interests. For Eichmann, he claims, the alternative to thinking in Arendt's terms was not thoughtlessness, but faith—he was a believer and lover, which she did not fully appreciate.[34]

This criticism is interesting, since Arendt was also criticized by others for her failure to understand the nature and importance of love and compassion—of course, in spite of the fact that her own doctoral work was on love in Augustine.[35] In an essay called "Suffering and Thinking. The Scandal of Tone in *Eichmann in Jerusalem*," Deborah Nelson, for example, argues

---

the political community"; see Kahn, *Political Theology*, 7–8.

33. Kahn, *Political Theology*, 153–54.
34. See Kahn's continuous engagement with Arendt in *Out of Eden*.
35. Arendt, *Love and Saint Augustine*.

that the negative responses to the book were also motivated by her tone, specifically by the fact that she "violated conventions of sympathy that were still incoherent, though deeply felt, and only later formalized."[36] The book irritated readers, Nelson claims, because it was a period when psychic pain was becoming one of the most prominent features of political and aesthetic discourse, but Arendt did not share those feelings and she did not take them into account. In fact, even in her writings Arendt was very critical of "sympathy and the politics of misery." She had strong ideas about the "disastrous" effects on politics and public discourse of emotions, specifically compassion, love, pity, and sympathy. Her friend Gershom Scholem accused her of "heartlessness" and meant by that a lack of compassion for the Jewish suffering, and she responded by embracing this heartlessness, saying "you are quite right—I am not moved by any 'love' of this sort . . . I have never in my life 'loved' any people or collective—neither the German people, nor the French, nor the American nor the working class or anything of that sort . . . I do not 'love' the Jews, nor do I 'believe' in them; I merely belong to them as a matter of course, beyond dispute or argument."[37] One may therefore indeed wonder whether Kahn's argument about the faith, hope, love, and imagination providing meaning to the nation-state and the rule of law would have impressed or convinced Arendt at all, since she was obviously deeply aware of those kinds of convictions and challenges, yet disregarded them. Still, Nelson comments, "she could not have been more out of step with the times."[38]

Yet, was she so out of step with the times—and with which times? Was her refusal not perhaps merely her resistance against forms of love which serve to exclude others precisely while and when and because they include some? Are there not perhaps forms of compassion which serve to divide people between "us" and "them" rather than uniting us? Do the problems not lie in the form of such love—racial, nationalist, sexist, patriarchal, homophobic, and many more, drawing boundaries and dividing lines—rather than in the fact of compassion itself?

In fact, was this not precisely the thrust of the parable of the Good Samaritan in Luke's account? After all, Jesus tells the story in response to the question of who my neighbor is. Does the rhetorical intention of the parable not become clear in the words "go and do likewise," suggesting "go

---

36. Nelson, "Suffering and Thinking," 220.

37. Nelson, "Suffering and Thinking," 224. For the letter from Arendt to Scholem, see her *Wahrheit gibt es nur zu Zweien*, 279–80. This collection of her letters to her friends in fact contradicts any claims that she was heartless, since friends describe and praise her as a remarkable gift of love and friendship.

38. Nelson, "Suffering and Thinking," 229.

and become a neighbor showing compassion across religious, cultural, and nationalistic boundaries, even across boundaries of traditional alienation and enmity"? This may be out of step with a present-day mood in the United States, as Kahn convincingly shows, and indeed in many other nation-states, religions, and cultures, but it does not seem to have been out of step with the intentions of Jesus in Luke's Gospel?

Such questions therefore lead back to yet a third reading of the parable of the Good Samaritan. Commenting on this parable, Calvin already claimed that the key lies in the fact that the character is a Samaritan.[39] For him, the parable is not merely about compassion that trumps law. The parable is rather about a specific form of compassion, namely a compassion that includes everyone—it is simply enough that the other one is a human person; not practicing this compassion toward everyone is barbaric, inhumane, disrespectful, cruel, hateful; practicing this compassion is based on respect for human dignity. For Calvin, the key to the parable lies in Jesus' deliberate reference to a Samaritan, showing that we are created for one another, not merely to pursue our own happiness, progress, and success. As human beings, we carry the responsibility to serve one another without any partiality. This form of compassion therefore trumps both law *as well as* our many more limited forms of compassion. This form of compassion calls for human dignity; for mutual service irrespective of who the others may be; for a will toward inclusion that ignores our everyday boundaries, customs, and practices; for an openness and availability that overcomes even our traditional enmities.

It is quite remarkable to see how the thrust of Calvin's description of our experiences and emotions when faced with the neighbor (recognizing both the image of God and our own flesh, for example in the 1559 *Institutes* III/7.6) differs almost word by word from the well-known description of our experiences and emotions when faced with our neighbor as danger and threat by Sigmund Freud in his *Civilization and Its Discontents*.[40] Indeed, "the notion of neighbor has lost its innocence" and we face the task "of rethinking the notion of neighbor in light of the catastrophic experiences of the twentieth century," but also of apartheid and contemporary globalization. "[I]n our own societies, is not the multiculturalist notion of tolerance, whose fundamental value is the right not to be harassed, precisely a strategy to keep the intrusive neighbor at a proper distance?"[41] This form of

---

39. See Calvin in Jansen, *Barmhartige Samaritaan*, 215–18.

40. Freud, *Civilization and Its Discontents*, 66–69.

41. Žižek et al., *The Neighbor*, 1–10; see especially, in the same publication, the contribution by Žižek, "Neighbors and Other Monsters: A Plea for Ethical Violence," 134–90.

compassion clearly calls for a different social imaginary than a world based on selfish desire (protected by law and without any sacrifice) or on selfish love (willing towards compassion and sacrifice, but a compassion limited by sovereignty and belonging).[42]

With that, the circle of the question has been completed. It may seem as if the gospel—including this parable—points to the importance of law, of human dignity accorded to all, irrespective of who and what and how they may be, and universal human rights, to which everyone have inherent claims. Universal law should trump our particularistic loves and desires. At the same time, we are aware that our everyday realities and practices—in our religious communities, traditions, cultures, nation-states, and sovereign political spheres—make us limit these rights in order to include only some and to exclude others—strangers, foreigners, exiles, refugees, asylum-seekers, non-citizens, migrants—and for these purposes of exclusion we again use our laws and regulations. The same laws that protect us and bind us together in shared identities and common love, for which we are willing to suffer, also make it possible for us to make others suffer and to threaten them, while excluding them from the circles of our identities and from our ways of belonging. Whenever this happens, the boundary-defying enemy-love of the parable again seems to challenge and trump our laws, our identities and our dangerous claims of sovereignty.

So Again, the Good Samaritan—And Globalization?

But how? Is globalization itself the boundary-breaking movement that will help us to overcome our exclusions, as some seem to think? Will the laws of the market achieve what the laws of countries and courts were unable to deliver? Or are these laws of the market creating new injustices, new forms of "us" and "them," new insiders and outsiders, new forms of belonging and new realities of staying behind or on the margins or outside in the dark? In which form will the love come, which will be able to break down these new boundaries? Which structures and which acts of compassion will be able to make real differences?

For South Africa today, the political theology of Kahn (and many others) certainly raises many serious questions. To mention only one, Kahn's fundamental thesis, namely that liberal democracy and its rule of law can only be understood against the broader background about the nature and

---

42. In the same spirit, Wolterstorff uses the gospel to argue for a culture of human dignity and human rights, for a spirit of justice, and *for* liberal democracy; for example, in *Understanding Liberal Democracy*.

claims—the imagination, faith, love, and hope—of the nation-state itself, points to a serious problem. In a widely known and influential essay from the time of public debates about the imminent transformation of South African society, the eminent political philosopher Johannes Degenaar addressed what he called "The Myth of a South African Nation."[43] Distinguishing between a number of ways in which "nation" and "nation-building" can be used, he proposed to reject them all regarding South Africa. He regarded any talk about "a South African nation" as a myth to be discarded. Instead of such a myth of the nation, he argued for the vision of a democratic culture. One could argue that, until today, this tension has not fully been resolved. It is not at all clear how South Africans envision "South Africa," what kind of society we imagine, believe in, dream of, love, are committed to, and are willing to sacrifice for—if we are willing to sacrifice anything for South Africa at all. Different "objects of our love" still compete and conflict in public and political discourses and are behind many of the tensions and struggles South Africa experiences today. Law alone is not able to resolve the tensions and struggles, according to Kahn only love will be able to do that, but love for whom and what? What does "South Africa" mean, for South Africans?[44]

Similar comments are probably applicable to contemporary debates about globalization. Some South African Reformed churches have been involved in the confessional process in the worldwide Reformed community, linked to the names Kitwe, Debrecen, and Accra. After Accra, churches from the North and South have jointly undertaken a study process, led by Allan Boesak, which produced a common description of the "empire" that Reformed believers discern at work in the global world, and later also a joint document called *Dreaming a Different World*. It could be instructive to study this process and document and the litany that was written as summary of the whole process, with a view to the questions of law as/and compassion.[45]

It is already informative that the findings were given in the form of a public prayer intended for use during worship, and that the title of the publication refers to "dreaming," thus calling forth allusions of imagination, faith, love, and hope. It seems to suggest that responses to globalization should be informed by such shared visions.[46] In fact, another outcome was the study that Cynthia D. Moe-Lobeda, who was invited to participate dur-

43. Degenaar, "The Myth of a South African Nation."

44. See my "Religion and Civil Society in 'South Africa'?"

45. For essays originating during this study project, see Boesak and Hansen, *Globalisation*; also Boesak and Hansen, *Globalisation II*.

46. For the final report of this joint study project between German and South African churches, including the litany used as press release, see Boesak et al., *Dreaming a Different World*.

ing the process, published as her own contribution, called *Resisting Structural Evil. Love as Ecological-Economic Vocation*. She similarly argues for ways of seeing—the devastation, the possibilities of what could and should be, but also the life-giving, life-saving mystery—and for ethics willing to meet the moral challenges of this time and place.[47] Similarly, one could read Allan Boesak's own recent book called *Dare We Speak of Hope? Searching for a Language of Life in Faith and Politics*, as an outcome of the same process, together with his even more recent *Kairos, Crisis, and Global Apartheid. The Challenge to Prophetic Resistance*. In both books, Boesak is also arguing for the importance of vision and hope and of love, commitment, and courage. Again, he most certainly takes law, justice, and power extremely seriously, but embedded in a broader vision—or in his case, rather a dream.[48]

Finally, these questions lead back once more—for a fourth time—to the parable of the Good Samaritan. During the 1970s, there was one meditation on the parable which impressed Allan Boesak so deeply that he returned to that meditation on more than one occasion over the years, until recently, when faced with the challenges of globalization.[49] During a conference in the Netherlands, the Catholic theologian Jean Cardonel said "(D)e man uit Samaria, de Naastenliefde komt past ná de strijd. De ellende van Caritas, Rode Kruis, Katholieke Hulp en wat al meer, is, dat ze zich niet om de oorzaken bekommeren ... Daarom stel ik de grote, de enige echte vraag: wat gebeurt er als de Naastenliefde niet ná, maar tijdens het gevecht aankomt?"[50] For the question of how to respond to the challenges of globalization, this perspective is crucial, since law and love tend to be important either after the violence when the victims need care and compassion or before the violence when potential victims can still be protected in time by law and regulation; but what if we have to respond while the violence is taking place? What if we arrive during the crime, the attack, rape, injustice, struggle? What if we are, after all, ourselves participants in the process, actors in the events, role players in the parable?

---

47. Moe-Lobeda, *Resisting Structural Evil*.
48. Boesak, *Dare We Speak of Hope?*; and Boesak, *Kairos, Crisis, and Global Apartheid*.
49. Boesak, "'For the Tyrant Shall be no More.'"
50. Originally in "Toekomst van de Religie," reprinted in Jansen, *Barmhartige Samaritaan*, 219–24. Roughly translated: "The man from Samaria, the Neighborly Love, arrives on the scene just after the conflict. The deficiency of Caritas, Red Cross, Catholic Aid, and many similar organizations is that they seldom care about the causes ... Therefore, I raise the main, the only true question: What happens if Neighborly Love arrives on the scene not after, but during the conflict?"

Bibliography

Arendt, Hannah. *Love and Saint Augustine*. Edited, translated, and reprinted with an interpretive essay by Joanna V. Scott and Judith C. Stark. Chicago: Chicago University Press, 1996.

———. *Wahrheit gibt es nur zu Zweien: Briefe an die Freunde*. Edited by Ingeborg Nordmann. Munich: Piper, 2013.

Bauman, Zygmunt. *Does Ethics Have a Chance in a World of Consumers?* Cambridge, MA: Harvard University Press, 2008.

Boesak, Allan A. *Dare We Speak of Hope? Searching for a Language of Life in Faith and Politics*. Grand Rapids: Eerdmans, 2014.

———. "'For the Tyrant Shall Be No More:' Reflections on and Lessons from 'The Arab Spring' in North Africa, the Middle East and the Civil Rights and Anti-Apartheid Struggles." *HTS Teologiese Studies/Theological Studies* 67 (2011). http://www.scielo.org.za/pdf/hts/v67n3/v67n3a31.pdf.

———. *Kairos, Crisis, and Global Apartheid: The Challenge to Prophetic Resistance*. New York: Palgrave Macmillan, 2015.

———. *Running with Horses: Reflections of an Accidental Politician*. Bloubergrandt: Genugtig!, 2009.

Boesak, Allan A., and Len Hansen, eds. *Globalisation—The Politics of Empire, Justice and the Life of Faith*. Stellenbosch, South Africa: Sun, 2009.

———. *Globalisation II—Global Crisis, Global Challenge, Global Faith: An Ongoing response to the Accra Confession*. Stellenbosch, South Africa: Sun, 2010.

Boesak, Allan A, et al., eds. *Dreaming a Different World: Globalisation and Justice for Humanity and the Earth: The Challenge of the Accra Confession for the Churches*. 2010. http://academic.sun.ac.za/tsv/downloads/Globalisation%20report%202010%20proof%203.pdf.

Botman, H. Russel. "'Dutch' and Reformed and 'Black' and Reformed in South Africa: A Tale of Two Traditions on the Move to Unity and Responsibility." In *Keeping Faith: Embracing the Tensions in Christian Higher Education*, edited by Ronald A. Wells, 85–105. Grand Rapids: Eerdmans, 1996.

Calvin, John. *Calvin's Institutes of the Christian Religion*. Translated by Henry Beveridge. Grand Rapids: Eerdmans, 1970.

Cardonel, Jan. "Toekomst van de Religie: Religie van de Toekomst?" *Tijdschrift Voor Theologie*, 1972. Reprinted in *Barmhartige Samaritaan in Rovershanden?*, edited by J. G. B. Jansen, 219–24. Apeldoorn: Semper Agendo, 1974.

Coplan, Amy, and Peter Goldie, eds. *Empathy: Philosophical and Psychological Perspectives*. Oxford: Oxford University Press, 2011.

Degenaar, Johannes. "The Myth of a South African Nation." *Occasional Papers 40*, IDASA, 1991.

Eagleton, Terry. *Trouble with Strangers: A Study of Ethics*. Oxford: Wiley-Blackwell, 2009.

Freud, Sigmund. *Civilization and Its Discontents*. Edited and translated by James Strachey. New York: Norton, 1989.

Hesselink, John. *Calvin's Concept of the Law*. Allison Park, PA: Pickwick, 1992.

Huber, Wolfgang. "Gerechtigkeit und Liebe." In *Gerechtigkeit und Recht*, by Wolfgang Huber, 199–221. Gütersloh: Gütersloher, 1996.

———. "Recht im Horizont der Liebe: Eine theologische Skizze." In *Konflikt und Konsens*, Wolfgang Huber, 237–50. Munich: Kaiser, 1990.
Jansen, J. G. B. *Barmhartige Samaritaan in Rovershanden*. Apeldoorn: Semper Agendo, 1974.
Jens, Walter. *Der barmherzige Samariter*. Stuttgart: Kreuz, 1973.
Kahn, Paul W. *Law and Love: The Trials of King Lear*. New Haven: Yale University Press, 2000.
———. *Out of Eden: Adam and Eve and the Problem of Evil*. Princeton: Princeton University Press, 2007.
———. "A Political Theology for a Civil Religion," 2012. http://www.eui.eu/Projects/ReligioWest/Documents/events/LecturesSeries/LectureKahn.pdf.
———. *Political Theology: Four New Chapters on the Concept of Sovereignty*. New York: Columbia University Press, 2011.
———. *Putting Liberalism in Its Place*. Princeton: Princeton University Press, 2005.
———. *Sacred Violence, Torture, Terror, and Sovereignty*. Ann Arbor: University of Michigan Press, 2008.
Kitcher, Philip. *Life after Faith: The Case for Secular Humanism*. New Haven: Yale University Press, 2014.
Makgoro, Yvonne. "Ubuntu and the Law in South Africa." *Potchefstroom Electronic Law Journal* 1 (1998). http://www.ajol.info/index.php/pelj/article/view/43567.
Mazamisa, Llewellyn Welile. *Beatific Comradeship: An Exegetical-Hermeneutical Study on Lk 10:25–37*. Kampen: Kok, 1987.
Moe-Lobeda, Cynthia D. *Resisting Structural Evil: Love as Ecological-Economic Vocation*. Minneapolis: Fortress, 2013.
Nelson, Deborah. "Suffering and Thinking: The Scandal of Tone in *Eichmann in Jerusalem*." In *Compassion: The Culture and Politics of an Emotion*, edited by Lauren Berlant, 219–44. New York: Routledge, 2004.
Niebuhr, Reinhold. *Moral Man and Immoral Society: A Study in Ethics and Politics*. New York: Scribner, 1932.
Nowak, Martin, and Sarah Coakley, eds. *Evolution, Games, and God: The Principle of Cooperation*. Cambridge, MA: Harvard University Press, 2013.
Post, Stephen G., et al., eds. *Altruism & Altruistic Love. Science, Philosophy, & Religion in Dialogue*. Oxford: Oxford University Press, 2002.
Radbruch, Gustav. "Gesetzliches Unrecht und übergesetzliches Recht." *Süddeutsche Juristenzeitung* 1 (1946) 105–8.
Schüssler Fiorenza, Francis. "Prospects for Political Theology in the Face of Contemporary Challenges." In *Political Theology: Contemporary Challenges and Future Directions*, edited by Francis Schüssler Fiorenza et al., 37–60. Louisville: Westminster John Knox, 2013.
Small, Adam. *Kitaar my Kruis*. Cape Town: HAUM, 1961.
Smit, Dirkie. "'Iets dat diepgaander is dan verplichting en gehoorzaamheid?' Een Zuid-Afrikaans verhaal over de erfenis van Calvijn." In *Het Calvinistisch Ongemak: Calvijn als Erflater en Provocator van het Nederlandse Protestantisme*, edited Bert de Leede et al., 117–36. Kampen: Kok, 2009.
———. "Religion and Civil Society in 'South Africa'? Searching for a Grammar for Life Together." In *Church and Civil Society. German and South African Perspectives*, edited by Michael Welker et al., 63–106. Stellenbosch, South Africa: Sun, 2017.

———. "'Whose Law?' South African Struggles with Notions of Justice." In *Religion and Human Rights: Global Challenges from Intercultural Perspectives*, edited by Wilhelm Gräb and Lars Charbonnier, 149–74. Berlin: de Gruyter, 2015.

Sober, Elliott, and David Sloan Wilson. *Unto Others: The Evolution and Psychology of Unselfish Behavior*. Cambridge, MA: Harvard University Press, 1998.

Strohm, Christoph. *Ethik im Frühen Calvinismus. Humanistische Einflüsse, Philosophische, Juristische und Theologische Argumentationen sowie mentalitätsgeschichtliche Aspekte am Beispiel des Calvin-Schülers Lambertus Danaeus*. Berlin: de Gruyter, 1996.

VanDrunen, David. "The Natural Law and Liberal Traditions. Heritage (and Hope?) of Western Civilization." In *The Law of God: Exploring God and Civilization*, edited by Pieter Vos and Onno Zijlstra, 64–83. Leiden: Brill, 2014.

Welker, Michael. "Justice—Mercy—Worship. The 'Weighty' Matters of Biblical Law." In *Concepts of Law in the Sciences, Legal Studies, and Theology*, edited by Michael Welker and Gregor Etzelmüller, 205–24. Tübingen: Mohr/Siebeck, 2013.

———. "The Power of Mercy in Biblical Law." *Journal of Law and Religion* 29 (2014) 225–35.

Witte, John. *The Reformation of Rights: Law, Religion and Human Rights in Early Modern Calvinism*. Cambridge: Cambridge University Press, 2007.

Wolterstorff, Nicholas. *Journey toward Justice: Personal Encounters in the Global South*. Grand Rapids: Baker Academic, 2013.

———. *The Mighty and the Almighty: An Essay in Political Theology*. Cambridge: Cambridge University Press, 2012.

———. *Understanding Liberal Democracy: Essays in Political Philosophy*. Oxford: Oxford University Press, 2012.

Žižek, Slavoj, et al. *The Neighbor: Three Inquiries in Political Theology*. Chicago: University of Chicago Press, 2005.

Poverty and Inequality in South Africa
What's Compassion Got to Do with It?

Nadine Bowers Du Toit

> "Overcoming poverty is not a gesture of charity.
> It is an act of justice."
>
> Nelson Mandela

Introduction

WHAT DOES THE LEGACY of apartheid have to do with compassion? If the university student protests over the past few years that raged throughout South Africa are anything to go by, then the answer may well be "not as much as one would think." These protests, originally framed within what one could call the "de-colonial turn" and the call to free universal university education in order to promote access, are now a symbol of the protest against the lack of transformation at the university—and dare I say larger society.[1] These stu-

---

1. The protests began at the University of Cape Town with calls for the removal of the colonist Cecil John Rhodes's statue from the premises of the University, but soon spread to other campuses, culminating in what was known as #RhodesMustFall. This later developed into what is currently widely referred to as the #FeesMustFall movement. This student movement is not only about advocating free universal tertiary education but also about the decolonization of South African universities. The discourse around transformation in higher education institutions in South Africa was articulated by students as "black pain," which centers on the indignity still faced by many black people due to the slow pace of transformation within the institutions of our society. The ideal of the "rainbow nation" is fragmenting, as heard in the opinion of one young student who critiqued Mandela's reconciliatory agenda: "I think dangerous precedents were set by Mandela and his leadership, that everything that needs to do with black pain needs negotiation whether valid or not"; Ramoupi, "Education Lessons."

dent protesters—and their poorer, more marginalized counterparts engaging in service delivery protests on the edges of the city—are all pointing to one thing and that is the lingering effects of systemic and race-related inequality in South African society.[2] It is a well-known fact that South Africa is one of the most unequal societies in the world and that despite growing intra-race inequality—inequality is still largely racially skewed.[3]

What these protesters are not looking for is compassion in its weak form: a kind of sympathetic response which recognizes the lack of equality and poverty suffered by the black masses, but does not take seriously the systemic nature of white privilege. It is alarming, however, that even this "weak" form of compassion—namely acknowledgement of the effects of the apartheid system on the situation in which many millions of largely black poor find themselves today—is lacking. This has become increasingly apparent in the past year—both in terms of the findings of the South African Reconciliation Barometer as well as in the social media: apartheid denialism and race polarization is on the rise.[4]

The church's response to these seismic shifts in society has been interesting to observe. For many years (and still to a large degree today), it is in this mode of compassionate acts of charity that the church in South Africa has largely been operating in response to the challenges of poverty and inequality. However well-meaning this response may be, it is widely recognized that welfare projects which merely attend to the symptoms rather than the root causes of poverty do not and cannot address the nature of systemic disadvantage.[5] Recent developments have, however, seen a rise (or perhaps reemergence) of groups (largely driven by national church leaders and academics) attempting to challenge an increasingly corrupt state as well as highlighting the need for the church to engage at grassroots level with issues of poverty and inequality.[6]

---

2. Of course, service delivery protestors are also pointing to the inability of the government to deliver. This paper, however, focuses more specifically on civil society. See Mottiar and Bond, "The Politics of Discontent," for a discussion on the nature of social protest in South Africa. Even the latest, horrifying xenophobic attacks have their roots in the discourse around the socioeconomic marginalization of the local black population. See also the report by the Centre for the Study of Violence and Reconciliation, "Understanding Current Xenophobic Attacks."

3. See Leibbrandt et al., *Trends*.

4. See Davis, "SA Reconciliation Barometer."

5. Swart and Venter, "NGOs and Churches."

6. Dongsung and Phiri, "Editorial," 249; Phiri and Dongsung, "Called to be a Diaconial Community," 253; Nordstokke, "Ecumenical *Diakonia*," 265. I am here mainly referring to the repositioning (or perhaps revival?) of the SACC (South African Council of Churches) and the emergence of the AHA (Authentic Hopeful Action) Movement,

What is missing, however, is the actual voice of the church at grassroots level with regard to issues that directly affect the ministry and members. This essay attempts to discuss the findings of a recent study with regard to their framing of concepts such as poverty and inequality against the background of our social context and a re-framing of a global understanding of diakonia in recent years.

Current Trends in Re-Framing Diakonia and Development

It is clear from the October 2014 edition of *The Ecumenical Review* that there is an upsurge of interest within the World Council of Churches (WCC) with regard to reconceptualization of an understanding of diakonia within a changing context.[7] Many of the articles within this edition all point to the notion that "diakonia has often been understood as service" and has been traditionally framed as "acts of charity and benevolence that have been conferred upon the less fortunate or needy in one's community."[8] Nordstokke traces what I would term a "weak" form of diakonia to theological ambiguity with regard to a clear understanding of the term within ecumenical circles, and points out that as a result it has often been separated from the mission of the church or viewed purely as "benevolent charity work."[9] In framing diakonia as "service" there is an immediate link to the term "compassion,"

---

which was launched in 2014.

7. It should be noted that it appears that, in this edition and in recent thinking within the ecumenical movement, the terms "diakonia" and "development" are sometimes used interchangeably, and at other times alongside each other. Within the South African context (in scholarly circles at least), the terms "development" and "transformational development" have been preferred. However, denominations such as the Dutch Reformed Church have a specific understanding of diakonia and appear to favor these terms; see Swart, *Research Report*, 122.

8. Phiri and Dongsung, "Called to Be a Diaconal Community," 253; Nordstokke, "Ecumenical Diakonia," 266.

9. Nordstokke, "Ecumenical Diakonia," 266. It should be noted that the evangelical stream has long preferred the term "transformational development" or "integral mission" to "diakonia," which keeps in tension both justice and love as dimensions of mission (see Samuel and Sugden, *The Church in Response* and *Mission as Transformation*; Myers, *Walking with the Poor*). In their attempt, there was a clear theological impetus to understand both the difference and relationship between individual and structural sin, which in turn lead to what Myers terms a "relational understanding of poverty." This relational understanding acknowledges the importance of personal change as well as the structural nature of injustice (addressed through what they refer to as "transformational development," which encompasses evangelism, charity/relief as well as advocacy). See also footnote 6 above.

as those who would seek to enact diakonia are motivated by compassion rooted in good neighborliness.

Herrmann explores the notion that words such as "mercy" and "compassion" often evoke the vision of a privileged Christian being gracious/merciful/compassionate to the disadvantaged, poor, and weak.[10] He makes the important point that while such words cannot be excised from our vocabulary (as many are biblical), we do need to carefully consider how we use words such as "compassion" or "mercy."[11] Herrmann then defines "compassion" to mean that "we too are 'needy' with self-sufficiency giving way to solidarity . . . we are all beggars."[12] This indicates that poverty does not only belong to the poor, as we are all poor and in need of love, solidarity, and dignity. Through the recognition of the wealthy of their poverty, room is created for questioning the power differential, which in turn makes space for compassion to be reciprocal rather than parochial.

Nordstokke highlights the fact that "ecumenical *diakonia* today requires a critical analysis of what causes poverty and human suffering, and bold action in defense of the excluded and their rights."[13] This move within ecumenical thinking towards highlighting the importance of diakonia as advocacy for justice and peace (rather than merely benevolent charity) is, of course, not new. It should also be noted, however, that it was liberation theology that made reference to the "preferential option for the poor" first and framed the church's action in terms of economic justice and solidarity.[14] Another contributor to the debate frames diakonia theologically in strong liberation theology terms when dealing with the issue of empire and economic justice.[15] Furthermore, Phiri and Dongsung also make a call for an understanding of *diakonia* within the framework of justice and peace, in which they draw strongly on the World Council of Churches (WCC) document "Theological Perspectives in the 21st Century": Diakonia seeking transformation is service that makes "the celebration of life" possible

---

10. Herrmann, "Compassion, Mercy, and Diakonia," 271.

11. This is key: I am not, therefore, advocating against the term or arguing its theological relevance, but rather the manner in which it has been appropriated by churches and development agencies in their response to poverty.

12. Herrmann, "Compassion, Mercy, and Diakonia," 272.

13. Nordstokke, "Ecumenical Diakonia," 266.

14. Of course, liberation theologians such as Gustavo Gutiérrez were extremely critical of purely economic and technocratic notions of development, preferring instead to opt for the term "liberation." This conception of development (termed "modernization theory") was appropriated by many churches and church agencies, and is also highly critiqued by Elliott, *Comfortable Compassion?*, 39–70.

15. See Chung, "Diakonia and Economic Justice," 302–3.

for all. It is not "limited to binding the wounds of victims or doing acts of compassion." Truly authentic and transformative diakonia "involves both comforting the victim and confronting the 'powers and principalities' (Eph 6:12). It must heal the victim as well as the one who victimises. Ecumenical diakonia that seeks transformation is 'prophetic action which also involves speaking truth to powers.' In this sense, service cannot be divorced from advocacy for justice and peace."[16]

We see here what I may term a "re-radicalization" of the theological discourse—a very clear move away from compassion as key framework toward what may be designated as "prophetic diakonia."[17] In this guise, diakonia is argued as needing to once again take seriously the issue of power.[18] Lupton notes that "mercy without justice degenerates into dependency and entitlement, preserving the power of the giver over the recipients."[19] A kind of compassionate charity that views the poor as inactive recipients with no agency can become what Lupton calls "toxic."

Re-exploring and reimagining the theology and tools provided by liberation theology in a new key presents a challenge to those from the South. Hewitt, a Caribbean theologian, contests in his contribution to Allan Boesak's festschrift that "liberational thinking and praxis remain an unfinished agenda" as South African black and Caribbean theology "have not fully awakened sufficient numbers of conscientized people to face the contemporary life-denying forces that are enslaving our people."[20] It has the potential to reposition those on the margins as subjects of their own development in confronting the powers that seek to oppress them, rather than as objects of benevolent charity who are powerless in the face of social, spiritual, and economic oppression.[21]

The latter is closely linked to another shift in perspectives on diakonia and development within the ecumenical movement, namely a renewed appreciation for the role of local congregations. In many instances, local

---

16. Phiri and Dongsung, "Called to Be a Diaconal Community," 255–56.

17. See Padilha, "Diakonia in Latin America," 289.

18. In his seminal work written during the late 1980s, Elliott (*Comfortable Compassion?*, 69) critiqued the ecumenical movement for their failure "to come to terms with a structural analysis of poverty at many levels—intellectual, ethical, political and existential" and claims that these issues were always marginal and "have never been owned by the main-line churches nor by their development agencies." It appears that one may say that this is shifting with the radicalization of diakonia, as illustrated by recent discourse.

19. Lupton, *Toxic Charity*, 41; See also Ham, "Colombo," 286–88.

20. Hewitt, "Black and Reformed," 167.

21. Documents such as the *Confession of Belhar* (see Article 4) certainly still give a theological voice to the pain of many on the margins.

congregations became the objects toward which diakonia projects were orientated and to which diakonia resources and expertise from the outside were given. As a consequence, ecumenical diakonia became more and more distant from the everyday life, witness, and ministry of local congregations. However, recent deliberations on the nature and theological foundations of diakonia have begun to reverse this paradigm by starting with the local congregations as the subjects of diakonia.[22]

This renewed appreciation brings the ecclesiological focus of diakonia back to the local congregation. However, this macro shift within world bodies such as the World Council of Churches will also need to see embodiment within the micro context of congregations. My own work over the past ten years has focused largely on local congregations as agents of change; a focus that stems from the fact that many South African congregations are indeed churches of the poor and marginalized. As such, they have the potential to be sites of own development.[23] It has also highlighted the inherent potential of partnering across racial divides in order to address poverty and inequality.[24]

Despite the fact that the local congregation has often been touted as key agent of mobilization for development, its potential for development has also been critiqued.[25] Much of this critique has related to the congregations' inability to move beyond a charity or welfare paradigm, and theology has been identified as a barrier in this regard.[26] In particular, what may be denoted as an appropriation of what I previously termed a "weak" understanding of compassion theologically, has been found to hinder congregations from moving beyond charity or relief. Within a context of inequality, failure to understand one's neighbor within the context of both social and economic reconciliation may result in a failure to confront the "complexities of neighborliness" in South Africa, "which require stepping beyond the boundaries of race and class."[27]

22. Dongsung and Phiri, "Editorial," 249–50.

23. Although South Africa has a vibrant FBO (faith-based organizations) sector, it does not conduct or understand diaconal work in the same manner as some of the European churches or Northern European diaconal agencies do. There is little contact or official sanction by ecumenical bodies or denominations as such, although some FBO's do originate from congregations and denominations.

24. Bowers and August, "Engaging Poverty," 422; see also Bowers Du Toit and Nkomo, "The Ongoing Challenge."

25. Swart, "Are the Rising Expectations Realistic?," 285.

26. Bowers Du Toit, "Theology and the Social Welfare," 262.

27. Bowers Du Toit, "Theology and the Social Welfare," 260; See also Bowers Du Toit and Nkomo, "The Ongoing Challenge", for a case study on the response of white-majority congregations to poverty and inequality against the background of reconciliation, restitution, and reparations.

Findings and Analysis

This section introduces the empirical component of this essay. It begins with the methodology used in obtaining and analyzing the data and then reports on the findings, which refer largely to the manner in which ministers as congregational leaders frame their understanding of poverty and inequality. The section does not discuss how churches are responding to poverty and inequality, despite the fact that this forms part of the broader study. In focusing on ministers' framing of poverty and inequality and the nature of their discourse, the hope is that the way in which congregational leaders voice the current nature of this challenge in South Africa will in turn point back to the title of this essay.

Methodology

The empirical findings of this essay are derived from a recent research project entitled "Meeting the Challenge of Poverty and Inequality in the Cape Metropole: Factors Impacting the Mobilization of Congregations in Their Response to Poverty and Injustice." The research was qualitative in nature, as the key thrust of the research is interpretive and explores the possible impact of variables such as theology, race, and socioeconomic status on the mobilization of churches with regard to poverty and inequality.

The original dataset was obtained from a faith-based organization that works in the area of church mobilization, and therefore congregations targeted by the study have all been exposed in some way (workshops, talks, events) to issues on poverty, injustice, division, and the need for the church's response to these issues. It was, however, not assumed that all congregations in the dataset would be actively mobilized regarding poverty and inequality.

This dataset was then sampled by a statistician at Stellenbosch University, using stratified random sampling in order to produce a sample that is broadly representative of theological traditions as well as a broad range of geographical areas (and race groups) within the Cape Metropole.[28] Denominationally, the congregations included those from the Anglican, Methodist, Dutch Reformed, Baptist, Independent Evangelical, and Pentecostal/Charismatic traditions. Geographically, there were churches from the suburbs and the townships,[29] covering all race groups[30] in the Western Cape.

28. Wagner et al., *Doing Social Research*, 91.

29. Areas covered include the following: Dunoon, Capricorn, Langa, Khayalitsha, Gugulethu, Manenberg, Rondebosch, City Center, Mowbray, Wynberg, Claremont, and Meadowridge.

30. It should be noted that poverty and inequality in South Africa is still directly

Fourteen interviews were conducted in total, thirteen of which were conducted with the minister as key respondent. As the research was qualitative in nature, semi-structured interviews were conducted with these respondents. These interviews were conducted with an interview guide, which was based largely on the research aims of the study. However, since the interviews were semi-structured in nature, the questioning strategy allowed for probing as well as flexibility in the order and manner in which questions were asked.[31] The interviews were subsequently recorded, transcribed, coded, and then analyzed, using ATLAS.ti.[32] Ethical clearance for this study was obtained from Stellenbosch University and all protocols were followed in this regard.

Findings

Poverty Framing is Nuanced

The ministers interviewed framed their understanding of poverty in a myriad of nuanced ways. When asked what their understanding of poverty was, not one respondent alluded to material or basic needs (such as food, clothing, housing, etc.) only. Several referred to poverty as having several facets, which included the mental, spiritual, and material (Rev. S; Rev. D; Rev. T; Rev. Z), and which indicates that they view poverty as a holistic phenomenon. Some respondents referred to poverty as a "cycle" or "trap", which keeps those caught up in it trapped (Rev. D; Rev. M; Rev. Z; Rev. R). One respondent noted, "...this whole cycle... it's ongoing all the time." This correlates directly to Robert Chambers's definition of what he calls "The Deprivation Trap."[33]

---

aligned with race, which is why this is specifically noted throughout the findings. It should also be noted that the term "Colored" is regarded as highly problematic by some who prefer the term "so-called Colored," or even disregard the term completely as they were afforded this designation by the apartheid state. However, for the purposes of this essay I will simply use the term "Colored" to refer to communities with mixed-race heritage.

31. Wagner et al., *Doing Social Research*, 134.

32. This is a Computer-Aided Qualitative Data Analysis Software; a tool that supports the coding of qualitative data. The data in this case was co-coded by both interviewers.

33. Chambers pioneered an understanding of the interrelated nature of household and individual poverty through what he called "The Deprivation Trap." His "trap" encompassed several dimensions, namely: isolation, powerlessness, vulnerability, physical weakness, and poverty. Each of these groups of deprivation interacts to form a trap and each of these clusters may interact and reenforce one another; Chambers in Swanepoel and De Beer, *Community Development*, 5.

Some respondents noted that mental poverty affected the poor's ability to escape the Deprivation Trap, as they felt powerless to escape the situation, and which in turn resulted in a lack of self-worth (Rev. D; Rev. Z). Others described poverty in terms of lack of access—largely to education, but also to other forms of access: "People who lack means in terms of education, in terms of access to transport, in terms of access to capital. . ." (Rev. T; Rev. R; Rev. A; Rev. M). This lack of access was referred to by one respondent as "being life-depriving" (Rev. A).

The relative nature of poverty in South Africa was also highlighted by one respondent who noted that, even if one perceives oneself as middle class, one is extremely rich in comparison to many poor in the country (Rev. D). Only one respondent (Rev. S) framed the roots of poverty as "laziness" and even then, this was not the sole manner in which he framed poverty. At least two respondents noted that poverty was not only economic and that those who may be identified as economically rich may be poor in other ways (Rev. A; Rev. B). Although only two respondents (Rev. A and Rev. C) used the term "poverty" as linked to the term "injustice," as the next section reveals, poverty was very much framed within the injustices of the past by many respondents.

Poverty is not Framed Chiefly in Theological-Ethical Terms

Although the ministers who were interviewed certainly referred to theological constructs and biblical texts during the course of the interviews, it is interesting to note that not many defined poverty in theological terms. One minister framed poverty in terms of a lack of dignity (which he related to the aforementioned lack of access) and some mentioned what they termed "spiritual poverty," which was most often noted in relation to other dimensions of poverty (Rev. A; Rev. D; Rev. S).

A black African Pentecostal minister referred to a "spirit of poverty"; however, this was not expanded upon and his major emphasis remains on mental poverty as the cause for individuals not breaking free from the poverty trap. Another black African minister noted, however, that the spiritual reality of poverty is greed. Not only does he frame this in socio-ethical terms, but he makes an astute link between what Walter Wink calls the "outer" and "inner" realities of systems: greed as the inner reality and inequality as the outer manifestation of it.

> The cause of poverty is those who have . . . the greed of those who have . . . inability to share with those who don't have. For me that's it. So world over . . . so whether in our country it manifested itself in a form of apartheid. In another country it

> manifest [sic] differently. So it will manifest in various forms but there's simple one thing because apartheid was . . . apartheid was not . . . was not driven by hatred it was driven by greed. Greed is right from the start of the Word of God in Genesis . . . the problem of greed was started (Rev. Z).

He also appears to link this soteriologically to the fall of humankind. Another white minister from an independent evangelical neo-reformed church also roots poverty soteriologically in the Fall (Rev. T). It is interesting to note that three of the five white respondents appeared to refer to poverty largely in relational terms. They made statements such as "wealthy communities; they are often relationally poor" or that the roots of poverty was a "broken relationship between God, human beings, and each other" (Rev. B; Rev. C). This is may be interpreted either socio-critically by engaging race and class, or through theological lenses. One could assume that due to race and class, white respondents were reluctant to tie poverty to categories of race and class (wherein they have relative privilege). One could also tie this to the fact that all three respondents find their roots in evangelicalism and, therefore, reference an evangelical understanding of poverty influenced by writers such as Bryant Myers.[34]

Poverty and Inequality Strongly Identified as Linked to the Historical Legacy of Apartheid

An overwhelming nine out of thirteen respondents mentioned apartheid as linked to poverty—or as the root of poverty—in South Africa. It should be noted that no questions were framed in terms of the effects of apartheid and that this finding emerged during the coding process as a key theme. It should also be noted that the respondents who mentioned apartheid as linked to poverty were across all racial lines. However, the analysis also reveals that black African and Colored respondents often mentioned this link as self-evident, whereas while several white respondents acknowledged the role of apartheid, their framing was more nuanced as they talked about it "separating people" or the city as "structurally divided" (Rev. B; Rev. B2).

It should be noted that it was the white Dutch Reformed minister who appeared to articulate the structural nature of the roots of poverty in South Africa, with "for one group there was huge development and for another group there were no opportunities offered for development so it contributed [to poverty]" (Rev. R). One minister in the township noted the following in

---

34. See footnote 12 for a brief discussion of this school of thought. Rev. C openly identifies the author as an influence elsewhere in the interview.

response to the question as to the roots of poverty: "Asking your question to an African person, definitely the obvious answer is apartheid" (Rev. Z). Another pointed out the following with regard to the link between poverty, race, and inequality:

> [I]f you go back to the apartheid system where blacks are on that side and the whites are on that side, then they got the opportunities and then the blacks they don't get the opportunities, and then there's injustice where they see and there are other people, the Colored people that get better opportunities than the blacks, so the apartheid has got an impact with [sic] poverty (Rev. M).

Inequities then, are not only black African versus white, but mention is also made of the Colored sector of the population. One Colored priest, nevertheless, noted: "We might have had '94 elections, but nothing has changed economically. The poor are still poor" (Rev. S). He then referred to the effects of what he perceived as continued white privilege and power: "You talk to white people; they know that you know, they hold the power economically and that gives them the power in other areas as well. And there is huge control..." Inequality, here, is then framed in terms of white power and privilege, and he takes his point further in identifying the past system's continuing legacy and effect on the present in terms of Galtung's theory of structural violence:

> They established a system that has been enforced by violence and it's not going to be got rid of without violence. You need something quite violent to get rid of that deep-seated stuff and ...uh...you know, black people are just gonna [sic] keep on being poor and keep on demonstrating (Rev. S).

His reference to apartheid in terms of structural violence is very revealing, as he connects it closely with the rising social discontent as evidenced by continuing social delivery protests. This was acknowledged by one of the white respondents, minister of a large congregation for mainly wealthy white people. He noted that while apartheid was no longer legal, its legacy and the deep race cleavages in society (which he saw reflected in his congregation's attitudes) has led to fear on the part of white people and frustration and aggression on the part of "people of color" (Rev. B). For others, the power that the previous system holds over their community is rooted in the Group Areas Act, which forcibly moved people of color to the geographical margins of the city on the Cape Flats, thereby marginalizing them socially and economically (Rev. M). The power of the past in maintaining the cleavages of race, class, and inequality remains, therefore, foremost in the manner in which ministers frame the state of poverty and inequality in the country today.

The Call for Equality

The respondents interviewed represented a wide range of socioeconomic demographics. Several churches—across racial lines—indicated gross levels of inequality within their congregations, while others referred to their congregations as either largely wealthy or living in absolute poverty. The latter, of course, correlates with the fact that although there is still high interracial inequality, intra-race inequality is on the rise. Ministers of "unequal" congregations struggled to deal with inequality in their congregations (whether they were black African, white, or Colored); but it is interesting to note that the manner in which they attempted to deal with it was through scripture.

While poverty and its roots were not framed chiefly in ethical-theological terms, it was interesting to note that there were direct scriptural references made to equity and sharing in such contexts. At least two respondents (one black African and one white) mentioned Acts 2 and 4, in terms of a gospel imperative (Rev. A; Rev. M). What is important to note here is that in terms of demographics, both these congregations have very poor as well as very rich members in the same congregation. Rev. M from Khayelitsha[35] noted the following:

> And I said also in the community, if everybody will say, the little that I have I will share with my neighbor who has nothing to eat and fortunately they do that, they share . . . You know a good example is the Acts, the book of Acts. You know they share everything together and there was not a single one who was poor because they share everything they have together.

It is, nevertheless, evident that, when looking at the cross section of respondents' congregations, inequality is still largely race-based. This is no more evident than in the contrast of one white congregation, which claimed to have one of the top ten richest people of the country as a member, to a black African township congregation where every member worked in jobs in the service sector/menial labor (Rev. Z; Rev. D).

All respondents, regardless of race or class, indicated concern and alarm with regard to the nature of inequality, and several reasons were provided for this (other than apartheid, but also linked to it). As previously identified, greed was also noted as a key reason for inequality. Some respondents noted that this was based on prejudice: "Because in the hearts of man [sic] prejudice arises quickly and . . . particularly when it comes to the production of income and means, there's a tendency for people to group together in their people groups or economic groups" (Rev. T).

---

35. A predominantly black African township in the Western Cape.

One white respondent noted that networks of opportunity perpetuated privilege in the white community, which did not exist as strongly in the black African community (Rev. B2). As previously mentioned, another respondent noted that white people still hold the power economically and that allowed them to "sit in their [sic] Constantias"[36] while the problem is "down in the townships" (Rev. S). In South Africa, there is a correlation between economic, racial, and spatial divisions, as indicated by the latter remark, and this only highlights the highly structural and historical nature of inequality. Perhaps the most powerful voice in this regard is from a minister located in Langa:[37]

> You can't deal with somebody who lives in Langa, who's poor, without dealing with somebody who lives in ... Camps Bay, who's super rich. That's what we're trying to do in this country; that's why we're not able to solve problem. Because somebody who's very poor lives in Langa, works for somebody who's rich, who's in Camps Bay, and they occupy the same land given to them by God (Rev Z).

His reference to them sharing the same "land given to them by God" is a significant theological marker in the discussion, as is the interrelatedness of all humanity: black African and white; rich and poor. It also simultaneously critiques the lack of socioeconomic reconciliation, and even subtly raises the issue of restitution.

One minister in a poor congregation for Colored people, for example, noted that he did not want "well-meaning" rich white people who performed acts of compassionate charity out of guilt. This, he said "does not help the people," as it creates a sense of dependency (Rev. M). While the white minister of an extremely wealthy congregation gives cause for hope in our divided society in his call for more equity, he also raises the issue of restitution:

> The fact [is?] that the church as believers must begin to think differently – that to affect more equality means that those who have more than enough should also say: how must we downscale and give away some of what we already have so that there can be more equality, so I think justice is a couple of things, but I think it is righting things that went wrong, it is the building of the new, it is also to help people's human dignity (Rev. B).

These comments highlight the complex nature of diakonia in South Africa and the need for a justice-based rather than a charity-based discourse.

---

36. Constantia is an extremely wealthy suburb located in the southern suburbs of Cape Town.

37. Another predominantly black African township in the Western Cape.

Conclusion

This essay has argued that there is an emerging radicalization (or re-radicalization?) of the poverty and inequality discourse. This has been identified within three perspectives or fields of possible analysis, namely: the sociopolitical context of South Africa, albeit briefly; the diakonia and development discourse within the global ecumenical movement, and the manner in which local congregational leaders at grassroots level frame poverty and inequality. Is this mere coincidence, or does it point to the intersectionality and complexity of the discourse, and thus the need to reposition the church's compassionate action?

If diakonia, as argued by the ecumenical discourse, must come from the grassroots level (i.e., congregations) then the way in which ministers (as congregational leaders) frame poverty and inequality must matter. Myers argues that the way in which poverty and inequality are framed will influence the manner in which the response takes place.[38] The fact that the South African response in the past has largely been in a charity or welfare mode has already previously been argued as due in part to a "weak" theological conceptualization. It is significant, therefore, that the findings of this study not only indicate that poverty and inequality are not chiefly framed in theological terms, but also that it is framed in clearly sociopolitical ones. It is also interesting to note that ministers expressed a nuanced understanding of poverty as more than material, which points to the need for a more nuanced response by the church to the complexities of these concepts within South Africa than compassionate charity.

The fact that the legacy of the past is so closely linked to poverty and inequality definitions and roots indicates that restitution and economic injustices are of interest to ministers. In other words, for many of them poverty is a justice issue that demands a radical response. In analyzing a number of responses it is evident that reconciliation as forgiveness, which ignores the structural nature of redress, is problematic. The question of who still holds to a large degree the social and economic power must be recognized. It is, however, also clear that within South Africa the power holders are shifting and greed is a role player too. Compassionate relief is, therefore, not sufficient to engage the complex nature of poverty and inequality, and brings into sharp relief the issue of power (and its intersectionality with race and class) in an unequal and radicalized society. As one minister pointed out, what was not needed was well-meaning white compassion that results in dependency by those on the receiving end of this kind of compassionate action.

---

38. Myers, *Walking with the Poor*, 58.

This shift is also indicated within global ecumenical discourse. The fact that ecumenical discourse has placed a marked emphasis not only on congregations, but on the need to frame diakonia as "not only binding the wounds of victims or doing acts of compassion" reflects its concern for the lack of engagement with the structural nature of poverty. In this way, its renewed focus on a more justice-based and advocacy-based discourse, which addresses the causes rather than the symptoms of poverty, recognizes the agency of the poor. It is also important to note that it also opens up avenues to problematize the material wealth (and power?) of the rich. It is no surprise, then, that liberation theology begins to emerge with its theological language. It may also, therefore, be suggested that it is exactly this kind of theological discourse that can perhaps enable South African clergy situated in situations of poverty and inequality to again give voice to their pain theologically.[39] Should there be whole-scale revival of this discourse? Must it be reimagined? What this will entail remains to be seen. What is nevertheless clear is that compassion (in its "weak" form) has very little to do with poverty and inequality in South Africa today.

Bibliography

Bowers, Nadine Francis, and Karel August. "Engaging Poverty: The Church as an Organisation of Change." *NGTT* 45 Supplement (2004) 416–27.

Bowers Du Toit, Nadine Francis. "Theology and the Social Welfare Practice of the Church: Exploring the Relationship in the Paarl Context." In *Welfare, Religion and Gender in Post-Apartheid South Africa: Constructing a South-North Dialogue*, edited by Ignatius Swart et al., 257–68. Stellenbosch, South Afrcia: Sun, 2012.

Bowers Du Toit, Nadine Francis, and Grace Nkomo. "The Ongoing Challenge of Restorative Justice in South Africa: How and Why Wealthy Congregations Are Responding to Poverty and Inequality." *HTS Theological Studies* 70 (2014) 1–8. http://www.hts.org.za/index.php/HTS/article/view/2022/4476.

Centre for the Study of Violence and Reconciliation. "Understanding Current Xenophobic Attacks and How South Africa Can Move Forward." http://www.eldis.org/go/home&id=50387&type=Document.

Confession of Belhar. http://urcsa-north.org.za/?p=55.

Chung, Paul S. "Diakonia and Economic Justice." *Ecumenical Review* 66 (2014) 302–12.

Davis, Rebecca. "SA Reconciliation Barometer 2014: The Struggle against Apartheid Amnesia." *Daily Maverick*. December 04, 2014. http://dailymaverick.co.za/article/2014-12-04-sa-reconciliation-barometer-2014.

Dongsung, Kim, and Isabel Apawo Phiri. "Editorial: New Perspectives on *Diakonia*." *Ecumenical Review* 66 (2014) 249–51.

---

39. Within a South African context, a "theology of liberation" was rejected in favor of a "theology of reconstruction" after the end of apartheid. I have recently argued in a paper presented at the Society for Practical Theology in South Africa, however, that a "theology of reconstruction" has not engaged sufficiently with the concept of power.

Elliott, Charles. *Comfortable Compassion?: Poverty, Power and the Church.* London: Hodder & Stoughton, 1987.

Ham, Carlos. "Colombo: Theological Perspectives on *Diakonia* in the Twenty-First Century." *Ecumenical Review* 64 (2012) 383–92.

Herrmann, Erik. "Compassion, Mercy, and Diakonia." *Concordia Journal* 37 (2001) 270–72.

Hewitt, Roderick. "Black and Reformed: Conversations with Caribbean Theology." In *Prophet from the South: Essays in Honour of Allan Aubrey Boesak*, edited by Prince Dibeela et al., 144–70. Stellenbosch, South Africa: Sun, 2014.

Leibbrandt, Murray, et al. "Trends in South African Income Distribution and Poverty since the Fall of Apartheid." OECD Social, Employment and Migration Working Papers 101, 2010. http://www.oecd.org/officialdocuments/publicdisplaydocumentpdf/?cote=DELSA/ELSA/WD/SEM%282010%291&doclanguage=en.

Lupton, Robert D. *Toxic Charity: How Churches and Charities Hurt Those They Help (And How to Reverse It).* New York: HarperCollins, 2011.

Mottiar, Shauna, and Patrick Bond. "The Politics of Discontent and Social Protest in Durban." *Politikon: South African Journal of Political Studies* 39 (2012) 309–30.

Myers, Bryant L. *Walking with the Poor: Principles and Practices of Transformational Development.* Maryknoll, NY: Orbis, 1999.

Nordstokke, Kjell. "Ecumenical *Diakonia* Responding to the Signs of the Times." *Ecumenical Review* 66 (2014) 265–73.

Padilha, Anivaldo. "Diakonia in Latin America: Our Answers Should Change the Questions." *Ecumenical Review* 46 (1994) 287–91.

Phiri, Isabel Apawo, and Kim Dongsung. "Called to Be a Diaconical Community through a Pilgrimage of Justice and Peace." *Ecumenical Review* 66 (2014) 252–64.

Ramoupi, Neo Lekgotla I. "Education Lessons from the Rhodes Statue's Fall." *Mail and Guardian*. April 17, 2015. https://mg.co.za/article/2015-04-17-lessons-from-the-rhodes-statues-fall/.

Samuel, Vinay, and Chris Sugden. *The Church in Response to Human Need.* Grand Rapids: Eerdmans, 1987.

———. *Mission as Transformation: A Theology of the Whole Gospel.* Oxford: Regnum, 1999.

Swanepoel, Hennie, and Frik de Beer. *Community Development: Breaking the Cycle of Poverty.* Lansdowne, South Africa: Juta, 2011.

Swart, Ignatius. "Are the Rising Expectations Realistic? Local Churches and Social Welfare in South Africa and Paarl." In *Welfare, Religion and Gender in Post-Apartheid South Africa. Constructing a South/North Dialogue*, edited by Ignatius Swart et al., 285–303. Stellenbosch, South Africa: Sun, 2012.

———. "Research Report: Meeting the Challenge of Poverty and Exclusion: The Emerging Field of Development Research in South African Practical Theology." *International Journal of Practical Theology* 12 (2008) 104–49.

Swart, Ignatius, and Dawid Venter. "NGOs and Churches: Civil Society Actors and the Promise of a Fourth Generation People-Centered Development in South Africa." In *Development: Theory, Policy and Practice*, edited by Jan K. Coetzee et al., 483–94. Cape Town: Oxford University Press, 2001.

Wagner, Claire, et al. *Doing Social Research: A Global Context.* London: McGraw-Hill, 2012.

Mercy and Justice

A Diaconal View on Compassion in a Changing Welfare State

HERMAN NOORDEGRAAF

Diaconia within the Protestant Church in the Netherlands

DIACONIA IS THE COMMITMENT, inspired by the gospel, of churches and other groups and movements to combat especially material and social needs. This commitment has existed from the earliest days of the Christian church, and has been described with the term *diaconia* or some other designation.[1] The position of *diaconia* in the organization of the church varies—if it has a formal place at all. This variety also applies to the views on the office of deacons. The latter is often defined more liturgically than socially. More frequently, the deacon has the function of serving as an assistant to higher placed officials such as priests or bishops. The office of deacon is frequently seen as a transition to a higher office.

The Protestant Church in the Netherlands[2] defines *diaconia* in its church order as essential for the being of the church. This view goes back to the view of John Calvin, the most influential reformer in the Low Countries. According to Calvin, we find in the New Testament an office of deacon that has not only liturgical but also social tasks; that is, to take care of people in need: the poor, the sick, and refugees (see, among others, Acts 6:1–6; Rom 12: 8; 1 Tim 3: 18–23). The office of deacon is important and therefore it has

---

1. Olson, *One Ministry*.

2. The Protestant Church in the Netherlands is the largest Protestant church in the Netherlands. It came into being in 2004 as a merger of two Calvinist orientated churches, namely the *Nederlandse Hervormde Kerk*, the *Gereformeerde Kerken*, and the Evangelic-Lutheran Church in the Netherlands.

a position within the organization of the church, with an own college of deacons and taking part in the church council.[3] We recognize this fundamental view of Calvin in the articles of the Protestant Church in the Netherlands church order on *diaconia*:[4]

1. The church order distinguishes three offices, namely that of minister, elder, and deacon. All three offices are equal. This equality is, among other things, expressed in the fact that deacons form part of the governing bodies of the church. At local level, there is the church council; regionally there is the classis, and nationally there is the general synod.

2. A distinct connection is drawn between the diaconate and The Lord's Supper, and a task for deacons is seen in the preparation of the intercessions.

3. Each congregation has a college of deacons that has a legal entity and its own financial means. Management of the diaconal funds and goods (sometimes buildings and land) is the task of the college of deacons.

4. *Diaconia* is not only the task of the deacons, but it is the responsibility of the entire congregation. That has to be the object of *diaconia*. From this perspective, the deacons are mainly the ones to promote awareness of the diaconal calling among church members, to actively involve them in diaconal activities, and to coordinate these activities. Hence the concept of "the diaconal congregation" has far-reaching consequences for the performing of the deacon's tasks.

5. *Diaconia* has to do with mercy and justice (Dutch: "barmhartigheid" and "gerechtigheid"). So, it seems that both in English and Dutch we have to use two words to characterize *diaconia*.

6. Aid and assistance is not only for the church members, but for all who are in need. That is why the church order mentions "the local church community" and "the world." Whether or not one is a church member is not the decisive point, but rather the question whether someone is needy and therefore needs help.

Diaconia also has distinct political and social dimensions: government and society must be called to account by the church regarding their calling to act justly. This is formulated in the church order with regard to the task of the deacons: "To serve the congregation and the church in its efforts with regard

---

3. McKee, *John Calvin on the Diaconate*; Noordegraaf, *De Diaconale C-Factor*.

4. *Church Order of the Protestant Church*; see Article V, paragraph 3; Ordinance 3, Article 11; Ordinance 8, Article 3; Ordinance 14, Article 9.

to social issues and to call upon the government and society regarding their responsibility in that respect."[5]

Behind this statement is the presupposition that it is the calling of the government to promote justice, while the church has the obligation to remind the government of its calling, should the government forsake this obligation. From this fundamental principle, I shall reflect on *diaconia* and compassion and on the calling of *diaconia* in the Netherlands within the context of a changing welfare state. It seems not to be self-evident any more that a welfare state should take responsibility to ensure a decent existence for its citizens by, among other things, realizing social security laws.

Mercy and Compassion

The title of this essay is "Mercy and Justice." I took this title from the church order cited above, but used my own translation. The Dutch words describe the ministry of diakonia as follows: "de dienst van barmhartigheid en gerechtigheid." I translate this expression as "the service of mercy and justice." The official translation reads: "the ministry of compassion and justice." Therefore, the word "compassion" is to be found in the church order of the Protestant Church. Perhaps the term "compassion" has to do with the fact that the word "barmhartigheid" (mercy) is considered old-fashioned.

In this regard, it may be helpful to look at the different ways in which various Bible translations have translated "eleos," which is the Greek word within the original text. The new Bible translation in the Netherlands (*Nieuwe Bijbelvertaling*, NBV, 2004) translates this word in the parable of the Good Samaritan (Luke 10:37) with "medelijden" ("pity"). In English, *The New English Bible* (1970) uses the word "kindness" as its translation for "eleos." The reason for difference in translation can be due to the fact that "mercy" and "compassion" have many overlapping meanings. These terms refer to a strong inner involvement with other people, especially people in need. The Latin term "*misericordia*" ("*miseria*" and "*cor*") also expresses this connotation. The word "*splaghnizesthai*" ("take pity on," "have mercy on") refers to the inner life (etymologically connected with "womb," "intestine"). This term is, moreover, used in Matt 14:14 (also Mark 6:34) with regard to Jesus, when he is said to see the crowd.

I prefer the translation of "mercy" for "elios," as this expresses the particular motivation through faith, and it refers to God being involved with and moved by people who are poor and socially excluded. With the term "compassion," we enter another, more general level of meaning. By making

---

5. Quoted from Ordinance 3, Article 11; see also Ordinance 14, Article 9.

clear, however, that there is an overlap in meaning, it is possible to communicate and work together with people of other faiths and with secular people who are moved by compassion because of their own background.

Mercy and Justice

In addition, it is significant to note that, as already mentioned, the church order of the Protestant Church in the Netherlands uses two words: "mercy" and "justice." The term "justice" was not used in older church orders; only "mercy" was taken up as a defining term for *diaconia*. It was only in what was called at the time "the new church order" of the *Nederlandse Hervormde Kerk* (one of the forerunners of the Protestant Church in the Netherlands) of 1951 that the concept of justice was used for the first time, referring to the task of the church to remind, if necessary, the government and society to practice according to their calling. "Mercy/compassion" was still considered to be the central concept in articles about *diaconia*, but now one found an attempt to foster a broader and deeper concept of *diaconia*.

This development has to do with the growing insight that traditional diaconal work in the field of *diaconia*, taking care of the poor, was not adequate any longer (if it had ever been) in view of the growing question of poverty, and more specifically, the fear of poverty: that one will become poor and dependent when faced with unemployment, illness, disability, old-age, or death of a parent/spouse, which may make families very vulnerable indeed. Since the first national Poor Law in the Netherlands in 1854, the care for the poor was primarily the task of the churches. But with the rise of industrial capitalist society, it became more and more evident that poor relief by the churches was not the real answer to the living conditions of many people. It was found that assistance was quite limited; the needy were fully dependent on what other persons decided and the requirements they put on the people in need. This assistance thus had to do with favors and not with rights. Individuals in need quite often experienced this assistance as humiliating. Moreover, there is a distinct asymmetry in power in terms of the relationship between giver and receiver. Thus, a vigorous debate emerged in Dutch society concerning how to move from a favor-based approach to a right-based approach, for instance, by introducing laws on social security. Especially the Great Depression of the 1930s revealed that the old-fashioned understanding of care for the poor was largely insufficient in order to guarantee a decent existence for everyone. It became evident that the government and society at large needed to take greater responsibility for caring of those in need.[6]

---

6. Many publications can be found on these discussions. Here I only refer to the survey work of Roebroek and Hertogh, "*De Beschavende Invloed des Tijds*."

Here, we see concurrence with the views of Nussbaum. When we speak about *diaconia* we should use two concepts: "compassion/mercy" and "justice." In her book *Political Emotions*, Nussbaum mostly focuses her attention on compassion, but as she stresses in her book, we need both: compassion and just laws and institutions. She actually underscores the important role of emotions in order to support and sustain laws and institutions when she argues: "My suggestion will be that the political culture needs to tape these sources of early trust and generosity, the erotic outward movement of the mind and heart towards the lovable, if decent institutions are to be stably sustained against the ongoing pressure exerted by egoism, greed, and anxious aggression."[7]

However, Nussbaum warns that emotions can be volatile, which makes it necessary to create laws and institutions. She writes as follows: "As Adam Smith rightly observed, people can be deeply moved by an earthquake in China, but then quickly diverted from that focus by a pain in their little finger. The attempt to run an ambitious program of social redistribution only on the basis of emotion is doomed to failure."[8]

Against the backdrop of these thoughts by Nussbaum, the following section will consider the question of what this connection between mercy/compassion and justice implies for diaconal action and the debate about the reconstruction of the Dutch welfare state.

The Dutch Welfare State in Reconstruction

After the Second World War, a welfare state was established in the Netherlands, and it became very well developed. The capitalist mode of production was kept, but it was combined with state interference: the state took responsibility for full employment, a just division of incomes, social security, and social welfare. The days of laissez-faire capitalism were gone. This formula was quite successful until the 1970s; it was possible to improve the lives of the population on both a quantitative and qualitative level. These were the "Golden Years."[9]

As in all Western societies, the welfare state in the Netherlands has for many years been, and still continues to be, under reconstruction. This development since the 1980s and onwards has been hampered due to financial problems and changing ideological views—some would say that the state

---

7. Nussbaum, *Political Emotions*, 177.

8. Nussbaum, *Political Emotions*, 135.

9. These words are used for post-war Western welfare state societies by Eric Hobsbawn in his *Age of Extremes*, chap. 9.

has taken too much responsibility and that has undermined the responsibility of individuals and civil society. Even though there is no blueprint for this reconstruction, some trends emerge in the cumulative effects of the measures that were taken by politics: First, less emphasis on providing income support to people without paid labor, and second, emphasis on social inclusion by participating in paid labor. These developments include measures to activate and force people to work (training, incentives, and sanctions), reductions in social benefits, privatization of public services, and a bigger role for societal organizations, among them the churches.

This reconstruction of the Dutch welfare state has far-reaching consequences for diaconal work. With this emerging understanding of the Dutch welfare state it had become the responsibility of the state to secure a minimum living level of existence. In terms of the Dutch welfare state claiming its public responsibility, churches were only involved in poverty relief in a restricted way. During the 1980s, however, rising unemployment and the reconstruction of the welfare state caused people who were dependent on minimum level benefits to fall into financial difficulty that sometimes led to poverty and social exclusion. This change in the way the Dutch welfare state functions raises anew the question of the churches' role in *diaconia*.

Poverty Again: Churches and Their Role

Since the 1980s, churches once more were confronted with poverty in their own country.[10] In 2016, the seventh report about aid by churches was published in the Netherlands. This report is based on research in a number of local churches: Orthodox and liberal Protestant, Roman Catholic, and Evangelical. One of the results of this report is that nearly eighty percent of local churches are involved in material aid in their diaconal work.[11] Apart from this aid to individuals and households, churches are supporting collective forms of aid that include, for instance, food banks that collect and distribute free food to people in need. The first official food bank in the Netherlands was founded in 2002. Nowadays, food banks form a vital aspect of Dutch society. Throughout the Netherlands there are 140 food banks with more than 70,000 recipients. Even though most food banks are not church-based organizations, more than eighty percent of congregations are shown to support a food bank in some way. These activities, mostly on a small scale, include, amongst other things, collecting food to be given to the

---

10. Noordegraaf, "Aid under Protest?"
11. Kerk in Actie en Andere Kerkgenootschappen: *Armoede in Nederland*.

food banks, providing volunteers, establishing distribution venues, giving financial support, and cultivating vegetable gardens.

Another aspect of the reconstruction of the welfare state is the cutting of spending in the field of care and welfare, and the decentralization of responsibilities from the national government to the local authorities. In order to understand the Dutch situation, it should be mentioned that all kinds of professional institutions that originated within the context of the churches, from the 1960s onward increasingly started to sever their links with churches and are now mostly non-church institutions. The situation in the Netherlands is quite different from the situation in, for instance, Germany, where many organizations continue to be church-based. Especially in some bigger cities in the Netherlands there are some instances in which churches are also active within professional organizations. For instance, one finds many church volunteers in relief centers for people struggling with addiction, as well as centers attending to those individuals who are homeless.

Most diaconal activities in local congregations are performed by volunteers on a small-scale basis. Research has shown that people who are active church members tend to do relatively more volunteer work than other groups. Churches offer an environment that is conducive to all kinds of social engagement in terms of the values, norms, and stories that are transmitted. In addition, church networks in which people are involved in face-to-face relationships offer the impetus for church members to engage in volunteer work.[12] To put it another way: Churches have a lot of "social capital." This is one of the reasons why churches are increasingly valued for the role they can play in fostering volunteer participation in the fields of care and welfare. Research shows that while churches offer professional services to specific target groups, they also are in a prime position to support vulnerable individuals and groups who are outside the view and reach of the official authorities and churches, by offering informal assistance and mutual support. Still, given the decentralization of local policy-making and the increased participation of church members in local networks, reorientation of local authorities and congregations is necessary.

With regard to the question of the ongoing quest in combatting poverty by means of an increased involvement in the field of care and welfare, an important question to ask is: Do churches fill the gaps left after the responsibility of the government ends? Diaconal boards on a national level take the position that one should firstly care for people in need and offer

---

12. Much research has been done on volunteering work, especially by the research center *Sociaal en Cultureel Planbureau*, an official advisory body of the government. See, among others, Dekker and De Hart, *Vrijwilligerswerk in Meervoud*; De Hart, *Geloven Binnen en Buiten Verband*.

assistance on a variety of levels. However, one should also raise awareness, within churches and society, of the needs of those who find themselves in poverty, below subsistence level, or faced with circumstances that place them in a situation of great precariousness.

These developments also challenge the churches to reflect on their response to the growing social problems. Churches have reacted in different ways: by way of the traditional charity model, but also by giving aid to people in need, by offering support to networks and organizations of the poor, by empowering individuals and communities, by raising awareness in the churches and society at large, by participating in public debate, and by engaging in advocacy for those who are in need.[13]

Diaconia, Mercy/Compassion and Justice

In conclusion, what are the implications currently for *diaconia* in churches in the Netherlands, when viewed in terms of both mercy/compassion and justice? Firstly, mercy/compassion has mostly to do with face-to-face relationships, or seeing and hearing people in need at a distance by way of the media. Also, *diaconia* is closely associated with relationships between people concerned with both fostering and sustaining relationships with people in need. These relationships should be based on respect and rooted in paying close attention to people, by listening and being receptive to their needs. It asks of individuals to relate to the lives of people, which includes both the personal and structural dimensions of their lives. In terms of the latter, one could include social relationships and institutions, the environment, accommodations, position of income, and the sources of such income (work and/or benefits). In terms of the subjective dimension, sense-making and perspectives that people develop through interaction come into play. *Diaconia* should preeminently be a life-world approach.[14] So, there should be attention to the objective living conditions of people and their interpretation of these.

Such an approach would imply paying close attention to the narratives, to the life stories of people, and the meaning and fragments of well-being and calamity, joys, and sorrows that can be discerned. This implies

13. See the reports on poverty, based on research among local churches, as mentioned in footnote 11. See the publications of Knooppunt Kerken en Armoede, for instance, *Betrokkenheid Troef*.

14. An entire theory of diaconal action is built up on this far-reaching point of view, namely, "the theory of being present." This is distinguished from "intervention that is problem-oriented," namely, to intervene to solve problems on the basis of a diagnosis. See Baart, *Een Theorie van de Presentie*.

that one builds up a relationship in which people can trust each other, and in which time is taken for real communication. Giving assistance should be more than reaching a target in a prescribed amount of time, as professional workers are obliged to do because of the rules of government. This approach demands a hermeneutic competency, to hear what is said in the stories people tell. This type of relationship has to be distinguished from a paternalistic approach, which can be described as charity in the bad sense of the word; for example, including doing favors to people, but under your own conditions.

Such an alternative approach moreover implies that we should also be critical of the way in which governmental organizations are functioning, the extent to which social politics is inspired by one-sided views of people who are entitled to benefits. They are submitted to a regime with fewer rights and more obligations. This then implies that the world of the people in need is not the starting point of social politics, but the aims of the government in the fields of employment and finances. Though, as the Israelite philosopher Margalit rightly points out in his book on a decent society:

> The charity society at its best is based on the principle of benevolence, the welfare state on the principle of entitlement. I claim that a society which assists the needy on the basis of their being entitled to the assistance is less humiliating in principle—whatever the application might be—than a society based on benevolence.[15]

It is important to note that experiences gained in diaconal work could be shared between churches and society in order to promote awareness and recognition of the needs in the community. Within this process, there is a number of different approaches that can be followed to get church members involved, including giving information through notices in the media, organizing encounters between church members and those in need, taking part in diaconal work, organizing public debate, etc. The important thing is for church members to get to know the world of the persons involved, through their life stories. Nussbaum speaks about the importance of encounter in changing mindsets. Without support for people in need, a politics that promotes just laws and institutions on behalf of people in need is not sustainable.[16] It is therefore very important that those individuals who find themselves in a situation of financial security know what it means to be poor. Moreover, *diacona* also implies advocacy that is committed to

---

15. Margalit, *The Decent Society*, 240.
16. Nussbaum, *Political Emotions*, 134–36.

speaking out to government and society, in order for them to take adequate policy measures essential for the improvement of people's life options.

Thus, the close connection between mercy/compassion and justice encourages churches to look after people in need, to build up and sustain relationships with those individuals and groups who find themselves in situations of precariousness, and to raise awareness within churches and society concerning these needs in close partnership. In this way, mercy/compassion and justice are, and should be, connected.

Bibliography

Baart, Andries. *Een Theorie van de Presentie*. Utrecht: Lemma, 2001.
Church Order of the Protestant Church. https://www.protestantsekerk.nl/actief-in-de-kerk/kerkorde/kerkorde-en-ordinanties.
De Hart, Joep. *Geloven Binnen en Buiten Verband. Godsdienstige Ontwikkelingen in Nederland*. The Hague: Sociaal en Cultureel Planbureau, 2014.
Dekker, Paul, and Joep de Hart, eds. *Vrijwilligerswerk in Meervoud*. Civil Society en Vrijwilligerswerk 5. The Hague: Sociaal en Cultureel Planbureau, 2009.
Hobsbawm, Eric. *Age of Extremes: The Short Twentieth Century, 1919–1991*. London: Joseph, 1994.
Kerk in Actie en andere Kerkgenootschappen. *Armoede in Nederland. Onderzoek Naar Hulpverlening door Diaconieën, Parochiële Caritasinstellingen en Andere Kerkelijke Organisaties in Nederland*. Kerk in Actie: Utrecht, 2016.
Knooppunt Kerken en Armoede. *Betrokkenheid Troef. Inspirerende Diaconale Initiatieven Tegen Armoede in Nederland*. Utrecht: Knooppunt Kerken en Armoede, 2016. https://www.knooppuntkerkenenarmoede.nl/wp-content/uploads/betrokkenheid-troef-web.pdf.
Margalit, Avishai. *The Decent Society*. Translated by Naomi Goldblum. Cambridge, MA: Harvard University Press, 1996.
McKee, Elsie A. *John Calvin on the Diaconate and Liturgical Almsgiving*. Geneva: Droz, 1984.
Nieuwe Bijbelvertaling. Haarlem: Nederlands Bijbelgenootschap, 2004.
Noordegraaf, Herman. "Aid under Protest?" *Diaconia* 1 (2010) 47–61.
———. *De Diaconale C-Factor. De betekenis van Calvijn voor het Diaconaat*. Groningen: Stichting Rotterdam, 2009.
Nussbaum, Martha C. *Political Emotions. Why Love Matters for Justice*. Cambridge, MA: Belknap, 2013.
Olson, Jeannine E. *One Ministry, Many Roles: Deacons and Deaconesses through the Centuries*. St. Louis: Concordia, 1992.
Roebroek, Joop M., and Mirjam Hertogh. "*De Beschavende Invloed des Tijds.*" *Twee Eeuwen Sociale Politiek, Verzorgingsstaat en Sociale Zekerheid in Nederland*. 's-Gravenhage: VUGA, 1998.
The New English Bible. Oxford/Cambridge: Oxford University Press/Cambridge University Press, 1970.

Cultivating Compassion

Cultivating Compassion?

Abigail's Story (1 Samuel 25) as Space for Teaching Concern for Others

L. JULIANA M. CLAASSENS

Introduction

In his speech to Nero Caesar, Seneca asks the following poignant question: "What . . . would living be if lions and bears held the power, if serpents and all the most destructive animals were given power over us?"[1] Martha Nussbaum reflects on this question in her essay "Equity and Mercy" when she contemplates the absence of compassion that so often characterizes individuals' and societies' engagement with one another:

> These serpents, lions, and bears, as Seneca well knows, inhabit our souls—in the form of our jealous angers, our competitiveness, our retributive harshness. These animals are as they are because they are incapable of receiving another creature's life story into their imagination and responding to that history with gentleness.[2]

For Nussbaum, it is this profound lack of imagination that is responsible for the inability of individuals and communities to show empathy with one another—a reality that may lead to hatred and violence and, in its most extreme form, the annihilation of the other.

Conversely, the way out of violence is to let the other into one's imagination, hence fostering a spirit of compassion and love. Nussbaum defines love as "a delighted recognition of the other as valuable, special, and

---

1. *Clem* 1.26.3, as discussed by Nussbaum in "Equity and Mercy," 183.
2. Nussbaum in "Equity and Mercy," 183.

fascinating; a drive to understand the point of view of the other," "gratitude for affectionate treatment, guilt at one's own aggressive wishes or actions," and finally, "trust and a suspension of anxious demands for control."[3] Few will disagree with these inspiring values that most certainly offer great potential for dealing with our most contentious interpersonal, interracial, interreligious, and international conflicts. But perhaps the more challenging question is: How does one go about fostering or cultivating these emotions of love and compassion?

Nussbaum over the years has been greatly interested in exactly this question of how societies and the individuals that make up these societies can become more compassionate in nature. For instance, in her recent book, *Political Emotions*, Nussbaum writes how the natural tendency of human beings is "to protect the fragile self by denigrating and subordinating others." She proposes that societies need to take great care to counteract such "forces [that] lurk in society" by means of "an education that cultivates the ability to see full and equal humanity in another person."[4]

This proposal relates to Nussbaum's longstanding interest in the role of literature, narratives, and I would also add motion pictures (and TV shows!), in order to cultivate compassion and love that extends beyond our own narrow "circle of concern." As she writes:

> We grieve for people we care about, not for total strangers. We fear damages that threaten ourselves and those we care about, not earthquakes on Mars ... But the ones who will stir deep emotions in us are the ones to whom we are somehow connected through our imagining of a valuable life, what I shall henceforth call our "circle of concern." If distant people and abstract principles are to get a grip on our emotions, therefore, these emotions must somehow position them within our circle of concern, creating a sense of "our" life in which these people and events matter as parts of our "us," our own flourishing. For this movement to take place, symbols and poetry are crucial.[5]

In this regard, I propose that narratives offer wonderful possibilities for cultivating compassion. Nussbaum, drawing on the work of Winnicot, suggests that the world of arts and culture can be considered as an act of play; i.e.,

    3. Nussbaum, *Political Emotions*, 176.
    4. Nussbaum, *Political Emotions*, 3.
    5. Nussbaum, *Political Emotions*, 11. Nussbaum herself explores how, for example, the poetry of the American poet Walt Whitman and the Indian poet Tagore has been able to evoke emotions in people, helping their respective communities that have been marred by anxiety and a fear of extinction to cultivate a sense of justice, "a spirt of love, inclusiveness, fairness, and human self-cultivation"; Nussbaum, *Political Emotions*, 13.

"an imaginative activity in which one occupies a 'potential space,' a realm of unreality that is peopled with stories that enact hypothetical possibilities."[6] Narratives offer a window into another's world—to put oneself for a couple of hours into another's shoes may go a long way of transcending the "me, myself and I" phenomenon that is so typical of human beings everywhere.

As I am writing this paper in the luxury of a sabbatical in Germany, I spent my evenings watching episodes of the greatly addictive television series *House of Cards*. I found myself utterly drawn into the narrative world of the wheeling and dealing that goes on in American politics; of the greatly ambitious Frank Underwood who holds a prominent position in the US Congress and is vying for the position of vice president and his equally ambitious wife, Claire Underwood, who has a parallel existence in her non-profit company that seeks to provide water to people in the developing world. This series is a great example of the power plays, "the jealous angers, the competitiveness, and the retributive harshness" of which Nussbaum spoke with regard to the opening quotation. But as a space for moral reflection, the lives of these "serpents, lions, and bears" offer the viewer much food for thought.[7]

As an Old Testament scholar, I believe that biblical texts are equally wonderful tools for forging what Nussbaum calls participatory imagination. Biblical stories, and perhaps specifically the tragic ones, possess the ability to draw the reader in, creating the space for conversation about what is good and what is right. In this encounter between text and context, the individual is bound to look anew not only at the narrative world created in the text, but also at the world in which the reader finds him-/herself.

One such story from the Old Testament that has recently caught my interest is the text that I focused on for my inaugural lecture,[8] the wonderful story of the clever and beautiful Abigail who in 1 Samuel 25 saves her household from a certain death by offering a lavish feast to David and his

6. Nussbaum, *Political Emotions*, 178–79.

7. In one of the most shocking opening scenes, the first scene of Episode 1 offers a revealing glimpse into the life of Frank Underwood. The scene starts with a car running a dog over, and Frank going out to see what he can do to help. Throughout the scene, the camera stays focused on the face of Frank, with a whimpering dog in obvious pain out of sight. As Frank first tries to comfort the suffering dog and later with his bare hands puts the dog out of his misery, Frank in one of his, what will become the trademark of the series, asides to the viewer makes the following statement that characterizes his life in Washington, DC: "There are two kinds of pain. The sort of pain that makes you strong, or useless pain. The sort of pain that's only suffering. I have no patience for useless things."

8. Claassens, inaugural lecture has since been published in "An Abigail Optic: Agency, Resistance and Discernment in 1 Samuel 25," Pages 21–37 in *Feminist Frameworks: Power, Ambiguity and Intersectionality* (ed. L. Juliana Claassens and Carolyn Sharp; Bloomsbury T&T Clark, 2017).

men. Abigail's act of generosity that saves the lives of her household stands in direct contrast to the actions of her foolish husband Nabal ("Nabal" in Hebrew literally means "folly"), who treats David with utter disdain when refusing him food and water. Moreover, her story occurs in a narrative world created by the book of 1 Samuel that matches the power plays and the lure of violent retribution seen in the *House of Cards*!

I found Abigail's story, which really is a story of compassion amidst a world void of compassion, fascinating indeed and much richer than I was able to convey in one lecture. For the purpose of this current essay, I propose that Abigail's act of compassion, in contrast to the failure of the other characters Nabal and David to show compassion, as narrated in 1 Samuel 25, offers a fruitful space for moral reflection. Particularly when read within the larger context of 1 Samuel 24–26 that tells of king Saul's pursuit of David, the story of Abigail's hospitality may serve as a means for cultivating compassion in its readers, both ancient and contemporary, who find themselves in fragile communities where violence threatens the common good.

Compassion and Agency

1 Samuel 25 is a classic story regarding compassion. Or perhaps, for the most part, the absence of compassion. So, 1 Samuel 25 starts with the narration of the profound lack of compassion on the part of two of the main characters: Nabal, the rich landowner in whose land the fugitive David and the four hundred outcasts who have gathered themselves around him find themselves, absolutely refuses to offer these hungry and needy men anything to eat or drink, even though they three times are said to come in peace (v. 6). Ignoring the familial language used by David, "your son," Nabal dismissively asks "Who is this David? "Who is this son of Jesse?" (v. 10). Nabal's words unequivocally communicates that David is no son of his—this inability to claim a familial connection being responsible for his inability to show mercy. Nabal's lack of compassion is strongly condemned by the narrator when he is said to be struck down by God in 1 Sam 25:38.[9]

Also David exhibits an acute lack of compassion. Slighted, fuming with anger, David vows to wipe out Nabal's entire household by morning (vv. 21–22). In Hebrew, the word used to describe all the male members of

---

9. Nabal's last meal is a self-indulgent drinking fest (mišteh in v. 36), which leaves him very drunk. Abigail waits until the next morning to tell Nabal about her act of providing food to David. In v. 37, it is said that Nabal's "heart died within him; he became like a stone." And in v. 38, the narrator adds that ten days later, God struck Nabal, and he died.

this household is the term "wall pissers," which serves the function of emphasizing the animal nature of these relations of Nabal. Of course, to portray individuals in nonhuman terms is a crucial step in dehumanizing them, which makes it easier to kill—a good example is the term "cockroaches" that was regularly used in the rhetoric of the Tstutsis in Rwanda when describing the enemy Hutus.

In both the case of Nabal and David, it is a lack of compassion that makes it possible for them to act in dismissive and potentially violent ways. Without food, David and his men would surely have starved. And if he had not been stopped, David would surely have massacred all the men in Nabal's household by morning, reminiscent of the terrible story told in 1 Samuel 22:6–19 in which Saul did go ahead, annihilating the entire household of Ahimelek when he commissioned Doeg the Edomite to massacre eighty-five priests of Nob for providing food to David and his men (vv. 18–19).

And then there is Abigail. Her gracious acts of hospitality offer a sharp contrast to the inhospitable and violent acts on the part of Nabal and David. When approached by a desperate servant of Nabal who complains of his master's stupidity that will most definitely lead to their demise, Abigail acts quickly. Her swift actions, gathering great quantities of food (two hundred loaves, two wineskins, five prepared sheep, five measures of parched grain, one hundred clusters of raisins, and two hundred cakes of dried figs, in 1 Sam 25:18) are driven by a deep sense of compassion. In the first instance, she acts on behalf of her family, having the faces of her sons and/or the sons of another mother in front of her eyes as she is repeatedly said to hurry (vv. 18, 23, and 34), gathering a huge amount of prepared food and sending it off to David and his men in a frantic attempt to avert war.[10] Abigail knows that if she does not act, these men and boys with faces and names and histories will most certainly be slaughtered if she does not intervene.

But Abigail also may be acting out of compassion for David and the four hundred landless, needy, men that are in desperate need of food. In response to the most basic cry of the desolate, "Help me!," Abigail responds by offering the hungry men generous portions of food. As Emmanuel Levinas describes this appeal of the other:

> In proximity the absolute other, the stranger whom I have "neither conceived nor given birth to," I already have on my arms, already bear according to the biblical formula, "in my breast as the nurse bears the nursling." He [sic] has no other place, is not autochthonous, is uprooted, without a country, not an

---

10. For an extensive argument regarding the nature and significance of Abigail's hospitality, see Claassens, "An Abigail Optic," 5–8.

inhabitant, exposed to the cold and heat of seasons. To be reduced to having recourse to me is the homelessness or strangeness of the neighbor. It is incumbent on me.[11]

Abigail indeed understands that "it is incumbent on [her]." Her actions that have the effect of averting a terrible tragedy are closely connected to her ability to hear the cry of those close to her as well as those strangers in her midst who find themselves in dire straits.

Abigail's deeds are accompanied by some powerful words. Ellen van Wolde points out that Abigail is the first person to call David a nāgíd; a divinely appointed leader who is committed to the well-being of the people (1 Sam 25:30).[12] The term nāgíd has not yet been used for David, not even at the time when Samuel anointed David in 1 Sam 16:11–13. Now, in the absence of the prophet Samuel, Abigail is showing David his true identity: a nāgíd of Israel who is called to be a shepherd to his people (see also Nathan's confirmation of Abigail's words in 2 Sam 7:8–9).[13] Abigail's words are reminding David that, to truly be the leader that he was meant to be, he not only has to refrain from having blood on his hands, but also has to learn to act compassionately and to attend to the needs of his subjects.

Abigail's actions and words speak of great wisdom–her act of providing food having been linked to the feast of meat and wine offered by Woman Wisdom in Proverbs 9:1–6.[14] As the quintessential embodiment of Wisdom, Abigail emerges as a prime example of what it means to do justice, to show kindness, in the process emerging much like Woman Wisdom as councilor to kings (Prov 8:15).[15] David acknowledges Abigail's role in averting bloodshed when he makes the following admission in vv. 32–34:

> Blessed be the Lord, the God of Israel, who sent you to meet me today! Blessed be your good sense, and blessed be you, who have kept me today from bloodguilt and from avenging myself by my own hand! For as surely as the Lord the God of Israel lives, who has restrained me from hurting you, unless you had hurried and come to meet me, truly by morning there would not have been left to Nabal so much as one male.

11. Levinas, *Otherwise Than Being*, 91.
12. Van Wolde, "A Leader Led by a Lady," 365–66.
13. Van Wolde, "A Leader Led by a Lady," 370–71.
14. McKinlay, "To Eat or Not to Eat"; Shields, "A Feast Fit for a King."
15. Shields, "A Feast Fit for a King," 54. In this regard, Shields argues that two feasts are contrasted in 1 Samuel 25: the "feast like a king" in which the foolish Nabal self-indulgently partakes (v. 36) and the lifegiving feast offered by Abigail to the future king David. As Shields argues: "While Nabal's feast 'like a king' ends in his death, the feast which Abigail offered, and which David accepted, was a feast fit for a king."

From David's revelation it is evident that Abigail's actions and words, which as we have said above are rooted in compassion, indeed had a transformative effect on the future king. But does this transformation extend beyond the narrow confines of 1 Samuel 25? I propose that the story of Abigail's hospitality exhibits a transformative role in the larger context of 1 Samuel 24–26 that outlines the contentious relationship between the current and future kings of Israel.

Transformative Compassion?

Several scholars have suggested that 1 Samuel 25 holds a unique position amidst the larger narrative found in 1 Samuel 24–26.[16] Both Chapters 24 and 26 narrate instances in which a fugitive David, fleeing for his life, comes close to killing his pursuer King Saul. However, in both chapters, David ends up sparing Saul's life.

So, Ellen van Wolde reads the narrative of 1 Samuel 25 on two levels: on a first level, as the story of Abigail's words and actions that prevent David from wiping out Nabal's household, and on a second, more metaphorical level, as referring to the broader David and Saul saga with Nabal representing Saul, and David envisaging the various options open to him in terms of his relationship with Saul.[17] Barbara Green offers a further interesting proposal when she argues that the Abigail-Nabal-David story told in 1 Samuel 25 constitutes a type of dream sequence dreamt by Saul, building on the literary concept of a sideshadow in which the author, narrator or character may contemplate a course of action that could be taken but then in the end is not.[18] As Green explains: "The episode involving David and the household of Nabal and Abigail opens a sideshadow to the more restrained chases of chs. 24 and 26, a road of overt violence contemplated imaginatively but ultimately not taken . . ."[19]

---

16. Polzin, *Samuel and the Deuteronomist*, 205–15; Green, "Enacting Imaginatively the Unthinkable"; Biddle, "Ancestral Motifs in 1 Samuel 25."

17. Van Wolde, "A Leader Led by a Lady," 365–66. See also Levenson's notion of 1 Samuel 25 as narrative analogy in which one part of the text is said to provide commentary upon another, in "1 Samuel 25 as Literature and as History," 23.

18. Drawing on the work of Bakhtin scholar Gary Morson, Green defines the notion of sideshadow as follows: "A sideshadow branches to sketch laterally what might have but did not take place. The term can be readily understood in reference to the more familiar concept of foreshadowing, where an author makes clear that certain events are bound to happen, have already been set, and are foreordained and foretold in various ways by events which precede them"; "Enacting Imaginatively the Unthinkable," 7.

19. Green, "Enacting Imaginatively the Unthinkable," 8.

Green thus argues that 1 Samuel 25 can be understood as a dream dreamt by Saul that parodies much of what has occurred thus far in terms of the interaction between Saul and David, "resembling but then also oddly inverting the familiar, as a nightmare can do."[20] According to her, the dream enacted in Chapter 25, and contemplated by David in Chapter 26 while Saul is asleep, has a distinct effect on the characters as the dynamic between the two of them changes, especially in 1 Samuel 26. By showing what potentially could have happened in Chapter 25 but did not, both Saul and David end up breaking the cycle of violence.[21]

While I am not convinced that 1 Samuel 25 is best understood in terms of Saul's dream, Green's suggestion of a sideshadow having a distinct effect on the characters in the rest of the narrative is intriguing. Particularly, in terms of Martha Nussbaum's suggestion that narratives may create the space for moral reflection, I propose that a story like the one told about Abigail-Nabal-David in 1 Samuel 25 may serve, as Nussbaum proposes, a "'potential space' in which roles and options can be tried out without real-life stress."[22] In this regard, it may well be that Abigail's acts of compassion and care extend beyond the confines of 1 Samuel 25 to impact the actions of both David and Saul whose hostile relationship is narrated in Chapters 24 and 26.[23]

In this regard, it is in the first instance important to note that both David and Saul are in a rather vulnerable situation. David is running for his life ever since Saul in 1 Samuel 19 vowed to kill him. And Saul, who has shown to be out of control in 1 Sam 22:18–19, killing eighty-five priests just for helping David and his men, has every intention of chasing David down and slaying him. But also Saul is portrayed in this narrative as being vulnerable. In both Chapters 24 and 26, the king finds himself in a precarious situation. In 1 Sam 24:3–4, David surprises Saul when he is using the toilet (see the Hebrew reference to Saul "covering his feet" in v. 3). This scene that is actually quite funny, with the mighty king caught with his proverbial pants around his feet has the purpose of underscoring the ultimate humanity of this great king who is shown using the toilet. However, instead of killing Saul, David cuts off a piece of the king's cloak that can be understood as a symbol of his royal power being violated. In 1 Sam 26:12, Saul is even more vulnerable when he is said to be sleeping, as "a deep sleep from the Lord

---

20. Green, "Enacting Imaginatively the Unthinkable," 6–7.
21. Green, "Enacting Imaginatively the Unthinkable," 9.
22. Nussbaum, *Political Emotions*, 181.
23. See also Polzin who argues: "Here, as in a morality play where a character's name may exemplify his or her inner character, David is protected from killing that Saul figure, Nabal the foolish one, through the providential persuasion of Abigail"; *Samuel and the Deuteronomist*, 208.

had fallen upon them." It would have been so easy for David to kill Saul at this time. Instead, David takes Saul's water bottle and his spear—essential elements for Saul to survive in the desert—only to later return the spear in an act of mercy (1 Sam 26:22).

Second, in the midst of this situation of great vulnerability, 1 Samuel 25 is playing out the worst possible possibilities, with David coming close to wiping out the whole house of Nabal, which really is a cypher for the house of Saul. 1 Samuel 25 dramatically shows just how close to the brink of mutual obliteration the characters are dwelling when David is depicted as losing it. Barbara Green rightly states that 1 Samuel 24–26 is characterized by "the nearness of violence, rather than the inevitability of the restraint."[24]

However, 1 Samuel 25 also contains the all-important figure of Abigail whose compassion, as we have seen earlier in this essay, plays a significant role in preventing David from falling over the brink into violence. Abigail's actions and her voice of reason, which may well be representing the prophet Samuel, as Ellen van Wolde[25] has argued, or perhaps Woman Wisdom, as was suggested earlier, the councilor of kings, not only saves the house of Nabal from David's murderous rage, but also rescues two powerful leaders from the fierce urge to annihilate the other. When David twice has the opportunity to kill Saul, who both times was finding himself in a most vulnerable position, he does not follow through with it.

David's restraint may have something to do with compassion. For a moment at least, David is able to let something of Saul's history into his imagination. In both Chapters 24 and 26, David tells his followers who have urged him to kill Saul that he cannot go through with it, for Saul is the anointed of God (1 Sam 24:6, 10; 26:11, 16). The fact that David calls Saul God's anointed suggests that David for the briefest of moments is able to recognize Saul as a person with a history, a person with a relationship with God. Rather than dehumanizing his adversary, David engages in an act of personalizing Saul, which has the effect of making it just a bit more difficult to kill him. Moreover, in his interaction with Saul, David reasons with the king, asking Saul why he is trying to kill him. Just who is it that Saul thinks he is pursuing, asks David in 1 Sam 24:14: "A dead dog? A single flea?" By using nonhuman language, David is trying to show Saul the absurdity of his pursuit, reminding him that he, David, is a *person* who currently is being hunted down like a dog, or to be quashed like a flea.

What is furthermore interesting about this narrative is the transformation that also occurs in Saul. Even though Saul is a deeply tragic character

---

24. Green, "Enacting Imaginatively the Unthinkable," 20.
25. Van Wolde, "A Leader Led by a Lady," 367.

whose life will end tragically in 1 Samuel 31, in 1 Samuel 24 and 26, David's restraint in killing Saul seems to have a transformative effect on Saul as well, compelling him to think twice about his own behavior. In Chapter 24, Saul admits that David has been more righteous than he (v. 17); even conceding that David will be king. Neither this admission, however, nor the reference that Saul went home at the end of Chapter 24, does not seem to convince David that Saul really had changed his mind. So, we read in 1 Sam 24:22 that David and his men went up to the stronghold, conceivably expecting further attacks. It is only after the transformative encounter with Abigail in Chapter 25 that the feud between these two men is ultimately resolved. In 1 Sam 26:21, Saul promises never to do harm to David again. The reason for this change of heart is, according to Saul, that by not killing him when he had a chance, David demonstrated to Saul that he considered Saul's life to be precious in his sight. David's actions are thus directly responsible for Saul realizing that he has made a mistake, and that he has been a fool—the same word used to describe Nabal in 1 Sam 25:25 (perhaps foreshadowing the fact that Saul will meet a similar fate than Nabal in 1 Samuel 31). Moreover, in response to Saul, David argues that just as he had held Saul's life in high regard, so his own life is precious in the eyes of God; David is thus putting his trust in God whom he professes to be the savior God. The mutual recognition of the value of life, and also each other's lives in the eyes of God, seems to be the game changer as the two rivals each go their separate ways, with Saul said to return to his place (1 Sam 26:25).

This end of violence that is the outcome of this narrative is rather remarkable, given the violence that marks the rest of the book. It seems as though David's interaction with Abigail in 1 Samuel 25 has helped both David and Saul to step out of the violent script that dominates the book of 1 Samuel and which, a couple of chapters earlier, has seen eighty-five priests violently slaughtered, so attesting to the transformative power of narratives.

Surviving in a Violent World

Thus far, we have contemplated the transformative effect of the story of Abigail's hospitality, as told in 1 Samuel 25, on the rest of the characters in 1 Samuel 24–26, when both Saul and David ultimately refrain from violence. On another level, though, the narrative of 1 Samuel 24–26 as a whole may similarly function as a space for moral reflection for the first readers, who after the Babylonian exile still may have been reeling from the trauma of seeing everything destroyed, including the end of the monarchy.

Indeed, the book of Samuel that likely received its final form after the exile portrays something of this uncertain world, a world marred by violence, a world in which the people have to come to terms with the loss of a king and the loss of their national identity.[26] Within in this context of precariousness, the readers enter a narrative world that mirrors the chaos they are experiencing, contemplating questions such as: How do individuals act within such a violent world that is characterized by the failure of leaders? What does it take for an individual to step out of the violent script that is normative in his/her society and instead chooses to refrain from violence?

In this regard, Martha Nussbaum offers us some hopeful perspectives when she reminds us that "cultures are not monoliths; people are not stamped out like coins by the power machine of social convention." Even though people "are constrained by social norms," Nussbaum argues that "norms are plural and people are devious." She proposes that even in the midst of communities tyrannized with ferocity and power struggles, "real men and women can also find spaces in which to subvert those conventions, resourcefully creating possibilities of love and joy."[27] Abigail's act of hospitality and David *and* Saul's decisions not to engage in violence seem to point to individuals who are able to resist violence and to dwell in peace.

It would, of course, have been nice if one could say that from this point in time David was a changed man. However, as *House of Cards* shows so incredibly well, within politics and power, human beings are deeply flawed and more often than not driven by their ambitions and their desire to control. The story of David's road to the throne (1 Samuel 16 to 2 Samuel 5) and the court narratives thereafter (2 Samuel 9–20) are no different when we see glimpses of a very human David. For instance, David shows great kindness to Mephibosheth, Saul's son who is crippled (2 Samuel 9). But then again there is the case of Bathsheba and Uriah, as told in 2 Samuel 11, in which a lack of empathy and compassion on the part of David has terrible consequences for all involved.[28] Indeed, as some of the most shocking power plays and even the murder of two of the main characters in the *House of Cards* remind us, the way in which the characters act within the narrative world created by literature (or by a TV show such as *House of Cards*) challenges

---

26. Jobling, "The Dead Father," 255–58. See also Polzin, *Samuel and the Deuteronomist*, 214–15.

27. Nussbaum, "Introduction," 14.

28. See Levenson's argument that the episode in 1 Samuel 25 is "the very first revelation of evil in David's character. He can kill." Moreover, Levenson continues that "the David whom we glimpsed ominously but momentarily in 1 Samuel 25 dominates the pivotal episode of Bathsheba and Uriah (2 Sam 11:1—12:25)"; "1 Samuel 25 as Literature and as History," 23.

the reader/viewer to reflect and perhaps to consider alternative ways of engagement that would be considered just or good. Within this process of contemplating what is good and right, characters like Abigail's hospitality goes a long way of reminding readers that an alternative way may be possible, which acts out of compassion and mercy and refrains from violence and retaliation.

Conclusion

In the opening quote to this essay, Martha Nussbaum has called our attention to the fact that lions, bears, and serpents have the propensity to lurk in us all. In her article, though, she does not say that we should just passively accept this reality as a given. "With Seneca," Nussbaum argues that we should "oppose the ascendancy of these more obtuse animals—and, while judging the wrong to be wrong, still cultivate the perceptions and capacities of mercy."[29]

The vibrant counter story of Abigail's compassion in a world where no compassion is the norm serves as one option for resisting the stronghold of the lions, bears, and serpents, both then and now. So, the transformative effect Abigail's example has on David and in turn also on Saul, which is responsible for a remarkable end of violence, raises some important questions for readers many centuries later: Can we respond to the history of others with gentleness? Can we receive their life story into our imagination? May we actively seek to cultivate perceptions and capacities of mercy so that we may live and live well? It is questions such as these that stay with us even after we have closed the pages of the Book of Samuel and after the closing credits of the latest episode of *House of Cards* have started rolling.

Bibliography

Biddle, Mark E. "Ancestral Motifs in 1 Samuel 25: Intertextuality and Characterization." *Journal of Biblical Literature* 121 (2002) 617–38.

Claassens, L. Juliana. "An Abigail Optic: Reading the Old Testament at the Intersections." Inaugural Lecture, Faculty of Theology, Stellenbosch University, March, 10, 2015. Stellenbosch: SunMedia, 2015. Published as "An Abigail Optic: Agency, Resistance and Discernment in 1 Samuel 25," in *Feminist Frameworks: Power, Ambiguity and Intersectionality* (ed. L. Juliana Claassens and Carolyn Sharp; Bloomsbury T&T Clark, 2017), 21–37.

Green, Barbara. "Enacting Imaginatively the Unthinkable: 1 Samuel 25 and the Story of Saul." *Biblical Interpretation* 11 (2003) 1–23.

29. Nussbaum, "Equity and Mercy," 183.

Jobling, David. "The Dead Father: A Tragic Reading of 1 Samuel 12." In *1 Samuel: Berit Olam: Studies in Hebrew Narrative & Poetry*, David Jobling, 250–81. Collegeville, MN: Liturgical, 1998.

Levenson, Jon D. "1 Samuel 25 as Literature and as History." *Catholic Biblical Quarterly* 40 (1978) 11–28.

Levinas, Emmanuel. *Otherwise Than Being, Or beyond Essence*. Translated by Alphonso Lingis. Pittsburgh: Duquesne University Press, 1998.

McKinlay, Judith. "To Eat or Not to Eat: Where Is Wisdom in This Choice?" *Semeia* 86 (1999) 73–84.

Nussbaum, Martha. "Equity and Mercy." In *Sex and Social Justice*, Martha Nussbaum, 154–83. New York: Oxford University Press, 1999.

———. "Introduction: Feminism, Internationalism, Liberalism." In *Sex and Social Justice*, Martha Nussbaum, 3–25. New York: Oxford University Press, 1999.

———. *Political Emotions: Why Love Matters for Justice*. Cambridge, MA: Harvard University Press, 2013.

Polzin, Robert. *Samuel and the Deuteronomist: A Literary Study of the Deuteronomistic History*. San Francisco: Harper & Row, 1989.

Shields, Mary. "A Feast Fit for a King: Food and Drink in the Abigail Story." In *The Fate of King David: The Past and Present of a Biblical Icon*, edited by Tod Linafelt, et al., 38–54. London: T. & T. Clark, 2010.

Van Wolde, Ellen. "A Leader Led by a Lady: David and Abigail in 1 Samuel 25." *Zeitschrift für die Alttestamentliche Wissenschaft* 114 (2002) 355–75.

"To the Wonder"

Finding God in the Most Unexpected Places

Charlene van der Walt

At the outset, when embarking on a new journey through an old landscape, expectations often exist that this time things will be better; this time the center will hold; this time the magic will not fade; these first steps are the beginning of a lifelong durable journey. This hope is possibly nowhere more evident than when we risk the hope of a life together with another in a romantic commitment, especially when coming to this commitment from a place of previous pain, disillusionment, and trauma. Within the sacred confines of relationship and intimate encounter with another, we often find a respite from experiences of fragmentation, disconnection, and isolation. When, however, despite our best efforts and intentions, communication breaks down and intimacy gets strained, we are often left disorientated and with deep experiences of despair. Where once a wordless union was possible, where days consisted of easy and effortless sequences of being, now fractured, no amount of words can express commitment, mend misunderstanding, and transform the house into a home. Who we are, who we want to be, who we aspire to be is complicated when our expectations of union are ruptured by pain, misunderstanding, and by the sting of the realization that there is something missing.

At the heart of this essay are two painful narratives of relational breakdown. These tragic tales of relational trauma form the backdrop for the essay's engagement with the theme of compassion. The complex notion of compassion is explored in relation to embodied experiences of vulnerability and isolation as expressed by the kindred prophet/priest characters embedded within the two narratives examined. Both of these vulnerably situated characters express a raw longing for God, for encounter, for connection.

As the narratives unfold, it seems that central to their experience of God's tangible presence is the embodied notion of compassion, expressed through acts of relational care.

The first narrative of relational breakdown is the 2013 film *To the Wonder*, brought to the screen by Terrence Malick.[1] This film, which offers a sharp contrast to the customary romantic comedy/drama-film success recipe, dramatically depicts the embodied breakdown of a second time around romance for both the unnamed characters, played in the film by Ben Affleck and Olga Kurylenko.[2] As Brody describes this film, "Malick constructs the story as the love story, as the story of stories, as a primordial archetype realized in practical and even familiar places, and he films his unnamed characters more or less without dialogue—but with plenty of language."[3]

This essay brings into conversation *To the Wonder*'s portrayal of lost love with a second narrative of relational breakdown as found in the book of Jeremiah. The agonizingly complex book of Jeremiah that engages with the disaster of the Babylonian invasions in the sixth century BCE reflects on the reasons for the occurrence of the traumatic event in the life of the people of Israel in terms of the breakdown in relationship between God and the people. According to Terence Fretheim,

> [t]he reasons these disastrous events took place is most basically rooted in the nature of the God-Israel relationship. The book stakes a theological claim that these events occurred, not because Israel's God was incompetent or uncaring, but because the people of God were unfaithful and their own God would not, indeed could not, remain indifferent, for the future of the *creation* was at stake."[4]

---

1. *To the Wonder*. Film directed by Terrence Malick, starring Ben Affleck, Olga Kurylenko, Javier Bardem, and Rachel McAdams, Magnolia Pictures, 2013.

2. Although Neil and Marina are named in the script and the subtitles of the film, their names are never mentioned in the classic Malick style voice-over dialogue.

3. Brody, "The Cinematic Wonder." The importance of the physical presence of bodies as explored by Butler in *Notes toward a Performative Theory of Assembly* broadens the theory of performativity beyond speech acts to include the concerted actions of the body. Assemblies of physical bodies have an expressive dimension that cannot be reduced to speech, for the very fact of people gathering "says" something without always relying on speech. The meaning, communicated beyond words by the character's embodied language, is a beautiful illustration of Butler's theory.

4. Fretheim, *Jeremiah*, 31.

A central metaphor in the book of Jeremiah is thus, in the words of Kathleen O'Connor,[5] a "family that comes undone."[6] The book of Jeremiah intervenes in a national disaster by employing the drama of God's broken family that have been ripped apart due to infidelity in order to try to find an adequate explanation for the occurrence of the tragic events of being invaded by an enemy empire.[7]

Both these narratives are set against the backdrop of the creation and all its splendor. For Malick, human existence is inseparable from the whole of creation, which is the planet's living body. More than a mere backdrop for the human drama unfolding in the film, nature emerges as humanity's proper home—a key player in our maturation process, both as individuals and as a species.[8] Malick's filmmaking brings to the screen something of the relational ethics between humanity and nature that one also finds in the book of Jeremiah. Fretheim remarks: "Jeremiah's relational God has created a relational world. An interrelatedness exists among all creatures for Jeremiah (and for Israel). The world could be imaged as a giant spider web. Every creature is in relationship with every other, such that any act reverberates out and affects the whole, shaking the entire web in varying degrees of intensity."[9]

Both the film *To the Wonder* and the book of Jeremiah notably do not speak of the relationship between humanity and creation in a mechanic or divinely determined fashion, but rather show something of humanity's capacity to have an impact on creation. The destruction that more often than not results from this interaction becomes poignantly clear as Neil, the male lead in *To the Wonder*, investigates some type of toxic poisoning of the water table, resulting in a grave threat to the people, crops, and animals in the area.

However, it is the theme of "compassion" that really forms the basis for bringing these two narratives together as we especially engage with the prophet/priest character embedded within the narratives of relational breakdown. In *To the Wonder*, Javier Bardem brings to life the complex and distressed character of Father Quintana, a Roman Catholic priest from Europe trying to make sense of God's involvement with humanity amidst all the pain and destruction that he witnesses in the course of his ministry. Painful laments

---

5. O'Connor, "A Family Comes Undone."

6. Jer 2:1—4:2.

7. These metaphors employed to justify God's judgment and punishment due to "infidelity" are, of course, highly problematic. Daniel Smith-Christopher remarks in his regard: "Theologies of 'God's punishment' . . . could lead to a destructive self-image and a sense of hopelessness in the reviewing or reviving a people's social and religious identity and existence"; Smith-Christopher, *A Biblical Theology of Exile*, 107.

8. Savu, "The Way to Grace," 105.

9. Fretheim, *Jeremiah*, 31.

develop from his personal experience of trauma and disillusionment as he yearns for the presence of God in the midst of pain and suffering.

To the Wonder received predominantly dismal reviews,[10] and especially the character of Father Quintana annoyed many reviewers. Even though just one voice amongst many, the priest's laments spoken in words "bordering on prayer"[11] struggled to translate into what is expected or acceptable to modern sensibilities. Father Quintana's voice, his tone, his posture is, however, reminiscent of the "weeping prophet" that we encounter in the book of Jeremiah. His painfully beautiful laments directed to God in voice-over are resonant of the so-called "confessions" of the prophet Jeremiah.

In reading Father Quintana as one who stands in the tradition of embodied lament by connecting him to the kindred spirit of Jeremiah, I hope to do justice to the remarkable movement that we observe within this character as he reflects on his own vulnerability and the fragility of the human condition. It is through the suffering and experiences of alienation on the part of both Father Quintana as well as that of the prophet Jeremiah that we find the following piece of paradoxical wisdom: It is amongst the broken and in the broken places that we may encounter life. Particularly in the striking development of the character of Father Quintana, we see something of the importance of embodied acts of compassionate care in the midst of our own experiences of isolation and disconnection. The encounter with God that Father Quintana longs for is not portrayed in terms of a dramatic Theophany, but rather as a consequence of "reaching out" to the other in acts of embodied care and compassion. It is in these acts of compassion that one recognizes something of the wonder of encountering God in precisely these unexpected places.

By reading Father Quintana within the context of the prophetic lament tradition, I am not trying to save his character from misunderstanding or shallow dismissal, but rather to enhance the reflective surface that we, as contemporary readers, encounter within the narrative. While facilitating a creative act of dynamic interaction between the two stories in question, my aim is to illustrate that these two narratives together serve as an important

---

10. Baskin, writing for the *Los Angeles Review of Books*, takes stock of the reviewers' description trends and states: "[T]he film may be described as 'substanceless' (Dana Stevens), 'puzzling' (A. O. Scott), 'unintentionally comical' (Stevens again), 'generalized woo woo' (Edelstein), and a 'self-parody' of the Malick films that are worth admiring (Steven Marche). Although not without its defenders . . . the majority of critics have dismissed *To the Wonder* in tones that have been withering, sometimes bitter, sometimes condescending, and often mocking"; Baskin, "Conversion Experience."

11. "Souls in Need."

reflective surface for contemporary readers and a space for the development of moral imagination, as Martha Nussbaum proposes.[12]

Truly engaging our own feelings of isolation and disconnection may seem such a daunting task that we rather choose to continue to live in superficial relationships, unable to find an expression for the longings of our heart. I would like to propose that the world of these interconnected narratives becomes a safe space for readers to confront complex and painful life realities. In the encounter with the characters, who find themselves to be isolated within the narrative, interpreters may be encouraged to reflect on their own experience of isolation as well as the embodied experiences of isolation of others. In contemplating the painful embodiment of the characters embedded within these narratives, and who come alive in new ways when brought into creative conversation with their intertextual counterparts, we might find a productive space to reflect on our own embodied realities and those of the community in which we are embedded.[13] The messy, complex, and painful world depicted in these narratives through the act of reading and interpretation becomes a dynamic space for ethical reflection and contemplation by contemporary readers. As Nussbaum argues, the narrative engagement serves as an important spark for empathy, and empathy forms the basis of moral imagination. As argued elsewhere, I believe that our sense-making capacity is deeply influenced and nurtured by our engagement with narrative, as it enhances our capacity for empathy.[14]

In the first part of this essay, I will turn my attention to the narrative landscape in which Father Quintana finds himself, and then in the second part of the essay shift my focus to embodied lament that we encounter in the person of the prophet Jeremiah and the confessions accredited to him. Through this creative encounter, the concluding part of this essay will reflect on some important perspectives that emerge from the combined broken relationships, narrative landscapes, and the priest/prophet characters that it gifts the reader/viewer with, in order to hopefully enrich our discussion on the contours of compassion. I propose that it is through witnessing the profound possibility for reconnection through acts of compassionate care in both these narratives that we may be confronted by our own frantic activities of longing for community and connection, so often conducted in isolation.

12. Nussbaum, *Sex and Social Justice*, 183.

13. Fodor argues that this act of reading is unavoidably bodily and communal in character when he states: "Reading is never simply a cognitive decoding of written signs, a logical assessment of linguistic content, or following an argument; it is also—and perhaps even primarily—a means of forming and disciplining the emotions and affections, offering an orientation, schooling dispositions, re-ordering desires"; Fodor, "Reading the Scriptures," 154.

14. See Van der Walt, "Is There a Man Here?"

To the Wonder—From Vulnerable Isolation to Compassionate Possibility

To the Wonder is Malick's sixth film, and the fourth in a sequence of what might be referred to, as Jon Baskin remarks, as "late Malick" films, since they have all appeared after the director's twenty-year hiatus from filmmaking.[15] Malick is something of an enigma to Hollywood filmmaking,[16] and Geoff Andrew describes him as "the modern American cinema's poet-philosopher,"[17] whose images . . . speak of a fascination with—and, perhaps a faith in the transcendent." In *To the Wonder*, Malick ventures where very few directors have dared to go as he organizes an entire film around "the spiritual practice of yearning and the multiple expression of human desire."[18] It is an unconventional film in the sense that the unnamed, yet credited, characters never really speak to each other, nothing really happens in the traditional sense of plot progression, and basically all the dialogue in the film is presented in the form of meandering voice-overs.[19] Considering Malick's unique style in film direction, it is probably not surprising that the final product is a tad unusual. The film was shot in natural light in various locations, from the coast of France to the Oklahoma Flatlands and, as Pinkerton remarks: "Malick does not film things because they are beautiful; they become beautiful because he films them."[20]

To the Wonder starts by exploring the beautifully complex love dynamic portrayed between Marina and Neil. Marina is a free-spirited old soul from Paris with a daughter from a previous marriage and Neil is an oil engineer from Oklahoma. More than specific individuals, we encounter in Neil and Marina types of characters: they represent opposites that

15. Baskin, "Conversion Experience."

16. Fech comments with regard to Malick's anti-establishment trends: "Malick's struggle is against currents of contemporary mainstream cinema which favors linear narrative and action-spectacle. His films eschew many Hollywood conventions to evince a fundamental conflict between the spiritual and the material"; Fech, "The Soul Announces Itself," 4.

17. Malick, who comes from the American midwest, completed a summa cum laude degree in philosophy at Harvard. He attended Magdalen College, Oxford, on a Rhodes scholarship, but did not finish his thesis on Martin Heidegger. Returning to the States, he taught philosophy at MIT and published a translation of Heidegger's *Vom Wesen des Grundes* as *The Essence of Reasons*. Instead of completing his PhD in philosophy, he attended the American Film Institute Conservatory in its inaugural year (1969), taking a Masters of Fine Arts degree in filmmaking.

18. Brussat and Brussat, "To the Wonder."

19. Ebert remarks with regard to the dialogue: "Although it uses dialogue, it's dreamy and half-heard, and essentially this could be a silent film"; Ebert, "To the Wonder."

20. Pinkerton, "Film of the Week."

attract.²¹ Film critics Frederic and Mary Anne Brussat write: "Malick has wisely structured the story around three main characters operating without a map and stumbling around in new territory. They are seeking love, sexual fulfillment, the comforts of home, the support of friends, connection with the bounties and the beauty of earth, and the presence of God."²²

We first encounter the couple in the ecstasy of love as they meander through the streets of Paris and visit the cathedral perched on a spire rock at Mont St. Michel on the French Coast. The voice-over dialogue speaks of belonging, a sense of completion in love, and is filled with snatches of laughter and shared thoughts. It is the beautiful carefree days of the relieved exhale within the embrace of newly found love. It is especially within Marina that we sense the joy and deep happiness of a yearning answered in the completion of love.

In a gallant haste to commit, Neil invites Marina and her daughter, Tatiana, to come and stay with him in the American Flatlands. Brody picks up an important technique employed in the film as the landscape shifts from the European coastal setting to a Middle-American town: "There is perhaps no film in the history of cinema that reveals such attention to light . . . Malick treats light as something of the main substance of the film, even the main subject of the film, as well as its crucial and deeply conceived metaphor."²³

The contrast between French and American light emphasizes the dramatic nature of the shift as the coast and the heartland, the cathedral and the town are contrasted. The move is indeed dramatic and in the first encounter, we find Marina searching for beauty in her new landscape, trying to connect with the vast horizon and the empty rooms with unpacked boxes.²⁴ The tone

---

21. www.bywayofbeauty.com picks up the distinctive type of characters when describing the plot: "What follows is a tug-of-war of human love between very distinct archetypes. Neil, stoic and silent, becomes increasingly glum, indecisive, and faithless; Marina, on the other hand, remains playful, impulsive, and ever hopeful. The two separate, re-connect, and separate again; fight, make love, and fight again"; "Souls in Need: The Journey 'To the Wonder.'"

22. Brussat and Brussat, "To the Wonder."

23. Brody, "The Cinematic Wonder." Beyond using the change of light to accentuate the contrast between the European and American settings, Urda remarks regarding the soundtrack: "Having employed gorgeous music to accompany the trio's time together both in France and during the early days in a stark Oklahoma suburb, he abruptly drops any musical accompaniment, and the silence is remarkable, or rather, it is remarkable that now we hear, as a result, the usual sounds of mundane reality—cars passing on a street, teeth being brushed. There is an emptiness that is immediately noticeable, and a harshness to these sounds in comparison to what we have heard"; Urda, "Eros and Contemplation," 136.

24. Urda notes: "Boxes are constantly being unpacked, or rooms stand vacant. The incompleteness becomes a symbol of the relationship itself, which also seems lovely but

of the film changes as Neil becomes distant and broody and Marina, without much success, yearns for connection. Before long, their sex life diminishes and Neil grows tired of Marina. She wants him to marry her, but Neil seems to have major commitment issues, or rather, he seems unable to make any sort of real decision. Baskin picks up on the stagnant muteness of Affleck's character: "In conspicuous contrast to the never-ending movement of the female characters who orbit him, his most characteristic action is to stand and stare, as if watching the film of his own life (which may be one 'reason' that Malick frequently positions his camera behind him)."[25]

The center cannot hold and we witness the painful disintegration of a bankrupt relationship. Tatiana speaks truth to the situation when she states that "something is missing," and before long Marina and Tatiana are on their way back to France.

The brief description above cannot do justice to the visual meditation on the breakdown of the relationship. The disillusionment, frustrations, silent moodiness, and painful isolation are tangible and leave the viewer with the realization that things can truly go horribly wrong, despite the very best beginnings and purest intentions. With Marina's departure, Neil hooks up with a childhood friend and sort of stumbles into a "relationship" with Jane, a mid-western rancher who is clearly more suited for him. She, also vulnerable, soon starts to talk of marriage and Neil, cognizant of his relationship with Marina, breaks the relationship off with Jane. In her devastation, she accuses Neil of debasing what they had together.

Marina returns to Neil, but this time without her daughter Tatiana. As her visa is soon to expire, Neil is confronted with a difficult choice.[26] Should he marry Marina or is he, in Peter Bradshaw's words, "in his heart, uneasy about this holiday romance with a dangerous and exotic French creature, in comparison with whom Jane is the obvious and safer bet?"[27] Perhaps, as compromise, Marina and Neil get married at the courthouse in a secular union.

Embedded within this painfully fragile depiction of searching and longing for connection and homecoming portrayed in terms of the relationship between Neil and Marina, we encounter the yearning presence of Father Quintana (Javier Bardem). This Spanish-speaking priest is suffering under the weight of his own crisis of faith, the vulnerability of his isolation,

---

lacking"; Urda, "Eros and Contemplation," 136.

25. Baskin, "Conversion Experience."

26. The obvious trauma of returning to the US without Tatiana is accentuated in the depiction of a Skype conversation between mother and daughter in which it is poignantly clear that although they might be able to see each other on a computer screen, the connection is not there.

27. Bradshaw, "To the Wonder."

and feelings of loss concerning his relationship with God and concerning those whom he encounters. In possibly the most beautifully haunting sequences of the film, we find Father Quintana ministering to the sick, poor, imprisoned, and disabled, visiting grotesque hidden-away shadows of human beings. We see him walking the streets of meth-devastated white ghettoes and listening to the incomprehensible murmurings of those long forgotten and never understood. He counsels those struggling in relationship, and this is also where his life intersects with that of Neil and Marina—this even while he is unable to make any real connection of his own. Father Quintana is longing for an embodied experience of God's presence and he voices his feelings of disconnection in vulnerability infused laments. Accordingly, he laments the devastation that he witnesses: he cries out to God in despair, he longs for an experience of God's presence in the midst of his terrifying isolation. These harrowing scenes find a soundtrack in voice-over laments: "Everywhere you're present, and still I can't see you. You're within me. Around me, and I have no experience of you. Not as I once did. Why don't I hold on to what I've found? My heart is cold. Hard."

He goes on to ask in language reminiscent of the lament tradition: "Why do you turn your back?" And as he is looking up to the heavens, specifically in the words of Jeremiah (see, for example, Jer 6:25), he mourns: "All I see is destruction. Failure. Ruin." Finally, from the dark night of the soul he exclaims, "Show me how to love you. Where are you leading me? Teach us where to seek you?"

The profoundly vulnerable tone of Father Quintana's laments mostly did not translate into something understandable to reviewers who describe the character as outdated, naïve, sentimental, and overly religious.[28] I propose, however, that if one were to dismiss the priest's laments the film loses its gravitas and the profound central movement slips beyond reach, unacknowledged.

Finding a Kindred Spirit in Jeremiah

The central theme of despair, disillusionment, isolation, and trauma that one can trace throughout Malick's film finds resonance in the prophetic book of Jeremiah that contemplates the disintegration of Israel's identity, as embedded in and derived from their relationship of care and protection with God. As described in the introduction of this essay, the people of Judah suffered three Babylonian invasions that devastated the community in the sixth century BCE. The land was occupied by invaders, loved ones

28. The blogspot www.bywayofbeauty.com further explores and reflects on the dismal reception of the character by reviewers; "Souls in Need."

were deported, communities fractured, leadership was suspended, and stabilizing institutions were dismantled. The foundational narrative of God's covenantal commitment to Israel and the promise of care, protection, presence, nation, and land, as established at Mount Zion, which was so central to Judah's identity, were shattered by their experience of trauma and disaster.[29] Kathleen O'Connor alludes to the devastating effects of this collective traumatic experience: "The effects of brute violence and destruction upon individuals and communities are to destroy speech, to isolate people in their traumatic state, to leave them overloaded with pain and mute with despair."[30]

Louis Stulman describes the devastating and all-encompassing nature of the occupation of Judah and the subsequent exile as a "cosmic crumbling."[31] Everything that was central to the people of Judah's identity and self-understanding had been refuted in terms of their experience of the Babylonian invasion, occupation, and exile. Judah can indeed be described as a deeply traumatized community.[32] Within this context of total collapse and disillusionment, we find the emergence of the prophetic voice in general, and specifically, the embodied lament of the prophet Jeremiah.[33]

The book Jeremiah does not only dare to speak the truth by naming situations of trauma, but it also tries to construct something tangible to enable the process of sense-making and to assist with the process of coming

---

29. Brueggemann, reflecting on the rootage of the book of Jeremiah, states the following: "at the deepest level the tradition of Jeremiah is rooted in the memory and the authority of the covenant at Sinai . . . [T]aken theologically, the awesome meeting at Mt. Sinai concerns the exclusive, uncompromising, nonnegotiable connection of Israel to YHWH." Brueggemann also continues to reflect on the theme of the rooting influence of the prophet Jeremiah by referring to the importance of the prophet Hosea, especially in the appropriation of the interpersonal imagery of marriage and divorce and the decisive link with the Book of Deuteronomy; Brueggemann, *The Theology of the Book of Jeremiah*, 10–11.

30. O'Connor, "Jeremiah as Ideal Survivor," 19.

31. Stulman, *Order Amid Chaos*, 7.

32. Abbott engages the difference between trauma and crisis: "Trauma, understood contextually, is a term integral to disaster response . . . [and] refers to the psychosomatic, social, and spiritual sequelae to events that overwhelm one's personal and/or communal coping mechanisms. Distinguished from a crisis, which assumes the individual will be able to reverse their temporary emotional paralysis within weeks, a trauma is more biologically and psychologically overwhelming, shatters integrity and induces powerlessness and estrangement, and is more prolonged"; Abbott, "Trauma, Compassion, and Community."

33. Stulman and Kim reflect on the nature of the genre of written prophesy: "[I]t is a meditation on the horror of war and its devastating repercussions. Not unlike contemporary art, it dares to broach the abyss with candor and fractured beauty. It courageously comes face-to-face with a world in disarray and fraught with moral ambiguity. And it refuses to retreat into denial"; Stulman and Kim, *You Are My People*, 6.

to terms with the devastation experienced. O'Connor argues that the book of Jeremiah is utterly concerned with disaster and in the process "it creates poetics and symbolic language to help traumatized survivors speak of their suffering and to begin to interpret it, cope with it, and to endure through it until that new day when life might again appear among them."[34] The metaphors developed, however traumatic, and the narratives told, however painful, aim at assisting the disorientated and the disenfranchised, to find a new vocabulary to name their experiences of trauma and to develop a new script for connection and community.

The book of Jeremiah is, however, exceedingly difficult to engage with and has been deemed by some as "unreadable."[35] Central to the intricacy of the book is the complexly constructed prophetic persona of Jeremiah whose presence almost seems to eclipse his message.[36] This impression may indeed precisely come about because of the deeply integrated and embodied nature of his prophetic message. Stulman remarks: "[A]s poet-prophet of the message of dismantling and rebuilding, Jeremiah functions as an archetypal figure who stands between two worlds—a country behind him and a county ahead of him—pronouncing the death of one and the birth of another."[37]

Jeremiah is at the same time embedded within the community and his suffering is an example of the people's fate, and intimately and profoundly

---

34. O'Connor, "Jeremiah as Ideal Survivor," 19.

35. Stulman and Kim, when reflecting on the nature of the book, note: "Taken in totality, the book of Jeremiah is a literary artifact of terror, a disturbing cultural expression of lament and chaos. Danger, disjunction, and distress bubble beneath the surface of virtually every text"; *You Are My People*, 98.

36. Besides the variety of conflicting and problematic metaphors employed within the book, Brueggemann identifies two main reasons for the complexity of the book: "First, the Book of Jeremiah consists of the swirling of several interpretative voices, each of which offers a strong reading of the historical-theological crisis that preoccupies the book." Rather than harmonizing these often contesting voices, the book permits several opposing and contrasting perspectives to exist next to one another. In addition, Brueggemann alludes to a second contributing factor, when he states, "[I]t is clear that the Book of Jeremiah is problematic because it stretches over several generations." A variety of contesting voices developing over a period in time gives rise to a book that reflects the ongoing engagement by various generations with the crises faced by the community of Israel and the demise of Jerusalem; Brueggemann, *The Theology of the Book of Jeremiah*, 1. Stulman picks up the diffuse and polyphonic nature of Jeremiah's persona as constructed in the narrative: "Jeremiah is represented in his book as a son of a priest, a messenger and spokeperson for God, an actor, a litigant, a gleaner, a sentry, a righteous sufferer, a covenant mediator, an iconoclast, a writer, a surrogate city, an impregnable wall of bronze, a confidant of kings, a prisoner and exile, a 'prophet to the nations,' an 'assayer and tester of the people's ways,' and a proponent and opponent of God"; Stulman, *Order Amid Chaos*, 143.

37. Stulman, *Order Amid Chaos*, 136.

connected with God.[38] Mary Mills remarks regarding Jeremiah's liminal position by arguing the following: "For the prophet exists on the borders of the world/God's world and on the margins of society by the virtue of his mission. The result of constantly embodying divine wrath . . . is that Jeremiah comes to exist on the edges of community activities."[39]

Reminiscent of the isolation that we encounter in Father Quintana, Jeremiah is called to a life of celibacy and thus lives his liminal existence without the social comfort and companionship that family can provide. Jeremiah's celibacy and consequential isolation is commanded by God and serves as a symbolic act, as Fretheim explains: "In obeying God's command in this respect, the prophet not only prefigured the end of these experiences for the people of Israel but also portrayed, indeed embodied what God's own experience of abandonment and the loss of community was like."[40]

Central, however, to the intertextual engagement constructed in this paper are the Laments/Confessions (11:18—12:6; 15:10–21; 17:14–18; 18:18–23; 20:7–13, 14–18) ascribed to the prophet Jeremiah. Nowhere else in the prophetic literature is the intimate conversation between God and a prophet so audible as in the Confessions of Jeremiah; as we hear the prophet cry out in pain, rage, sorrow, and grief that emerge in the midst of suffering and the experience of alienation.[41] Jeremiah, utterly grounded in his prophetic calling, laments his experience of vocational meltdown. He complains to God about the pain and suffering that he has to endure and directs his blame to the sins of the people, the failure of leadership, the wickedness of the enemy; but ultimately, Jeremiah's confessions blame God.[42]

Jeremiah, deeply connected to his prophetic calling, deems himself innocent. However, ironically, it is precisely his prophetic calling that causes

---

38. O'Connor remarks: "Jeremiah's absolute loyalty to God creates a counterpoint to the behavior of the community whom he accuses of abandoning YHWH to follow after other gods . . . Jeremiah's relationship with God is unbroken and enduring despite his suffering and his anger at God. God and he continue to be 'made known' to one another . . . he converses with God and clings to God in his suffering"; O'Connor, "The Prophet Jeremiah," 138.

39 Mills, *Alterity, Pain and Suffering*.

40. Fretheim, *Jeremiah*, 15. O'Connor continues along the same lines when stating, "there will be no more giving and taking in marriage, no voice of gladness, no voice of bride or bridegroom . . . His solitary state serves as an icon of the devastation of daily domestic life in the land"; O'Connor, "The Prophet Jeremiah," 137–38.

41. See McEntire, *A Chorus of Prophetic Voices*, 98–99.

42. McEntire identifies three possible interpretations of the identity of the "oppressor" that Jeremiah addresses in his accusing laments, namely Babylon, YHWH using Babylon, or the leaders of the people of Judah who enraged YHWH, who then uses the Babylonian Empire as tool of oppression; McEntire, *A Chorus of Prophetic Voices*, 101.

him great anguish as his commitment to God and the message that he has to proclaim causes the recipients of his prophecy to hate him and to conspire to bring about his demise. In the midst of this traumatic experience, Jeremiah clings to God and affirms his need for connection. Jeremiah's lament does not communicate the prophet's desire to sever the connection with God, but rather it is in the honest wrestling and raw expression of embodied vulnerability that the connection is reinforced, deepened, and developed.

By articulating his lament, Jeremiah becomes an "ideal survivor/emblematic sufferer" for the suffering nation.[43] O'Connor states: "For readers who live in the hungry maw of disaster, Jeremiah's prayers express their desolation, misery, and doubt. Although the confessions appear on the surface to be purely personal, they actually enact in the life of one person Judah's shattered faith."[44]

Jeremiah shows the way to a people disorientated and disconnected. By voicing his pain, by bringing all his feelings of despair and misery to the surface through protest, blame, complaint, and resistance, Jeremiah is modeling a path to re-connection, re-orientation and re-membering of the community. Through this stripped expression of pain and protest, it becomes possible for people to see their own devastating vulnerabilities, and in the process perhaps also to develop the compassionate capacity to see the vulnerability of others.[45] Embodied understandings of vulnerability as experienced and voiced by both Jeremiah and Father Quintana, and especially in relation to the absence of God, seem to form the basis for the process of finding ways to reconnection and the establishment of community.

Further, in the expression of his vulnerability, Jeremiah becomes the embodiment of God's vulnerability. As Fretheim remarks, "rather the prophet's experience of rejection and his lamenting his situation was understood to mirror God's experience at the hands of the people. Even more, because the prophet not only spoke God's word, but embodied it, God's experience becomes Jeremiah's experience."[46]

---

43. See O'Connor, *Jeremiah: Pain and Promise*, chap. 8; O'Connor, "The Prophet Jeremiah," 130–40; O'Connor, "Jeremiah as Ideal Survivor," 19–24.

44. O'Connor, *Jeremiah: Pain and Promise*, 84.

45. Ackermann, reflecting on the trauma of contemporary reading communities in the light of a devastating rape culture and the realities of those living with HIV and Aids, hints at the value of the genre of lament: "I suggest that the ancient language of lament offers a vehicle for expressing the raw emotions . . . The language of lament also offers the Body of Christ the opportunity to say: 'We are suffering, we stand in solidarity with all who suffer, we lament while we believe that there is hope for all in the Good news,'" Ackermann, *Tamar's Cry*, 25.

46. Fretheim, *Jeremiah*, 15.

Hidden in Jeremiah's expression of vulnerability through the language of lament we find God's presence. Jeremiah 8:18—9:22 offers a profound expression of God's vulnerability, when the voice of the prophet becomes the lament of the "weeping God."[47] It is in God's tears that we encounter God. As Juliana Claassens argues: "For liberation to take place, God has to feel the people's suffering. Only the weeping God can feel the people's pain; only the suffering God can help."[48] The brokenness expressed by the prophet is simultaneously and complexly an expression of the brokenness of the people and the fragile vulnerability of God. In the raw lament of the prophet, we encounter the manifestation of vulnerability, the weakness, exposure, and brokenness of the prophet, the people, and God is made audible and visible; paradoxically, it is in this place of vulnerability that the possibility for community becomes possible. Vulnerability and the expression thereof in lament sparks the possibility for connection and community when those vulnerable reach out and compassionately care for others recognized in similar dispositions of vulnerability.

Vulnerable Communion

By interpreting Father Quintana's devastating isolation, embedded within his ruined community, in addition to his raw longing for an experience of God in terms of the embodied lament that we encounter in the prophet Jeremiah, it becomes possible for us to witness something of the mystery of vulnerability that Malick brings to the screen in the final movement of the film. In arguably one of the most profound sequences in all of Malick's oeuvre, we find Father Quintana in suspension between mourning and wonder. Serene Jones, in her theological reflection on trauma in a ruptured world, writes: "To mourn and to wonder, that is what the spirit yearns for when it stands in the midst of trauma and breathes the truth of grace. Mourning and wonder—neither one answers the question that trauma poses to grace. They are, instead, states of mind, if nurtured, open us up to the experience of God's coming into torn flesh, and to love's arrival amid violent ruptures."[49]

Father Quintana, deeply aware of his own vulnerability, is portrayed as engaging with those most vulnerable in his society through acts of compassionate care to the poor, needy, and disenfranchised. Woven into these deeply

---

47. The voice of the "I" in the poem has been debated, and while some continue to accredit it to the prophet Jeremiah, I take my cue from scholarship finding God as the principal speaker. See especially Brueggemann, *To Pluck Up, to Tear Down*, and O'Connor, "The Tears of God."

48. Claassens, *Mourner, Mother, Midwife*, 26.

49. Jones, *Trauma and Grace*, 161.

moving scenes are images that inspire wonder: the landscape, the sky, a child running. In voice-over, Father Quintana delivers his final monologue by partially quoting the prayer on the St. Patrick's Breastplate: "Where are you leading me? Teach us where to seek you? Christ, be with me. Christ before me. Christ behind me. Christ in me. Christ beneath me. Christ above me. Christ on my right. Christ on my left. Christ in my heart. Thirsting we thirst."

By masterfully combining the audio and visual, Malick presents us with the mystery that our deep longing for connection with God is not found in isolation or in the expectation of a dramatic Theophany, but in the realization of our embodied vulnerability and the mysterious wonder of a community born through acts of compassionate care. The priest's existential question: "Where is God?," is hauntingly answered by Malick in image and voice-over when he shows the viewer that God is found in acts of compassion and care for those who are vulnerable and downcast.

Malick brings to life through film more than the mere communal recognition of vulnerability, as also expressed by the prophet Jeremiah when, in Jer 8:22—9:1, the tears of the prophet become the tears of the people, and also transform into the tears of God. Malick hints at the connection and community that is possible when vulnerability ceases to be an experience of isolation, but rather becomes the spark for community through acts of embodied compassion.

Melissa Raphael offers a similar insight in her book, *The Female Face of God in Auschwitz*, when she argues that God's presence becomes a reality in the simple re-humanizing acts of compassionate care when feeding, washing, clothing, and comforting those who are vulnerable.[50] She beautifully describes the nurturing practice of washing the body as women communally cared for each other's broken and malnourished bodies within the camp.

To the Wonder was the last film that the acclaimed film critic, Roger Ebert, ever reviewed. In his final sentence, he reflects: "There will be many who find 'To the Wonder' elusive and too effervescent. They'll be dissatisfied by a film that would rather evoke than supply. I understand that, and I think Terrence Malick does, too. But here he has attempted to reach more deeply than that, to reach beneath the surface, and find the soul in need."[51]

Malick offers us an understanding of love transformed when he contrasts, in the words of Father Quintana: "There is love that is like a stream that can go dry when rain no longer feeds it," and continuing: "But there is a love that is like a spring coming up from the earth. The first is human love, the second is divine love and has its source above." And in the final analysis,

---

50. Raphael, *The Female Face of God in Auschwitz*.
51. Ebert, "To the Wonder."

it seems that what Malick is mystically hinting at is that we encounter this second source of love in the realization of our own vulnerability, the vulnerability of others, and, most deeply, in compassionate acts of relational care. Love, community, a life together seems possible if it springs from the Source. This possibility of enduring love that Malick hints at sparks hope for the possibility of life together, even for those most devastated and isolated, and it inspires those most vulnerable to reach out to others in order to connect through acts of compassionate care, and in the process to find God in places most unexpected.

Bibliography

Abbott, Roger. "Trauma, Compassion, and Community: Reconciling Opposites in the Interests of Post-traumatic Growth." *Practical Theology* 5 (2012) 31–46.
Bywayofbeauty. "Souls in Need: The Journey 'To the Wonder.'" www.bywayofbeauty.com/2013/04/souls-in-need-journey-to-wonder.html.
Ackermann, Denise. *Tamar's Cry: Re-Reading an Ancient Text in the Midst of an HIV/AIDS Pandemic*. Stellenbosch, South Africa: Ecumenical Foundation of Southern Africa, 2001.
Baskin, Jon. "Conversion Experience: Terrence Malick's 'To the Wonder.'" *Los Angeles Review of Books*, May 12, 2013. https://lareviewofbooks.org/article/conversion-experience-terrence-malicks-to-the-wonder/.
Bradshaw, Peter. "To the Wonder—Review." *The Guardian*, February 21, 2013. http://www.theguardian.com/film/2013/feb/21/to-the-wonder-review.
Brody, Richard. "The Cinematic Wonder of 'To the Wonder.'" *The New Yorker*, April 10, 2013. http://www.newyorker.com/culture/richard-brody/the-cinematic-miracle-of-to-the-wonder.
Brueggemann, Walter. *The Theology of the Book of Jeremiah*. Cambridge: Cambridge University Press, 2007.
———. *To Pluck Up, to Tear Down: A Commentary on the Book of Jeremiah 1–25*. Grand Rapids: Eerdmans, 1988.
Brussat, Frederic, and Mary Ann Brussat. "To the Wonder." http://www.spiritualityandpractice.com/films/reviews/view/24896.
Butler, Judith. *Notes toward a Performative Theory of Assembly*. Cambridge, MA: Harvard University Press, 2015.
Claassens, L. Juliana M. *Mourner, Mother, Midwife: Reimagining God's Delivering Presence in the Old Testament*. Louisville: Westminster John Knox, 2012.
Ebert, Roger. "To the Wonder." April 6, 2013. http://www.rogerebert.com/reviews/to-the-wonder-2013.
Fech, William J. "The Soul Announces Itself: Terrence Malick's Emersonian Cinema." Master's thesis, Oregon State University, 2013.
Fodor, Jim. "Reading the Scriptures: Rehearsing Identity, Practicing Character." In *The Blackwell Companion to Christian Ethics*, edited by Stanley Hauerwas, and Samuel Wells, 141–69. Sussex: Wiley & Sons, 2004.
Fretheim, Terence E. *Jeremiah*. Macon, GA: Smyth & Helwys, 2002.

Jones, Serene. *Trauma and Grace: Theology in a Ruptured World.* Louisville: Westminster John Knox, 2009.

Mills, Mary E. *Alterity, Pain, and Suffering in Isaiah, Jeremiah, and Ezekiel.* Library of Hebrew Bible/Old Testament Studies 479. New York: T. & T. Clark, 2007.

McEntire, Mark. *A Chorus of Prophetic Voices: Introducing the Prophetic Literature of Ancient Israel.* Louisville: Westminster John Knox, 2015.

Nussbaum, Martha C. *Sex and Social Justice.* New York: Oxford University Press, 1999.

O'Connor, Kathleen M. "A Family Comes Undone (Jeremiah 2:1—4:2)." *Review & Expositor* 105 (2008) 201–12.

———. "Jeremiah as Ideal Survivor." *Journal for Preachers* (Lent 2005) 19–24.

———. *Jeremiah: Pain and Promise.* Minneapolis: Fortress, 2011.

———. "The Prophet Jeremiah and Exclusive Loyalty to God." *Interpretation* 59 (2005) 130–40.

———. "The Tears of God and Divine Character in Jeremiah 2–9." In *Troubling Jeremiah*, edited by A. R. Pete Diamond, et al., 387–401. Journal for the Study of the Old Testament Supplement Series 260. Sheffield: Sheffield Academic, 1999.

Pinkerton, Nick. "Film of the Week: To the Wonder." *Film Forever*, February 10, 2015. http://www.bfi.org.uk/news-opinion/sight-sound-magazine/reviews-recommendations/film-week-wonder.

Raphael, Melissa. *The Female Face of God in Auschwitz: A Jewish Feminist Theology of the Holocaust.* London: Routledge, 2003.

Savu, Laura. "The Way to Grace: Terrence Malick's Ecotheological Vision in The Tree of Life." *University of Bucharest Review* 2 (2012) 97–106.

Smith-Christopher, Daniel. *A Biblical Theology of Exile.* Minneapolis: Augsburg Fortress, 2002.

Stulman, Louis. *Order Amid Chaos: Jeremiah as Symbolic Tapestry.* Sheffield: Sheffield Academic, 1998.

Stulman, Louis, and Hyun Chul Paul Kim. *You are My People: An Introduction to Prophetic Literature.* Nashville: Abingdon, 2010.

Urda, Kathleen E. "Eros and Contemplation. The Catholic Vision of Terrence Malick's To the Wonder." *Logos: A Journal of Catholic Thought and Culture* 19 (2016) 130–47.

Van der Walt, Charlene. "Is There a Man Here? The Iron Fist in the Velvet Glove in Judges 4." In *Feminist Frameworks and the Bible: Power, Ambiguity, and Intersectionality*, edited by L. Juliana Claassens and Carolyn J. Sharp. 117–132. London: Bloomsbury T. & T. Clark, 2017

Passio—Compassio
J. S. Bach's Passions Transformed into a Passion Transcending Christianity

MIRELLA KLOMP

A Contemporary Passion in a Changed Religious Landscape

EVERY YEAR IN JUNE, *Holland Festival* (HF) takes place in the Dutch capital.[1] This festival—first held in 1947 to rebuild a positive interaction between the Netherlands and its surrounding countries after World War II—defines itself as "the leading international performing arts festival in the Netherlands."[2] Offering a broad scope of international performing arts with a mix of performances and concerts from all corners of the world, the festival seeks to feature established names as well as new talent, showing innovation in art and exploring new types of venues and forms of theater.

One of the performances in the 66th edition of HF was *Passio-Compassio*, a contemporary passion especially seeking positive interactions. It was performed in the concert hall *Muziekgebouw aan het IJ* on June 12, 2012, for an audience of some three hundred to four hundred people.[3] The piece, created in 2010, drew from Johann Sebastian Bach's *St. Matthew Passion*, his *St. John Passion*, Oriental early Christian songs, as well as Turkish Sufi songs (i.e., expressions of Islamic mysticism). It was performed by *Ensemble Sarband*, a

---

1. The author wishes to thank Prof. Dr. Robert Vosloo and Dr. Nadine Bowers-du Toit for their reflections and constructive comments on previous versions of this text.

2. https://www.hollandfestival.nl/en/about-hf/vision-of-the-holland-festival/.

3. The author was part of the audience at this concert. A fragment of this performance can be found on www.youtube.com/watch?v=fgsbnbi_jrg. Also see the website of the ensemble for more information on the work: sarband.de/Prog_PassioE.html.

German ensemble led by an artistic director originating from Bulgaria, who as a young boy migrated to Germany with his mother.[4] His ensemble

> unites performers from widely different cultures and musical backgrounds. The cooperation in the ensemble is not a fashionable crossover, but conceived as a continuous dialogue on equal terms. All the artists unrestrictedly contribute their native traditions, their personal histories and their own creativity to the programs, so that Sarband also becomes a musical training ground for communication and tolerance between different cultural identities.[5]

A quote from a press review, prominently placed on the ensembles' homepage, reads: "For many years now, Sarband have been building breath-taking bridges between cultures and religions. . ."[6] To connect seems to be their mission; this also speaks from the name of the ensemble that literally means "connection." Their aim is to show that music is a medium that can express mutual respect. They show this with diverse performers and to a diverse audience, all coming together in the performance, binding them "to cultural experiences previously perceived as alien."[7] *Passio-Compassio* is one of their projects that intend to build bridges.

Passio-Compassio is also one of many contemporary passions performed in concert halls in the Netherlands. In Dutch late modern society, the passion (a large musical form rooting in the Christian liturgical tradition), like other forms of Christian material and immaterial heritage (e.g., religious language, symbols, narratives, objects, and practices) has over the last century increasingly been transferred: it migrated from the enclosed domain of the institutional churches to other domains, and changed. This process is characterized as a transfer and a transformation of religion and/or the sacred.[8] Particularly after the year 2000, new passions have been creatively and freely composed and transformed: modern composers, artistic and musical directors of ensembles, and even broadcasting companies have actualized the passion narrative of Christ, commented on it, deconstructed it, combined it with other narratives and discourses, and so forth. Obviously, the notion

---

4. sarband.de/Vladimir.html.
5. sarband.de/artists.html.
6. sarband.de/index.html.
7. sarband.de/english_introduction.html.

8. On the transfer and transformation of immaterial religious heritage, see De Hart, *Keeping the Faith?*; Sengers, *The Dutch and Their Gods*. Also (in Dutch language): De Hart, *Maak het Nieuw*; Post, "Heilige Velden"; Borgman, *Metamorfosen.*; Van de Donk, *Geloven in het Publieke Domein.*; Frijhoff, *Heiligen, Idolen, Iconen.*

of "transformation" is not unproblematic, because there is no such thing as a "standard passion:" There has never been an *editio typica*, a fixed passion structure, or even a fixed narrative that should be seen as a standard. Yet, most passions throughout history were created in a Christian societal context, and therefore show and share in a dominant Christian discourse. What is new in the little rise of contemporary passions, is the fact that it has taken place in a society where the religious landscape has changed dramatically over the last decades. "Depillarization" since the 1960s[9] has crumbled the politico-denominational segregation of Dutch society: the "vertical" division into "pillars" according to different Christian denominations or ideologies in general no longer exists. Ongoing de-churching and people calling themselves less and less religious and spiritually interested[10] diminish the role of church in society, change the role of the church in peoples' lives, and influence the presence and interpretation of Christian ideas and values in Dutch society. Today, many people find the sacred when performing or participating in rituals in the areas of nature, art, music, wellness, and sports.[11] At the same time, like other European countries, the Netherlands is seeing an influx of refugees from Muslim countries, which invokes a sentiment of fear for a growing Muslim presence in a country that was long permeated with Protestantism. All in all, the Dutch religious landscape and its artifacts have seen an enormous change, which also influenced the appropriation of notions kernel to Christianity, such as "passion" and "compassion."

The art practice *Passio-Compassio*, understood against the backdrop of the socioreligious context mentioned above, leads to the question: *What is the connection between passion and compassion in Passio-Compassio as performed by Ensemble Sarband at HF in Amsterdam in 2012, and how can this relation be evaluated from a Christian theological perspective?* In search of an answer to this question, I will engage in a theological discussion with myself, with (representations of) my own experiences, tradition, and theology, all influenced by the cultural context in which I was brought up and live. With the help of other scholars and disciplines, I enter into a conversation with ritual knowledge, for the benefit of retrieving compassion that enhances living together in a globalizing world.[12] "Compassion" here is taken as the act of connecting with the suffering other, reaching out, and allowing or even welcoming her/him with their pain into one's own life. In our multicultural

9. Frijhoff and Spies, *Dutch Culture*, 325.
10. Bernts and Berghuijs. *God in Nederland*.
11. Post, "From Identity to Accent."
12. Ritual knowledge, according to Jennings, is "to know reflectively what is known ritually, to re-cognize ritual knowledge"; see Jennings, "On Ritual Knowledge," 333.

and multireligious society, compassion with "the other" is often far off. Sentiments such as fear, discontent, and distrust currently seem to grow. In this context, compassion is a complex concept. Yet, in order to be able to live together, it is crucial to rediscover what compassion is about.

Interrogating Passio-Compassio

My research on *Passio-Compassio* is empirical in nature and principally based on participatory observation during the concert in 2012.[13] When applying participatory observation as a data collection method, positionality is important: aspects of our identities such as gender, social class, race, education, etc., are markers of relational positions rather than essential qualities.[14] This influences our epistemology: knowledge "is valid when it includes an acknowledgement of the knower's specific position in any context, because changing and contextual and relational factors are crucial for defining identities and our knowledge in any given situation."[15] Hence, as a practical theologian specializing in ritual-musical ethnography, I must spend a few words on my own particularity as a researcher prior to the description of any performance, including *Passio-Compassio*.

> I am a white, female Dutch theologian in her thirties, and an ordained minister in the Protestant Church in the Netherlands. I was born in a Lutheran family, and raised in that tradition. I was trained for the ministry both at the Dutch Evangelical-Lutheran Seminary and at the Vrije Universiteit. Already at a young age I became familiar with Bach's music: in church, and at the Lutheran choir camps for children that my parents had me attend, as well as during the organ lessons they had me take from the age of seven. I learned to play all the famous chorales, and when I became a teenager, our church organist (who was my teacher) sometimes had me accompany the congregation in their hymn singing.

These particularities influence my description, the collected data, the language and concepts that I use, and how I see the ontology of the performance

---

13. Additionally, I used the following sources: the printed program booklet with lyrics and explanations, YouTube clips on the performance, texts on the webpage of the performing ensemble by the musical director, quotations from press reviews selected by the musical director published on that website, a specific document on the passion downloaded from that website, as well as texts on the webpage of the performing ensemble on how they work.

14. On positionality, see Alcoff, "Cultural Feminism."

15. Maher and Tetreault, "Frames of Positionality," 118.

and the empirically obtained data: I have no other access to the ritual than by way of the research data that I generated through participatory observation of the performance.[16]

In case of *Passio-Compassio*, these particularities are even more crucial, because my autobiography strongly influenced the listener experience of *Passio-Compassio*. Therefore, this contribution includes an important autoethnographic angle. Autobiographic and autoethnographic theology starts from life as it has developed and as it is developing in its connections with others, instead of well-ordered and systematically arranged knowledge.[17] It is a method that takes *the other* as well as *difference* very seriously. It has been said that an autoethnography "lets you use yourself to get to culture,"[18] and by analogy, I claim that it "lets you use yourself to get to theology." Considering the role and position of *the other* in compassion, the following autoethnographic overtone serves as a "key" in the conversation on compassion developed below.

> *That night too, we went to church, like we used to do every Holy Week. We had always done so with the entire family. That year on Good Friday my father stayed at home to pack his suitcase. My sister and I knew that he would leave our family the next day, and we had every reason to hope that he would never return. That evening, my mother drove the three of us to celebrate the liturgy in the small but sturdy "High Church" Lutheran congregation that we belonged to. She took her normal place between the other sopranos in the church choir; by way of exception, that night my sister and I sat left and right of her. During the worship service the passion narrative was being read, and,* in alternatim *with the congregation, the choir sang four-part chorales from Bach's passions with which I was so familiar. At the end of the service, some choir members cried with us. I was thirteen and filled with a mix of pain, sorrow, and sheer relief. The passion was about me. Choir members comforted my broken family. The music offered consolation. God was next to me in the choir stalls.*

This experience, and—being raised with music that, according to Luther, is after all *optimum Dei donum*—several other experiences connected to music, ritual performance, suffering, compassion, and consolation, influenced my investigation of the performance *Passio-Compassio*. It deeply influences the conversational structure and nature of this contribution.

---

16. Barnard, "Dots on a Blank Sheet," 43–44.
17. Barnard, "My Father's Tobacco-Jar," 2.
18. Pelias, "The Academic Tourist," 372.

The Performance of Passio-Compassio

Description

On the aforementioned evening in 2012 in the modern concert hall, the performers on stage sit and stand in a semicircle: a vocal double quartet, and some fifteen musicians with their reed flutes, violins, a fiddle, saxophones, a bass clarinet, psalteries, harpsichord, organ, and two soloist singers in the front. Among them, the director of Ensemble Sarband, Vladimir Ivanoff, playing frame drum, and the Lebanese alto, Fadia el-Hage. The music they perform has a very Eastern sound and performance practice, considering the frequent use of prepared suspensions, passing tones, and embellishing tones. The piece consists of a musical introduction followed by twenty-one parts that, when listed, make clear how this passion was put together: like a patchwork of different elements.[19] Elements taken from Bach's *St. Matthew* and *St. John Passion* and even his *Christmas Oratorio* are mixed with thirteenth-century mystical texts by Rumi, and combined with spiritual songs from early Christianity. The lyrics are in German, Turkish, Arabic, Aramaic, and Syrian. Songs are either sung in the original language or in translation, and some are performed in more than one language. During the performance, every now and then text fragments are projected on the black screen behind the performers, in the background of the stage.

Some forty-five minutes after the performance has started, all of a sudden five men in black capes with tall brown hats enter the stage one after another: dervishes from the Sufi Mevlevi Order originating from the Golden Horn (a historic inlet of the Bosphorus dividing the city of Istanbul in Turkey). They are also known as whirling dervishes due to their whirling practice, which is a form of remembrance of God. The dervishes remove their capes, and in a white robe and wide skirt start pivoting around their left feet, using their right feet to push off with, turning counterclockwise around their own axes and whirling for seven minutes; starting slowly, building up, and returning to slow again. Their eyes are closed, their heads with the tall hats held at slight angle. This dance of the Mevlevi Order, according to the program booklet, is a form of prayer: it is a ritual that

> represents a mystical journey in which the dervish gradually leaves his or her ego and personal desires behind and through love and truth touches perfection. After returning from this journey, a person is more adult and better capable of serving creation and of loving. The continual whirling of the dervishes

---

19. The appendix at the end of this essay contains an overview of the elements that the piece comprises.

is thus a way of going into ecstasy and in that manner becoming closer to God. The desired state (*wajd*) is by no means reached in every celebration of a ritual, however, and it is strictly forbidden to feign it ... When they reach momentum, they open and raise their arms, turning their right palm upward and their left palm downward: to receive the blessing of God, and to pass that blessing to the world.[20]

Summarizing the performance, we may say that *Passio-Compassio* was a multisensory *mishmash* (given the Oriental influence in the performance, the use of the Yiddish word seems appropriate) of languages, words and sounds, of textual and melodic quotations, of Oriental and Occidental instruments and styles of singing, a mix of cultural elements, rituals and religious traditions, of the passion of Christ, of human suffering, and love.

Listener experience

As a participant observer, I was moved by the new way in which "old music" that is obviously very dear to me was brought into this concert. I often attend concerts of classical, mostly choral, music (in the Amsterdam *Muziekgebouw aan het IJ* and elsewhere) and I am in favor of contemporary classical music that creatively appropriates Christian musical forms. The connections with contemporary Western culture that are often made in these performances shed new light on these forms—light that generates new meaning. As a listener I appreciated *Passio-Compassio* in its effort to make connections between styles, cultures, and religions, and to bring Bach in a new and surprising manner: by means of Bach's choral work, Ivanoff had treated the passion narrative of Christ in a creative way, opening it to the suffering of other people (potentially every human being). He thus created a multicultural as well as a multireligious passion.

Particularly because of the latter, I also felt confusion and a certain estrangement. Whirling dervishes inserted a strange element into Bach's obviously Christian passion narrative: an Islamic religious practice. These feelings were reinforced by the concert hall seating plan: the position of the chairs was opposite the stage. Looking at the dervishes created a distance: it was "them on stage having their ecstatic experience with their eyes closed" versus "the audience passively watching this practice." There was no interaction. The connections that *Passio-Compassio* tried to make—between words, styles, languages, instruments, sounds, practices, cultures, and religions—mainly appear to be made on stage. My confusion was enhanced

20. Quote from program booklet *Passio-Compassio* (page 14–15).

by the explanation of the piece in the program booklet, where passionate emotion and suffering were seemingly conflated and linked to *passio*:

> Judaism, Christianity and Islam refer to messages of salvation preceded by severe ordeals, sacrifices and passions. All human beings experience suffering regardless of their religious and cultural background. Suffering, like love, results in passion. Passionate emotion itself, experienced in love for human beings or for God, can again lead to suffering. Art and religion are both capable of transcending the cycle of suffering and passion. Then, the pure emotion of passion is transformed into a universal sphere of awareness, of perception of the other. Passio becomes Compassio.[21]

Obviously, the essence of art is creativity and artistic freedom, so it needed be no surprise that the artist wrote a text based on creative associations of "passion" and "compassion." But, unable to turn off the theological resonances of these notions and the Christian framework of my theology, I found myself left with the following conundrums: how was the audience involved in this transformation of passion and compassion? And were the whirling dervishes on stage taking over Christ's role to make the connection between God and those who suffer? Did the performance not lose sight of the particularity of the Christ narrative, in which passion and compassion are (concepts) inextricably linked, and in which the other is included rather than excluded? Was Christ's passion transformed into a universal message of love and respect? How to evaluate the move from the Christian passion to a passion transcending Christianity?

My listener experience (a mix of sympathy and alienation), combined with my theological gut feeling on compassion led to the idea that *Passio-Compassio* ended in a vague multireligious art practice where conversation and consensus would only be made possible when bracketing our particular religious identities. I was only prepared to go halfway across the bridge that Ensemble Sarband was trying to build. The performance did not appeal to my compassion for those who suffer in this world, nor did I experience any compassion with my own suffering. Did this performance show anything about compassion, or a compassionate God?

---

21. Quote from program booklet *Passio-Compassio*, 28.

The O/other in the Interreligious Dialogue

"Autoethnography lets you use yourself to get to theology," I wrote. Although I was incapable of theological wording at the time, the Good Friday liturgy with the Bach chorales and the passion narrative from my teens had left an experience that intimately connected our personal suffering with God's suffering, and the compassion of the choir members around me with God's compassion. *Passio-Compassio*—an art performance in the secular settings of a concert hall and Holland Festival, that brought Bach's Christian passion music into conversation with other cultural and religious traditions, of which the Islamic ritual practices were most striking—questioned my ideas about passion, compassion, and the relationship between the two. The performance particularly made clear that the globalizing world is a multi-religious world in which we cannot escape the other. Both the encounter with "different" Islamic ritual practices in this performance and the fact that compassion always implies the involvement of another living creature, demand theological reflection on the O/other.

The openness or hospitality towards other languages and particularly other religious practices raises the question whether hospitality and compassion are endless. At what point does the other (religion, culture, person) become so important that one loses oneself? What conditions does the hospitality of the piece require, provided that one does not want to lose sight of the compassionate God?

In her book *Fragile Identities*, Marianne Moyaert discusses the tension between openness and identity in interreligious dialogues, stating that dialogue partners are often expected "to unite the attitude of faith *commitment* on the one hand and *openness* on the other,"[22] whereas it remains unclear what precisely these concepts entail. She agrees with Hans Küng that it is theology that should clarify why openness is appropriate (or not). Thus, the tension between faithfulness and betrayal that comes with hermeneutical openness does not only relate to one's own religion, but also to God. This tension, by the nature of the case, must not be transcended or removed:

> The moment theology no longer wrestles with the religious other is the moment the strange other is reduced to the same or is deleted as a *totaliter aliter*. The moment the theologian no longer wrestles with his faith commitment to God is the moment he [sic] has fixed God to the familiar or deleted God as the mysterious, unknowable *Real*.[23]

---

22. Moyaert, *Fragile Identities*, 2.
23. Moyaert, *Fragile Identities*, 276.

Moyaert employs Paul Ricoeur's hermeneutics to think through hospitality from a theological viewpoint. She gives two motivations for hospitality.[24] First of all, bearing in mind that we ourselves were strangers—and she refers to several biblical narratives where Jews and Christians are strangers—leads to hospitality towards other strangers: only by acknowledging the strangeness of our own identity we can open ourselves to the strangeness of the other. This also implies that we must acknowledge the fragility of our own identity, as well as the vulnerability of our religious meanings: we are never completely at home with ourselves; our religious meanings are never complete, never perfect. Identity and otherness are not opposed. Secondly—again she refers to biblical narratives—there is the idea that God reveals himself in the stranger:

> "God enters the picture as a God *incognito*, to whom we offer or do not offer hospitality. God reveals and conceals himself in the stranger and, without knowing whom we are dealing with, we discover with surprise and only later the attitude with which we met God" (Jansen 2002:299). But people can receive God in the stranger only when God is no longer fixed to the known and the familiar.[25]

Qualities of Compassion

Beyond the Me, Myself, and I

Moyaert's argument opens our eyes to the inclination to consider Bach's passions and the Christian passion narrative as "ours" and "owned." My listener experience was deeply influenced by an easy identification with both, supported by my religious upbringing and theological education. But in that I was overlooking the distance between myself, the text(s), and the musical works, which also have aspects of strangeness. The strange and uncanny effect of *Passio-Compassio* can actually help to understand the strangeness also of Bach's passions: to recognize the foreign in the familiar. The religious language of Bach's libretto and the words of the chorales surely differ from our God-talk today. And Jesus' suffering to the point of death remains an incomprehensible religious truth, no matter our familiarity with the narrative. To recognize the foreign in the familiar, in turn, makes us more

---

24. Moyaert, *Fragile Identities*, 262–64.

25. Moyaert, *Fragile Identities*, 264. The citation from Jansen is taken from Jansen, *Talen naar God*, 299, and was translated into English by Moyaert.

hospitable to the foreign other: only by acknowledging the strangeness of our own tradition, religious objects, and practices, we can open ourselves to the strangeness of other traditions, religious objects, and practices. Hospitality towards the "other" practices of the whirling dervishes could then have led to a movement deeper into these ritual practices, breaking open a love and compassion transcending my own (religious) particularity. It could have actually deepened or strengthened my core convictions. It could have led to acknowledge that the whirling dervishes in their strangeness whirled for me, prayed for me, blessed me and every other human being in my and their suffering, using their ecstatic union to bring or even tie us to God. Locking up God's compassion in the particularity of the suffering Christ means being in God's way. Compassion requires openness: as Moyaert said, we can only receive God in the stranger when God is no longer fixed to the known and the familiar.

Thus compassion demands a shift from self-centeredness to other-centeredness for those who have compassion. This may seem obvious, but it is not. What looks like compassion is sometimes just focused on the self: when people show compassion in order to make them feel better about themselves, it is not other-centered and thus not compassion. From those who suffer, compassion requires at least an openness that allows the other to connect with you, to reach out to you, and to welcome you with your pain into their life. In either position, compassion is getting beyond the me, myself, and I.

A Manifestation of Divine Love

Passio-Compassio raised the question of how the move from a Christian passion to a passion transcending Christianity should be evaluated. This question is obviously related to my teenager experience that Christ's suffering and compassion and human suffering and compassion were deeply connected. It is also connected with a Lutheran theology that has a strong Christological focus.

Moyaert points to the fact that interreligious dialogue implies the possibility of not only a gain in meaning, but also a loss of meaning: "Interreligious dialogue . . . also presupposes the work of mourning. A discourse that speaks one-sidedly of interreligious dialogue as a source of enrichment ignores the vulnerability of religious meanings."[26] What applies to interreligious dialogues also applies to multireligious art practices, I think: these also include the work of mourning. The performance *Passio-Compassio*

26. See Moyaert, *Fragile Identities*, 277.

"pointed away" from Christ, and Bach's passions were transformed into a passion transcending Christianity. This may feel like a loss. Yet, the question is whether this "transcending Christianity" actually *excludes* God, and if so, whether this is problematic. When we turn to Scripture, at this point, we discover that this kind of "pointing away" is not unfamiliar to Christ himself. He did not come "to be served, but to serve, and to give his life a ransom for many" (Matt 20:28), and "being found in human form, he humbled himself and became obedient to the point of death—even death on a cross" (Phil 2:8). He became "the Lamb that was slaughtered, to receive power and wealth and wisdom and might and honor and glory and blessing!" (Rev 5:12). Christ went to the end, to death. He kenotically emptied himself to the point where no life was left, in order to make humanity more fully human. This means that in his suffering he did (and still does) not exclude humanity, but in essence included humanity.

In line with this, we may say that, as a passion transcending Christianity, *Passio-Compassio* did not leave, lose or exclude, but rather included God. Wherever people suffer, Christ suffers. This should, however, not be a reason to glorify suffering: it is not our suffering that is salvific, not through our suffering that our life is renewed; it is through the suffering of Christ that we regain life. Only a suffering God can help. Similarly, his passion is the ground of Christian compassion. Wherever people show compassion, they become—I say with Martin Luther[27]—as it were, a Christ to the other. Here, I think, lies a key to retrieve compassion: the compassion of the other is the compassion of the Other. It is exactly for this reason that people through the ages have prayed: "Erbarme Dich," "have mercy."

The basis of Christ's compassion is divine love. Christ's suffering and his death are manifestations of divine love, and these make the passion salvific. This is how Bach understood the passion: because his *St. Matthew Passion* interprets the passion and death of Christ as a manifestation of divine love, one also finds that references to the bridegroom and bride abound, e.g., in the powerful opening choir where the daughters of Zion admonish the faithful to behold the bridegroom.[28] When reexamining *Passio-Compassio*, it appears that Vladimir Ivanoff also understands that compassion roots in love. In his multireligious performance, many of the mystical Sufi texts and spiritual songs he interwove with parts from Bach's passion are about love: "A heart that loves rises up to the canopy of heaven" (*#intro*); "Love means

---

27. Luther, *The Freedom of a Christian*: "Hence, as our heavenly Father has in Christ freely come to our aid, we also ought freely to help our neighbor through our body and its works, and each one should become as it were a Christ to the other that we may be Christs to one another"; 367–68.

28. Rathey, *Bach's Major Vocal Works*, 117–29, esp. 117–18.

letting go of one's self over and again" (#1); "Every moment I hope that love will kill me; Ah never shall such sweet pain come into the weak heart" (#17). At the end of the performance, like in Bach's *St. Matthew Passion*, we hear the aria *Erbarme Dich*:

> Have mercy, my God,
> For the sake of my tears.
> Behold,
> Heart and eye are weeping before you
> Bitterly.
> Have mercy, my God.[29]

In *Passio-Compassio*, this area was accompanied by the mystical Sufi text:

> Oh brother, hear, do not be deaf to love!
> Let love change you![30]

With this text, Ivanoff tied the *Erbarme Dich* aria even closer to God: the call to the brother reinforced the call to God to show his mercy. At the same time, Rumi's text could be taken as a call for compassion of a human brother: "Have mercy, let love change you." *Passio-Compassio* thus connected God's compassion with human compassion, emphasizing the importance of love, suggesting that any manifestation of compassion is a manifestation of divine love.

Conclusion

Our globalizing world is characterized by the interchanging of world views, products, ideas, and also religious practices and beliefs. The reality of the religious other has come closer and it touches upon our daily living together. In this essay, I showed that the performance *Passio-Compassio* initially led to feelings of estrangement and a wrestling with my faith commitment to Christ (rooted in my religious and theological upbringing, as well as the practices of whirling Dervishes that presented the religious other). The performance intended to transform passion into compassion, but I was unable to open myself to the way the performers seemed to be offering compassion. My fear of multireligious vagueness that betrayed Christ was in the way, likely influenced by former experiences in which suffering, compassion, Bach's passions, and Lutheran liturgy were profoundly linked.

29. Quote from program booklet *Passio-Compassio*, 24.
30. *Passio-Compassio*, 24.

The autoethnographic angle let me use myself to get into a theology based on (interreligious) hospitality. The theological reflection on passion and compassion made clear that sufferers at least need to be a little open to the other in order to be able to experience compassion. In this, it is helpful to recognize that the self also has foreign aspects: one is never complete, never fully at home with oneself. Otherwise, when showing compassion, one needs to be focused on the other rather than the self. Either way, compassion transcends the me, myself, and I.

Further theological reflection showed that compassion is inextricably linked with the passion of Christ, even when this is not obvious. All human compassion is anchored in the suffering of Christ that brought and brings new life to humanity. In compassion, it is not the glorification of suffering that renews life, but the fact that all suffering is about Christ's suffering. At the heart of compassion thus lies divine love. God is found in the act of connecting with the sufferer, and in the act of letting others connect with oneself. I started this essay with a description of "compassion" as the act of connecting with the suffering other, reaching out, and allowing or even welcoming her/him with their pain into one's own life. In conclusion, I would like to rephrase that description of compassion, because I seem to have excluded Someone. "Compassion" is the act of connecting with the suffering other—and in that, by that, and through that, with the love of the suffering Other—reaching out and allowing or even welcoming her/him with their pain into one's own life. In retrospect, *Ensemble Sarband* with their performance of *Passio-Compassion* at Holland Festival indeed managed to build bridges, in my theology.

Appendix

Intro, with projection of text by thirteenth-century Persian poet and theologian Rumi.

1. Aria "Können Tränen meiner Wangen nichts erlangen" (*St. Matthew Passion*, sung in Arabic), followed by instrumental interlude with projection of text by Rumi.
2. Chorale "Wie soll ich Dich empfangen" (Paul Gerhardt, sung in German and Turkish).
3. Turba "Wir haben ein Gesetz" (Instrumental with projection of text by Rumi).
4. Evangelist "Und weinete bitterlich" (Instrumental with projection of text by Rumi).

5. "Qoló dHut" (Spiritual song, sung in Syriac).
6. "Abo dKochto" (Spiritual song, sung in Aramaic).
7. Syrian-Orthodox chant: "Amano Morio" (Spiritual song, sung in Aramaic).
8. "Yawno Tlito" (Spiritual song, sung in Aramaic).
9. Hicaz Ilahi "Nur-I cemali" (instrumental prelude with projection of text by Rumi).
10. Muslim spiritual song (sung in Turkish).
11. Turba "Jesum von Nazareth" (instrumental with projection of text by Rumi).
12. "Aljaum" (Maronite liturgy, sung in Arabic).
13. Aria "Von den Stricken meiner Sünden" (*St. John Passion*, sung in Arabic).
14. "Acem İlahi" (Muslim spiritual song, sung in Turkish).
15. Chorale "Wenn ich einmal soll scheiden" (instrumental prelude with projection of text by Rumi, chorale Paul Gerhardt, sung in German and Arabic).
16. Chorale "Befiehl du deine Wege" (chorale by Paul Gerhardt, sung in German and Turkish).
17. "Es ist vollbracht" (instrumental prelude with projection of text by Rumi, aria *St. John Passion*, sung in Arabic).
18. "Dörcüncü Selâm" (from the ritual of the Mevlevi, sung in Turkish).
19. Son Pesrev (instrumental).
20. Son Yürük Semai (instrumental with projection of text by Rumi).
21. Aria "Erbarme Dich" (*St. Matthew Passion*, sung in Arabic, with projection of text by Rumi).

Bibliography

Alcoff, Linda. "Cultural Feminism versus Post-Structuralism. The Identity Crisis in Feminist Theory." *Signs* 13 (1988) 405–36.

Barnard, Marcel. "My Father's Tobacco-Jar, Church Square Pretoria and Freedom Park: An Autoethnographical Exploration." *Verbum et Ecclesia* 35, no. 2, Art #882 (2014). http://dx.doi.org/10.4102/ve/v35i2.882, 7 pages.

———, et al. "Dots on a Blank Sheet. Procedures in Ritual and Liturgical Research." *Jaarboek voor Liturgieonderzoek* 25 (2009) 35–46.

Bernts, Ton, and Joantine Berghuijs. *God in Nederland 1966–2015*. Utrecht: Ten Have, 2016.

Borgman, Erik. *Metamorfosen. Over Religie en Moderne Cultuur*. Kampen: Klement/Pelckmans, 2006.

De Hart, Joep. *Keeping the Faith? Trends in Religion in the Netherlands*. The Netherlands Institute for Social Research 2014-10. The Hague: Sociaal en Cultureel Planbureau, 2014. https://www.scp.nl/english/Publications/Summaries_by_year/Summaries_2014/Keeping_the_faith.

———. *Maak het nieuw. Over Religieuze Ontwikkelingen en de Positie van de Kerken. Een Persoonlijke Geschiedenis*. The Netherlands Institute for Social Research 2011-34. The Hague: Sociaal en Cultureel Planbureau, 2011.

Frijhoff, Willem. *Heiligen, Idolen, Iconen*. Inaugural address, Vrije Universiteit, Amsterdam. Nijmegen: SUN, 1998.

Frijhof, Willem, and Marijke Spies. *Dutch Culture in a European Perspective: 1950, Prosperity and Welfare*. Assen: Uitgeverij Van Gorcum, 2004.

Jansen, Mechteld. *Talen naar God: Wegwijzers bij Paul Ricoeur*. Gorinchem: Narratio, 2002.

Jennings, Theodore. "On Ritual Knowledge." In *Readings in Ritual Studies*, edited by Ronald L. Grimes, 324–34. Upper Saddle River, NJ: Prentice-Hall, 1996.

Luther, Martin. "The Freedom of a Christian." In *Luther's Works 31: Career of the Reformer: I*, translated by W. A. Lambert, and edited by Harold J. Grimm, 343–77. 4th printing. Philadelphia: Fortress 1979.

Maher, Frances, and Mary Kay Tetreault. "Frames of Positionality: Constructing Meaningful Dialogues About Gender and Race." *Anthropological Quarterly* 66 (1993) 118–26.

Moyaert, Marianne. *Fragile Identities: Towards a Theology of Interreligious Hospitality*. Currents of Encounter 39. Amsterdam: Rodopi, 2011.

Pelias, Ronald J. "The Academic Tourist: An Autoethnography." *Qualitative Inquiry* 9 (2003) 369–73.

Post, Paul. "From Identity to Accent: The Ritual Studies Perspective of Fields of the Sacred." *Pastoraltheologische Informationen* 33 (2013) 149–58.

———. "Heilige Velden. Panorama van Ritueel-Religieuze Presenties in het Publieke Domein." *Tijdschrift voor Religie, Recht en Beleid* 1 (2010) 70–91.

Rathey, Markus. *Bach's Major Vocal Works. Music, Drama, Liturgy*. New Haven: Yale University Press, 2016.

Sengers, Erik, ed. *The Dutch and their Gods. Secularization and Transformation of Religion in the Netherlands Since 1950*. Hilversum: Verloren, 2005.

Van de Donk, Wim B. H. J., et al., eds. *Geloven in het Publieke Domein. Verkenningen van een Dubbele Transformatie*. WRR Verkenning 13. Amsterdam: Amsterdam University Press, 2006.

www.ingramcontent.com/pod-product-compliance
Lightning Source LLC
Chambersburg PA
CBHW062023220426
43662CB00010B/1446